FINAL FANTASY IX

OFFICIAL STRATEGY GUIDE

BY DAN BIRLEW

AUTHOR ACKNOWLEDGEMENTS

Big thanks to Tim Cox, my editor, for his great support on this guide. Sincerest thanks to Leigh, David, and Janet for handing me such a great project. To my wife Laura, for making me take breaks occasionally and for keeping me healthy. And also, thanks to Squaresoft for continuing and, most certainly, improving the FINAL FANTASY series. One of my favorite videogames is now a whole lot more fun. To Rick, Fernando, and the rest of Square's staff, thank you very much for the help and the support.

ABOUT THE AUTHOR

Dan Birlew is the author of numerous strategy guides, mostly about Squaresoft games. He operates "President Evil's Archive," where he updates a collection of professional and amateur videogame strategy guides

BradyGAMES also owes a big thank you to Wes Ehrlichman for all of his hard work.

BradyGAMES would like to extend an extra special thanks to the entire Squaresoft team. This strategy guide is unique in that it takes a totally new direction from other strategy guides on the market. It is the result of a LOT of hard work from a large group of dedicated individuals who invested a lot of time and energy on this project.

In particular, we would like to thank Jun Iwasaki, Kenji Mimura, Keiko Kato, Patrick Cervantes, and Andrew Shiozaki. Also, we must thank Steven Wright and Heather Dougal-Wright (Beeline Group), and Shaun Collins and Natasha Olivieri (Virtual Interactive, Inc.).

Lastly, thanks to Rick Thompson, Mark Abarca, Ryan Riley, Fernando Bustamante, Ryosuke Taketomi, Maki Yamane, Brody Phillips, Richard Amtower, Matthew B. Rhoades, and Yutaka Sano. Also, thanks to David "Ribs" Carrillo, Jeff Love, Chris Manprin, Dana Kwon, Michelle Elbert, Michael A. Erickson, Aaron J. Adams, Jennifer L. Mukai, Kelly Chun, Bryan Chen, Stephen Wong, Jesse Cheek, and Kenji Nakamura.

BRADYGAMES STAFF

Publishing Director
David Waybright

Creative Director
Robin Lasek

Editor-In-Chief
H. Leigh Davis

Marketing Manager
Janet Eshenour

CREDITS

Title Manager
Tim Cox

Screen Shot Editor
Michael Owen

Production Designers
Bob Klunder
Jane Washburne
Lisa England
Paul Belcastro
Tracy Wehmeyer

Book Designer
Ann-Marie Deets

FINAL FANTASY IX
OFFICIAL STRATEGY GUIDE

LEGAL STUFF

Brady Publishing
An Imprint of
Macmillan USA, Inc.
201 W. 103rd St.
Indianapolis, IN 46290

Please be advised that the ESRB rating icons, "EC", "K-A", "T", "M", and "AO" are copyrighted works and certification marks owned by the Interactive Digital Software Association and the Entertainment Software Rating Board and may only be used with their permission and authority. Under no circumstances may the rating icons be self-applied to any product that has not been rated by the ESRB. For information regarding whether a product has been rated by the ESRB, please call the ESRB at (212) 759-0700 or 1-800-771-3772. Please note that ESRB ratings only apply to the content of the game itself and do NOT apply to the content of the books.

ISBN: 0-7440-0041-6
Library of Congress No.: 00-136090

Printing Code: The rightmost double-digit number is the year of the book's printing; the rightmost single-digit number is the number of the book's printing. For example, 00-1 shows that the first printing of the book occurred in 2000.

03 02 01 00   4 3

Limits of Liability and Disclaimer of Warranty: THE AUTHOR AND PUBLISHER MAKE NO WARRANTY OF ANY KIND, EXPRESSED OR IMPLIED, WITH REGARD TO THESE PROGRAMS OR THE DOCUMENTATION CONTAINED IN THIS BOOK. THE AUTHOR AND PUBLISHER SPECIFICALLY DISCLAIM ANY WARRANTIES OF MERCHANTABILITY OR FITNESS FOR A PARTICULAR PURPOSE. THE AUTHOR AND PUBLISHER SHALL NOT BE LIABLE IN ANY EVENT FOR INCIDENTAL OR CONSEQUENTIAL DAMAGES IN CONNECTION WITH, OR ARISING OUT OF, THE FURNISHING, PERFORMANCE, OR USE OF THESE PROGRAMS.

TABLE OF CONTENTS

INTRODUCTION

Now that you have the OFFICIAL FINAL FANTASY® IX strategy guide in your hands, we should explain something to you. This guide is the first of its kind, as we've taken a brand-new approach in creating an innovative type of gaming experience.

This guide is unlike any other strategy guide ever created. The guide is structured in a unique way to help maximize your gaming experience. So, what exactly does that mean? Let us explain.

As the front cover states, this guide is enhanced by the PlayOnline.com site. If you're not familiar with PlayOnline.com, it's the premier site for everything about FINAL FANTASY IX. Just log on to www.playonline.com to find out what it's all about. You'll find a complete walkthrough, area maps, vital weapon and armor stats, a detailed bestiary, plus much more!

Our guide was created with the PlayOnline.com site in mind. In fact, it was developed in unison with our good friends at SQUARESOFT. In essence, this strategy guide covers the key elements to get you through the game without giving too much away or revealing any plot "spoilers." Then to take it a step further, the guide provides a few occasional teasers where you'll find information exclusive to PlayOnline.com. Also, the PlayOnline.com site serves to supplement strategy contained in our guide. When used together, you will be rewarded with the most complete FINAL FANTASY experience.

USING THIS BOOK

The key element to look for in this book is the PlayOnline.com icon and note box. For your convenience, they always appear in the same place. It consists of a few key items that you must learn about, which are illustrated on the following page.

Each PlayOnline.com callout has a "KEYWORD" associated with it. The "KEYWORD" is very important; it determines how the book interacts with PlayOnline.com. When you log on to PlayOnline.com, enter the "KEYWORD" in the PlayOnline.com search window and PlayOnline.com will send you to an appropriate part of the online guide that provides additional strategy or tips.

Also, each callout has a bar that indicates the subject matter for the callout. Therefore, you can quickly scan the callout and see if it's something that you're looking for. If so, enter the "KEYWORD" on PlayOnline.com to get more information.

For example, in this sample you'll notice that the "KEYWORD" is CSTONE1, while the subject matter is SPECIAL ITEM. Knowing this, you can type in CSTONE1 and expect to receive additional information on this special item.

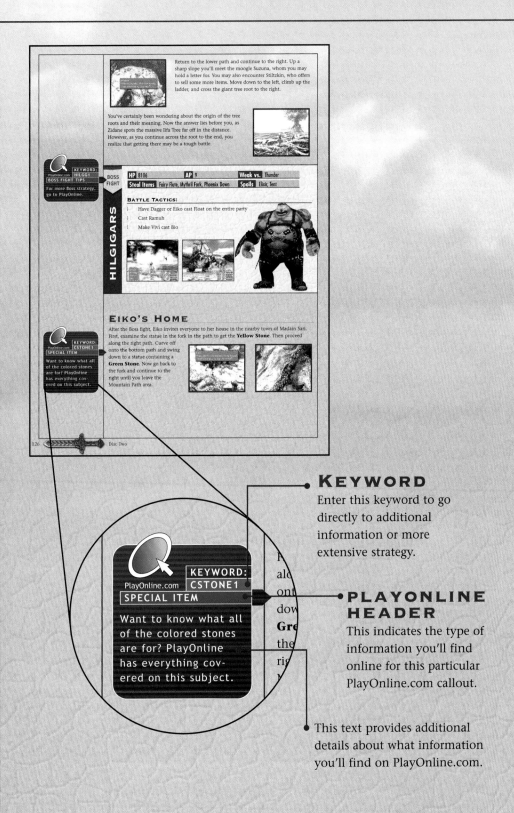

KEYWORD

Enter this keyword to go directly to additional information or more extensive strategy.

PLAYONLINE HEADER

This indicates the type of information you'll find online for this particular PlayOnline.com callout.

This text provides additional details about what information you'll find on PlayOnline.com.

It's all really pretty simple. You can use the book on its own, or use it in conjunction with PlayOnline.com. The choice is yours. Without a doubt, this new approach will provide a new aspect to your gaming experience. We hope you enjoy it.

With this information in hand, it's time to begin your ultimate quest!

GAME BASICS

This section is here to help warm up beginners and advanced RPG veterans alike. The game system changes from one *FINAL FANTASY* to the next, so all players must roll with the changes.

If you are new to RPGs, welcome to a whole world of fun! Don't let the complexity of the exploration and combat control turn you off. Just focus on the basic aspects to start, and then concentrate on the specifics after you've played the game for a few hours. That's the way I became so engrossed in this genre!

Most of the information explained in this section is also contained in Mogster's tutorial. Of course, we've attempted to expand on Mogster's points to make things even simpler. You can learn from Mogster any time you visit a Qu's Marsh anywhere in Gaia. Also, several interludes occur during the first few hours of the game, where Mogster steps in to explain a few points.

BASICS OF EXPLORATION

FINAL FANTASY IX is an RPG (Role-Playing Game). The general idea is to search the world presented in the game, looking for powerful or valuable treasures and fighting evil monsters to save the planet.

Control of the game is managed by moving one character around an area. The one character represents the entire party, although the other characters may not appear on-screen. To see who is in the party, press the Triangle button to access the Main Menu. There will be opportunities for you to determine which characters are in the party, but sometimes there isn't a choice because of the situations of the game.

Either the directional pad or analog stick will move the character in the direction desired. As you get close to objects or areas of interest, a Field Icon appears above the character's head. The Field Icon is further explained in this section. Press the X button to search these areas to find useful items or important clues about how to proceed.

Talk to the citizens of towns and areas to learn about the world in which the characters live. You might gain important clues from these conversations about the enemies and areas that lie ahead, or about optional side quests that might be of benefit. Some people have little to say, or once they've said a lot to you they will only repeat their last sentence over and over. After searching any one area and speaking to all the people, it's time to move on to the next location.

Some special events or mini-games that occur during the adventure will have specific controls. The game includes instructions that are displayed at the beginning of each special event, each time you attempt it.

BASIC CONTROLS (AREA/WORLD MAP)	
Button	**Function**
X	Confirm/Talk/Action/Search
Circle	Cancel/Run
Triangle	Open Main Menu
Square	Talk/Search/Challenge to a card game/Call for moogle
L1, R1	Rotate camera angle left or right
L2	Set camera angle behind
R2	Change camera perspective top down/angle
START	Pause
SELECT	Toggle mini-map/map diagram

WORLD MAP, AREA MAP

Any town, dungeon, castle, or cave that the party explores is considered a Field Map. The characters must also travel across the world from area to area. This is called traveling the World Map. You can travel the Field only on foot, but you can travel the World on foot, by vehicle, or on a chocobo (a little yellow bird that runs around yelling "KWEH!").

While visiting a well-populated town, random battles will not occur. However, when exploring a deserted castle, a wilderness cave or a dark dungeon, random battles with the monsters that reside in the area will occur.

Upon leaving a town or an area, the character emerges onto the World Map area. Random battles occur while traveling the world. The type of monsters encountered depend on the terrain and the geographic location of the area. Monsters are indigenous to their terrain. The terrain also determines the frequency of random battles. To avoid random battles with monsters, the party must travel in a vehicle or ride a chocobo. You can dismount a chocobo on any landmass other than mountains, whereas you can only land and disembark from a vehicle at a beach or a grassy, hospitable area. You can only disembark from a sea boat at a beach, port, or harbor.

Area Map

World Map

Crossing World Map on vehicle

You can only cross water and mountains by the use of the appropriate vessel, or a chocobo with the proper abilities. You can only land or disembark from chocobos and vehicles on certain types of terrain and never on mountainsides.

TERRAIN TYPES

Type	Frequency of Encounters	Disembark Vehicle?
Grassy	Normal	Boat, chocobo, or Airship
Swamp	High	Chocobo or Airship
Beach	Normal	Boat or chocobo
Forest	High	Chocobo
Desert	High	Chocobo or Airship

HELP MENU

Point the hand cursor at anything in the Main Menu and press SELECT to get some help from Mogster. When you do this, small blue windows will appear with descriptions of whatever the cursor is pointing at in the menu.

The moogle tells you the special abilities of items or the function of menu commands. You can also use the Help option during battles to learn more about what skills or tricks your characters can use.

FIELD ICON

During your adventure, the characters will move past a lot of suspicious or curious things in a given area. That's when a Field Icon might appear over the character's head. When you see the icon, press the X button to make something occur.

There are some areas where you might not be able to see your character on-screen. When this happens, pop out the HERE Icon, which is a large hand that points at the character's head. To call the HERE Icon, press SELECT. The default setting causes the HERE Icon to appear only when you enter an area or when you press SELECT. You can turn on/off the icon from the Config menu.

SAVE MOOGLES

Cute and friendly little moogles appear in almost every area that you explore in the world. They will save your game progress on a MEMORY CARD, or allow you to use a Tent to partially restore everyone's HP and MP (outside of KO'd characters) and remove some status abnormalities.

The Mognet option enables you to receive letters from other characters. The moogles also like for you to deliver letters from one moogle to another. To see if a moogle has any mail for you to deliver, choose the Mognet option, and then choose Cancel. If the moogle has a letter, you will get the option to deliver it.

Fortunately, the moogle to whom the letter is addressed is somewhere up ahead on the suggested path. To deliver the letter, talk to the moogle and select Mognet. An option should appear to deliver the letter.

Delivering letters between moogles is advantageous, because some moogles will give you Kupo Nuts or other rewards in return. You can give Kupo Nuts to the moogle family at Gizamaluke's Grotto to receive useful items.

While crossing the World Map, press the Square button and Moguo will rush to your aid. However, if you call him and then cancel, he'll get angry with you!

ITEMS

As you explore the world and conquer areas, you will acquire an incredibly large number of items. Items that have a "key" purpose in the game are kept in a different inventory from the rest of the "regular" items.

To see the purpose of any item, highlight it in the menu and press the SELECT button to bring up the Help Menu. To view the inscription on a Key Item, place the hand cursor over that item and press the X button. Inscriptions on items often provide a clue as to their use.

When equipping a character with items, only the kinds of items that the character is capable of using or wearing will be available to equip on them. You can find many pieces of equipment for free while exploring new areas, so carefully explore before purchasing items at shops. On the other hand, there are some weapons and armaments that are only available at shops, so save your Gil!

Some items are consumable, meaning that they are subtracted from inventory when used. You can restock some items, such as medicines, from specialized shops in towns and cities throughout the world. Keeping a good supply of all these items is essential to keeping the party effective and efficient in battle. Also, you can damage some enemies during battle by using these items against them.

You can also use gems and jewels to restore a certain amount of HP on the battlefield. You can use these items as equipment to learn powerful spells and abilities. Make sure that all of your characters learn the abilities contained in a stone before you use it to restore HP.

CONSUMABLE ITEM FUNCTIONS

Item	Use
Potion	Restores 100 HP in the field, 150 HP in battle
Hi-Potion	Restores 300 HP in the field, 450 HP in battle
Phoenix Down	Recovers a character from KO (zero HP)
Echo Screen	Cures Silence status
Soft	Cures Petrify and Gradual Petrify
Antidote	Cures Poison and Venom
Eye Drops	Cures Darkness
Magic Tag	Cures Zombie status
Vaccine	Cures Virus
Remedy	Cures various status impairments
Annoyntment	Cures Trouble status
Tent	Restores a large amount of HP and MP, removes some status effects

BATTLES

Most of the fun of playing an RPG lies in challenging and defeating powerful monsters and villains. Most battles that occur happen randomly, meaning that the characters are suddenly swept into a fight from time to time while traveling a certain area or while moving on foot across the world.

However, sometimes a monster is introduced, or it introduces itself. These creatures are usually enemies that you must fight to proceed in the game. They are commonly referred to as *Boss enemies*. You can expect Bosses to be much tougher, much more intelligent, and much trickier to defeat than all of the other enemies. Overcoming Boss monsters requires brilliant and sometimes risky strategies.

Battles usually don't occur in towns or cities, unless they are part of some kind of tournament or contest to win prizes. Most of your battles will occur suddenly as you are exploring dark and mysterious areas, where villains and evil lie in wait for young heroes.

When you enter the battle screen, your party will be aligned against an enemy party of one to four monsters. All characters have an opportunity to strike, which is their "combat turn." When all of the characters have attacked and the enemy has retaliated, one combat round is complete. Battles can go on for several rounds, until all of the enemies or all of the characters are dead or incapable of continuing to fight.

A character gets to fight when it becomes his/her turn. This is determined by a time gauge. When the character's time gauge fills up, you can choose commands for that character to execute. The eight playable characters in *FINAL FANTASY IX* all have different and unique abilities to utilize in battle. You must use the characters' skills so that the party functions as a team. Oftentimes, the magic-users are required to cast status-changing spells that will let the characters who can't use magic attack more effectively.

After each battle, characters may gain EXP, AP, Gil, and spoils. EXP is a measure of experience and allows the characters to gain levels and become more powerful. AP are Ability Points that are applied to each skill or ability that the characters are trying to learn. Thus, if you are trying to learn five abilities and you defeat a monster that yields 2 AP, then 2 points are applied toward learning *each* ability. Characters who are not in the current party do not gain EXP or AP.

Gil is money that can be used to purchase new items, equipment, and supplies. You can also use it to gamble, stay the night at an Inn, or bid on auction items. Monsters also drop spoils after the battle, which are items of all sorts including medicines, weapons, armor, equipment, Add-ons, and key items.

BASIC BATTLE CONTROLS

Button	Function
X	Confirm
Circle	Cancel
Triangle	Cycle to the next ready character when ATB gauge is full
Square	Hold down to hide menu
L1, R1	Select single/multiple targets
L2	Turn the target window on/off
START	Pause
SELECT	Turn on/off help

ATB

Time during battle is managed by the ATB System. ATB stands for "Active Time Battle." There are two ATB modes: *Active* and *Wait*. You can select the mode you prefer in the Config Menu. If you're new to RPGs, you should choose *Wait*. Selecting *Active* allows enemies to strike while you're trying to choose items or spells for your characters.

Active: Always real-time; time never stops during battle

Wait: Time stops while selecting magic and items

DAMAGE POINTS

Numbers and details pop up during battle whenever your HP and MP change. Numbers appear in two different colors. With HP, white numbers indicate damage, while green numbers indicate recovery. With MP, white numbers also indicate loss or drain, while green numbers indicate MP recharge.

DAMAGE DETAILS

Note	Definition
Miss	The attack misses. No damage inflicted or sustained.
Critical	Attack deals greater damage than usual. Sometimes twice the normal amount.
Death	Instant KO. Character must be revived with item or magic.
Guard	Status attacks or elemental assaults have no effect, due to some ability that is equipped or an inherent strength of the enemy.

ORDER

The positions and lineup of your characters on the battlefield is an important aspect of combat not to be overlooked. Outside of battle, you can change the order and the row of your characters using the Order option on the menu. To change your lineup, select the character you want to move, and press the X button. This causes another hand cursor to appear. Move the second hand cursor to the character you want the first character to change places with, and press the X button again to switch them.

Row is an even more important factor of positioning characters on the battlefield. There are two rows: the front and the back. In the front row, you can dish out big damage with a physical attack, but you may also receive a higher amount of damage. In the back row, characters can only cause a small amount of damage with the Attack command, but they will receive less damage from enemy attacks.

The rows automatically switch when a Back Attack occurs. This is when an enemy sneaks up on the party from behind. Damage to all characters will be greater in this situation. Those who are normally positioned in the back row are now in the front row, and vice versa. You can switch between front row and back row while in the battle menu by holding the directional button to the left. The Change option will appear, and this command will let your characters use their turn to change rows.

Characters who inflict greater damage with physical attacks should be placed in the front row, while characters who are more inclined toward magic use should be placed in the back. This is because spells cause the same amount of damage whether they are cast from either the back row or the front row. For those characters who dish out more damage with physical attacks, there are long-range weapons that enable fighters to cause as much damage from the back row.

When the character named Quina is recruited, s/he should be placed in the front row to start off. After Quina eats several monsters and learns a plethora of spells and abilities, you should start using Quina more as a magic-user, because his/her physical attacks inflict such a random amount of damage.

ABILITIES

Characters can learn and equip a variety of abilities from the weapons and items they receive. These abilities enable them to cast magic, cure status or damage, cause status or damage, and summon Eidolons to wreak havoc on the entire battlefield.

However, you can learn abilities that prevent the character from being afflicted by certain status ailments. Also, there are other abilities that can boost your characters' power in battle. Abilities are a complex subject, so please check out the **Abilities** section for more details.

TRANCE

Trance is something that occurs to characters who have sustained a lot of damage in battle. Most characters have a red Trance gauge, which indicates just how close they are to Trancing. You can view the Trance gauge during battle and when viewing the Status screen for any character. The gauge increases as the character takes hits from an enemy. This gauge doesn't increase if the character is struck by a fellow party member, since no hostility is ever intended between comrades. If afflicted with Zombie status, the Trance gauge is reduced to zero. When the Trance gauge fills completely, the character becomes an engine of destruction.

When Trance occurs, the character transforms. Powers increase while a character is under Trance. In addition to greater physical attack power, a new set of battle commands may also become available. Skills or special abilities that the character uses regularly gain a greater chance to strike effectively.

The time that the character stays in Trance is measured by the Trance Gauge. When the character under Trance performs actions, the gauge decreases. When the gauge reaches zero, Trance ends. Trance also ends when the battle ends.

STATUS EFFECTS

Status refers to a character's condition. There are good status effects and bad ones. Some go away at the end of a battle, while you must cure some with certain medicines or magic.

In addition to the ones listed in this section, there are Doom and Gradual Petrify. When these are cast or inflicted, a countdown from 10 to 1 occurs over the character's head. If the countdown reaches 0 and no cure has been administered, the character dies or turns to stone. You can cure Gradual Petrify by administering a Soft, or using the Stona or Esuna spells.

KO status (Knocked Out) is considered to be the status when a character is reduced to 0 (zero) HP. They will fall down unconscious, but you can revive them by using a Phoenix Down, a Phoenix Pinion, or by casting Life or Full-Life on them.

If all the characters are stricken with Stop, Petrify, Venom, or KO status, the game will end. Characters who are stricken with KO, Petrify, Virus, or Zombie do not receive EXP or AP when the battle is over.

Enemies can use status effects to make your battles much more difficult. Strategy is required to defeat such enemies, so you must equip the proper abilities before fighting such monsters. The Walkthrough provides some tips on which abilities to equip before certain battles so that you can avoid negative Status Effects.

The Reflect status causes spells cast to bounce from the target. Spells can only be reflected once. Thus, if an enemy is protecting itself with Reflect, cast Reflect on one of your characters and have your magic-users aim spells at that comrade. The spell will bounce off the fellow party member and attack the enemy.

You can use "good" status effects to increase a character's attack power or protective abilities. Enemies will use these types of status effects to their advantage as well. When a good status effect is achieved by casting a spell on a character, the effect will wear off after 2 or 3 combat rounds. Good statuses that are achieved by equipping support abilities on characters (such as Auto-Haste or Auto-Regen) will never wear off. The exception is Auto-Life, which only brings back the character from KO'd status once during each battle.

You can prevent many bad and very bad status effects by equipping preventative abilities such as Locomotion, Bright Eyes, Clear Headed, Antibody, etc. See the **Abilities** section for more details.

BAD STATUS EFFECTS (DISAPPEAR AT END OF BATTLE)

STATUS	EFFECT	SYMPTOMS	CURE
Confuse	Lose control of the character.	Character spins in position.	Physical Attack, Esuna
Berserk	Strength increases, control of character is lost.	Character turns red and fumes.	Gysahl Greens
Stop	Character cannot move.	ATB bar grayed out, stops moving.	Remedy, Dispel
Poison	HP gradually decreases.	Purple cloud over character's head.	Antidote, Esuna, Panacea, Remedy, Angel's Snack, effect expires
Sleep	Character cannot move or attack.	"Zzzz" appears over head.	Physical Attack, effect expires
Slow	ATB Gauge fills up slowly.	ATB is gray, arrows pointing downward over head.	Dispel, Haste, effect expires
Heat	Terrible burns cause KO if the character takes any action.	Character turns red, head is on fire.	Esuna, effect expires
Freeze	Character becomes frozen, instant KO upon impact.	Character turns blue and stops.	Esuna, effect expires
Mini	Character shrinks, reducing power and Defense.	Character reduced in size.	Mini, Remedy, Esuna, Quina's Angel's Snack

VERY BAD STATUS EFFECTS (REMAIN AFTER BATTLE)

STATUS	EFFECT	SYMPTOMS	CURE*
Petrify	Character turns to stone and cannot move.	Character becomes gray and still.	Soft, Stona, Remedy
Venom	HP and MP gradually decrease, and character cannot move.	Black and purple cloud over character's head.	Antidote, Remedy, Panacea, Esuna, Angel's Snack
Virus	Character cannot gain EXP or AP after battle.	Only visible in status menu.	Vaccine
Silence	Character cannot use magic.	Ellipses appears over character's head.	Echo Screen, Esuna, Remedy, Angel's Snack
Darkness	Character's vision impaired, reducing attack accuracy.	Dark cloud in front of character's face.	Eye Drops, Esuna, Remedy, Angel's Snack
Trouble	The damage an afflicted character receives transfers to other characters.	Trouble icon appears over character's head.	Annoyntment
Zombie	Healing items and magic cause damage/ KO to the character.	Character turns darker color.	Magic Tag

*Some Cures can be applied during or after battle to remove status

GOOD STATUS EFFECTS (INCREASE EFFECTIVENESS DURING BATTLE)

STATUS	EFFECT
Auto-Life	Character revives from KO automatically, once during battle.
Regen	HP gradually restored.
Haste	ATB Gauge fills up faster.
Float	Character floats off ground, does not receive Earth damage.
Shell	Damage from magic attacks decreases.
Protect	Damage from physical attacks decreases.
Vanish	Character invisible, cannot be hit by physical attacks; reappears if hit by magic or when the effect expires.
Reflect	Magic is reflected back at the caster. (Some magic cannot be reflected.)

ELEMENTAL PROPERTIES

Characters and enemies can use magic and weapons that are imbued with elemental properties to gain an advantage in combat. This occurs when a weapon or spell calls upon some element found in nature or the environment to cause damage to an enemy. Most spells and summoned Eidolons employ elemental properties to inflict damage.

The elements are in constant conflict, and one element is always strong or weak against another elemental type. Because enemies use elements to make themselves strong against your attacks, it's important to master the use of elemental properties so that your attacks have more power and your spell casters' MP is not expended unwisely.

There are a total of eight Elemental Properties: Fire, Ice, Thunder, Earth, Water, Wind, Holy, and Shadow. There is also a non-elemental property, which is not affected by any other elemental property.

ELEMENTAL PROPERTIES

Element	Property
Fire	Effective against Ice and undead monsters
Ice	Effective against insects, large enemies, Fire, and dragon-type monsters
Thunder	Effective against enemies near water
Earth	Ineffective against flying monsters
Water	Effective against Fire monsters
Wind	Effective against flying monsters
Holy	Effective against shadow monsters
Shadow	Effective against holy monsters

SHOPS AND SYNTHESIS

As you defeat enemies, your party starts to amass a large quantity of money, called Gil. In almost every town or city you explore, you'll encounter a variety of shops where you can purchase consumable medicines and supplies and buy or sell weapons and equipment. Spend heavily on armor and Add-ons, and spend cautiously on weapons.

As you continue to explore new and dangerous areas, you will find free equipment in treasure chests. Sometimes you can purchase an item at a shop long before it becomes available in a dungeon or monster-filled castle, giving your party the extra edge.

In addition to regular shops where you can buy and sell items, there are synthesis shops. These are places where you can combine items to create new items. All you need are two items and a few Gil to cover labor. The items you need and the amount of money you pay vary for each synthesized item. There is a Legendary Synthesist in the game who can create unique and extremely powerful items. His location and his list of items to create are divulged in the **Side Quests, Mini-Games, and Secrets** section.

Avoid selling extra or useless items to shops until very late in the game. Although some items are worth a lot of money and provide a good way to make some quick Gil, you need many of the weapons and armors you find to synthesize new items that aren't available anywhere else but a synthesis shop.

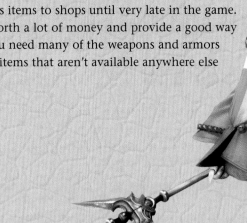

CHARACTERS

ZIDANE TRIBAL

Zidane is a thief and a member of the Tantalus theater troupe. All of the other actors/thieves seem to look up to Zidane as a kind of older brother. He is also the favorite of his boss, Baku.

Zidane equips two daggers to attack, or he can wield a dual-bladed polearm. Zidane can use his MP to perform powerful, non-physical Thieves' Skills. He is also the first of the party members to discover the powerful Trance ability, which causes his learned Thieves' Skills to become powerful, over-the-top "Dyne" attacks, which cause anywhere from 2000-9999 HP damage!

STEALING ITEMS

Zidane can steal items from enemies, and he can improve and refine this skill by learning certain abilities. He can eventually steal better items first (Master Thief), and inflict damage while stealing (Mug). Until you learn such abilities, use the Detect skill to spot any items the enemies may possess.

KEYWORD: ZIDN1
ABILITIES

For more details on Zidane's abilities, go to PlayOnline.

PRINCESS GARNET TIL ALEXANDROS 17TH (AKA, DAGGER)

Princess Garnet of the Royal House of Alexandria is the heir to the throne, and the daughter of Queen Brahne. From a very young age, Garnet has taken a keen interest in the legendary Eidolons. In her pre-teen years, she learned that the ability to summon several different Eidolons lay dormant within her.

When the princess is kidnapped by Zidane and Tantalus, she decides to use the opportunity to travel the world and learn more about her latent powers. To keep a low profile while away from the castle, she adopts the alias "Dagger." Her friends use this nickname fondly. Dagger attacks with either rackets or rods, but her true power lies in her use of White Magic.

KEYWORD: GARN2
ABILITIES

For more details on Dagger's abilities, go to PlayOnline.

SUMMONING EIDOLONS

The princess can learn to summon powerful Eidolons by equipping gemstones until she gains enough AP to summon the deity on her own. Most of her summoning involves powerful elemental and non-elemental attacks. Eidolons will not always appear during a summons. They always appear the first time you summon them, and thereafter the chance of them appearing during the summons is random. Usually, they just send their weapons to do the dirty work.

When the Eidolon appears during the summon animation, the attack is nearly twice as powerful. When Dagger goes into Trance, there is a much stronger chance that the Eidolon will appear. Dagger can summon the Eidolon to appear each time by learning the Boost ability.

SUMMONING SECRETS

Dagger's Odin summons has a certain percentage chance to cause instant death to an enemy. However, if Odin fails to cause death, no damage is inflicted whatsoever unless the "Odin's Sword" support ability is equipped. This causes wind damage to all enemies in case instant death fails to occur.

The Atomos summons has a different attack percentage depending on whether the full animation or just the partial animation is shown. The strength of other summons depends on the type and number of jewels in your inventory.

KEYWORD: DAGSUMM6
SUMMON SECRETS

Uncover Dagger's summoning secrets at PlayOnline!

CAPTAIN ADELBERT STEINER

PlayOnline.com
KEYWORD: STENR3
ABILITIES

For more details on Steiner's abilities, go to PlayOnline.

Steiner is the Captain of the Knights of Pluto, a cadre of misfit soldiers serving Queen Brahne of Alexandria. It is Steiner's sworn duty to protect the Queen and the Princess, and he holds that solemn oath in higher regard than all other priorities.

You can only equip Steiner with heavy armor and knightly swords. He can learn a variety of skills that damage as well as reduce an enemy's strength. In addition, Steiner can perform magical sword attacks when Vivi is in the party. This enables Steiner to attack with the added effect of the Black Mage's magic. When Steiner Trances, his regular physical attacks cause almost twice the normal amount of damage!

VIVI ORUNITIA

PlayOnline.com
KEYWORD: VIVI4
ABILITIES

For more details on Vivi's abilities, go to PlayOnline.

Vivi is a young Black Mage who is asked by Zidane to join the party. Although his past is a mystery even to himself, Vivi struggles to learn about the nature of the world and his destiny. Vivi can learn Black Magic attack spells by equipping items, but the staves that he wields are extremely low in physical attack power. This means that Vivi depends on having a hefty amount of MP at the beginning of all battles.

BLACK MAGIC

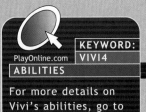

The very nature of Black Magic is to destroy or attack. Vivi learns most of his spells from wooden staves that you can find or purchase as the game progresses. Vivi should start each major battle by using his first couple of turns to "Focus" his magical powers. This is a command on his battle menu, and it can sometimes double the power of his spells!

Vivi learns some incredibly powerful magical attacks, but because his physical strikes are so weak, he depends on spell-casting to an extreme. Thus, Vivi's abilities are practically negated if the enemy casts a Reflect spell. To counter this, a White Mage (like Dagger or Eiko) must cast Reflect on a party member, and then Vivi can bounce spells off of him or her at the enemy.

Arguably, Vivi's most powerful spell is the Doomsday spell, which inflicts Shadow damage upon everything on-screen. Prepare your party accordingly when Doomsday is cast, and learn how to use it effectively against enemies.

FREYA CRESCENT

PlayOnline.com
KEYWORD: FRYA5
ABILITIES

For more details on Freya's abilities, go to PlayOnline.

A member of the Royal Dragon Knights of Burmecia, this mysterious female warrior has left her homeland to search the world for her lost love. Learning of the events transpiring around Gaia, she is compelled to join Zidane and the party.

Freya attacks with giant lances and spears. She can also learn the skills of a Dragon Knight, which enable her to restore and protect the party, as well as perform some other devastating attacks.

JUMPING AND DRAGON KNIGHT SKILLS

While her normal physical attack is mediocre in power, the Jump command can be used to make Freya leap high into the air, where she gathers enough power to perform her devastating Spear attack. While in the air, Freya cannot be attacked or inflicted with negative or positive status effects. If Regen has been cast on her prior to Jumping, she will continue to regain HP while off-screen. When Freya Trances, command her to Jump and she will remain in the air, showering all enemies with a hail of spears!

Freya learns powerful and extremely helpful Dragon Knight abilities by equipping various lances and spears. However, since these are considered *skills* and not magic, she can still use these abilities in places where magic is negated!

QUINA QUEN

You can recruit this strange and funny creature from his/her home on the Mist Continent Qu's Marsh. Quina is a Qu, and his/her language is a bit primitive. Being a gourmand, Quina wishes to travel the world with Zidane and find good things to eat. This desire enables Quina to consume enemies on the battlefield. Not only does this remove the enemy, but Quina may learn a Blue Magic ability by eating it!

Because Quina's physical attacks cause an unpredictable amount of damage on each strike, it's important to teach Quina as many useful skills as possible. Eventually, the Qu should be treated more like a Blue Mage than a fighter, and should be placed in the back row in your party's order.

KEYWORD:
PlayOnline.com QUIN6
ABILITIES

For more details on Quina's abilities, go to PlayOnline.

EATING BLUE MAGIC

During any battle, Quina can attempt to Eat an enemy; however, the enemy must be in a weakened state (near death) for this to succeed. After selecting the Eat command, Quina will tell you whether the monster is ready to be eaten. If the enemy is weak enough, Quina will simply eat it. As the monsters you encounter become more powerful, it becomes difficult for Quina to eat them and learn abilities. Use Dagger's Scan ability to determine the current HP of each monster. When their HP gets low, only have your weakest attackers strike and then keep trying to eat the monster each round. Casting spells such as Slow or Mini will aid in the digestion process.

Quina can eat almost any kind of monster, and even some Boss monsters too. The abilities that Quina learns enable you to perform some tricks that will help you kill monsters and confront Bosses more effectively. Since some monsters only appear up to a certain point in the game, try to eat various monsters as you encounter them to learn as many abilities as you can.

FROG CATCHING

In addition to Quina's Eat ability, Quina will also ask if s/he can catch frogs whenever you enter the frog pond area of a Qu's Marsh. There is one Qu's Marsh on the Mist Continent, one on the Outer Continent, and two on the Forgotten Continent. Quina can catch frogs in any of these ponds.

KEYWORD:
PlayOnline.com QUFROG1
SIDE QUESTS

Frog catching for fun and profit. Details at PlayOnline.

> **QUINA & "FROG DROP"**
> *The number of frogs s/he catches determines how much damage the "Frog Drop" attack causes. More on frog catching is detailed at PlayOnline.*

KEYWORD:
EIKO7
ABILITIES

For more details on Eiko's abilities, go to PlayOnline.

EIKO CAROL

Eiko lives alone in her home village of Madain Sari. She is the last of the "summoners" who once dwelt there. But now she lives in her house amongst the ruins, in the company of her moogle friends.

When Eiko meets Zidane and the party, she demonstrates her awesome summoning powers in battle. Eiko comes along with the adventurers because Dagger is very interested in learning more about summoning, and Eiko has set her sights on making Zidane her new boyfriend!

SUMMONING EIDOLONS

Eiko can learn to summon powerful Eidolons by equipping gemstones and other Add-ons until she gains enough AP to summon the being on her own. Her summons involve powerful elemental and non-elemental attacks, and also protective and restorative magic that affects the whole party at once.

Eidolons will not always appear during a summons. They always appear the first time you summon them, and thereafter the chance of them appearing during the summons is random. When the Eidolon appears during the summon animation, then the effect is nearly twice as powerful. When Eiko goes into Trance, there is a much stronger chance that the Eidolon will appear. Eiko can make the Eidolon appear each time by learning the Boost ability.

SUMMONING SECRETS

While Eiko only learns to summon four Eidolons throughout the course of the game, you can make some of these beings perform various spells and attacks depending on what Add-on Eiko equips. As you play through the game, you'll see that Eiko actually has just as many summon variations as Dagger.

In addition, once Eiko learns how to summon Phoenix from a Phoenix Pinion, there is a chance that Phoenix will completely restore the party if everyone gets KO'd. You can determine the percentage chance of this occurring by dividing the total number of Phoenix Pinions in stock by 256. So don't use or sell those Phoenix Pinions; they're hard to come by!

KEYWORD:
AMARN8
ABILITIES

For more details on Amarant's abilities, go to PlayOnline.

AMARANT CORAL

The Flaming Amarant is the willful and independent bounty hunter assigned to stop the heroes. When he sees the power Zidane possesses, he agrees to join in the mission to save Gaia. However, Amarant continues to be competitive with Zidane and dismissive of the others, and his attitude can only be viewed as hostile. He's a real mystery. Why does Amarant have such an attitude, and why does he remain with the party?

THROWING WEAPONS AND FLAIR

Amarant rips enemies with sharp claws or pounds them with hard knuckles. When properly equipped and taught the proper skills, he can be the fiercest warrior on the battlefield. In addition to his fighting skills, Amarant can inflict incredible amounts of damage to a foe by throwing various weapons at them (another reason not to sell your items). Although your extra weapons will cause great amounts of damage, the best items to throw are Pinwheels, Rising Suns, and Wing Edges. You can buy these weapons at most equipment shops in any town.

Amarant is a skilled assassin, but he can cast magic and perform skills to crush monsters and protect and revive his fellow party members. See, he's not such a dark loner after all!

ABILITIES

Abilities are special powers that characters possess. There are a ton of different abilities, but generally they fall into 2 categories.

Action Abilities: Signified with a red jewel icon, these are magic spells and special moves you can use in battle. Oftentimes, it consumes MP to use them.

Support Abilities: Signified with a blue-green jewel icon, these are special abilities that support and protect characters during battle.

To be functional, you must equip support abilities with magic stones. Similar to MP, the maximum number of stones a character can use to equip abilities increases as the character levels up. The Main Menu shows two numbers for magic stones: the remaining number and the maximum number. The first number shows the remaining stones, and will decrease as you equip support abilities. The second number indicates the maximum number usable by the character, and increases as a character levels up.

To set magic stones on support abilities, select *Ability* in the Main Menu and then select *Equip*. There are circles next to each support ability. The ability is equipped if a magic stone appears to fill the slot. The menu shows which support abilities have been equipped. A darker icon indicates that the ability is not equipped.

> **REMEMBER THIS!**
> *It should be noted that you only need to enable Support Abilities using magic stones. Action Abilities are functional if the ability has been learned, or as long as the proper items are equipped.*

LEARNING ABILITIES

In general, you must equip items to learn abilities. Most items hold special powers that help draw out a character's inborn abilities. Select Equip in the Main Menu to check which abilities a character can learn from items. The abilities that a character is incapable of learning from the item are grayed out.

You can use action and support abilities as soon as you equip the item. However, you can't use them if the item is removed or replaced with another. To use abilities without equipping items, the character must learn them by gaining enough AP (Ability Points) for each ability. You earn AP by winning battles.

Each ability has an AP Gauge. This shows how many AP have been earned toward permanently learning the ability. When the ability is being learned, a green bar fills the gauge to a certain point and a ratio indicates exactly how many points have been gained toward learning that ability. If the gauge appears in red with three stars, then the character has gained enough AP to use the ability without equipping an item.

You can press the X button while in the Status Menu to view all of the abilities that a character has learned or is learning. Continue to press the X button to page through the abilities.

KEYWORD: SUPPTA2

ABILITIES

More extensive coverage of Support and Action abilities is available at PlayOnline.

The amount of AP to learn each ability is different. The same item that teaches one character an ability may not teach all other characters the same ability. In most cases, the other character must equip a different type of item such as an Add-on to learn the ability. Also, one character may learn an ability for 30 AP, whereas another character may need 50 AP to learn the same ability. It all depends on the affinities of the character and the ability's purpose in the game.

SUPPORT ABILITIES

Name	Function	Name	Function
Auto-Reflect	Automatically casts Reflect in battle	Bandit	Raises success rate of Steal
Auto-Float	Automatically casts Float in battle	Boost	Raises strength of Eidolons
Auto-Haste	Automatically casts Haste in battle	Chemist	Doubles the potency of medicinal items
Auto-Regen	Automatically casts Regen in battle	Concentrate	Raises the strength of spells
Auto-Life	Automatically casts Life in battle (once per battle)	Counter	Counterattacks when physically attacked
Auto-Potion	Automatically uses Potion when damaged	Cover	You take damage in place of an ally
HP+10%	Increases HP by 10%	Distract	Lowers enemy's physical attack accuracy
HP+20%	Increases HP by 20%	Eye 4 Eye	Raises Counter activation rate
MP+10%	Increases MP by 10%	Flee-Gil	Receive Gil even when running from battle
MP+20%	Increases MP by 20%	Gamble Defense	Raises Defense occasionally
Bird Killer	Deals lethal damage to flying enemies	Guardian Mog	Mog protects with unseen forces
Bug Killer	Deals lethal damage to insects	Half MP	Cuts MP use by half in battle
Stone Killer	Deals lethal damage to stone enemies	Healer	Restores physical attack target's HP
Undead Killer	Deals lethal damage to undead enemies	High Jump	Jump higher to raise jump attack power
Devil Killer	Deals lethal damage to demons	High Tide	Allows you to Trance faster
Beast Killer	Deals lethal damage to beasts	Initiative	Raises chance of Preemptive Strike
Man Eater	Deals lethal damage to humans	Long Reach	Back row attacks with same power as front row
Ability Up	Character learns abilities faster	MP Attack	Character uses MP to raise Attack Power
Level Up	Character levels up faster	Mag Elem Null	Nullifies magic element
Accuracy+	Raises physical attack accuracy	Master Thief	Steal better items first
Add Status	Adds weapon's status effect (Add ST) when you attack	Millionaire	Receive more Gil after battle
Alert	Prevents back attacks	Mug	Damages enemy when you steal
Antibody	Prevents Poison and Venom	Odin's Sword	Attacks with eidolon Odin
Body Temp	Prevents Freeze and Heat	Protect Girls	You take damage in place of a girl
Bright Eyes	Prevents Darkness	Power Throw	Raises the strength of throw
Clear Headed	Prevents Confusion	Reflectx2	Doubles strength of Reflected spells
Insomniac	Prevents Sleep	Reflect-Null	Nullifies enemy's Reflect status when attacking with magic
Jelly	Prevents Petrify and Gradual Petrify	Return Magic	Returns magic used by enemy
Locomotion	Prevents Stop	Restore HP	Restores HP automatically when Near Death
Loudmouth	Prevents Silence	Steal Gil	Steal Gil along with items
Absorb MP	Absorbs MP used by enemy	Power Up	Raises the strength of Chakra
		Dragon Killer	Deals lethal damage to dragons

We also have included a complete list of items and the abilities you can learn from them. The following table provides this information.

ITEM	ABILITY		
Dagger	Flee		
Mage Masher	Detect	Flee	
Mythril Dagger	Bandit		
Gladius	Annoy	Lucky Seven	
Zorlin Shape	Flee		
Orichalcon	Detect		
Butterfly Sword	What's That!?	Protect Girls	
The Ogre	Soul Blade		
Exploda	Sacrifice	Lucky Seven	
Rune Tooth	Lucky Seven		
Angel Bless	Thievery		
Sargatanas	Annoy		
Masamune	Sacrifice		
The Tower	Lucky Seven	Thievery	
Ultima Weapon	Flee		
Broadsword	Beast Killer		
Iron Sword	Minus Strike		
Mythril Sword	Armor Break		
Blood Sword	Darkside		
Ice Brand	Mental Break		
Coral Sword	Charge!		
Diamond Sword	Power Break		
Flame Saber	Magic Break		
Rune Blade	Iai Strike		
Defender	Thunder Slash		
Save the Queen	N/A		
Ultima Sword	Stock Break		
Excalibur	Climhazzard		
Ragnarok	Shock	Thunder Slash	
Excalibur 2	Minus Strike	Climhazzard	Stock Break
Javelin	Dragon Killer		
Mythril Spear	Reis's Wind		
Partisan	Lancer	High Tide	
Ice Lance	White Draw		
Trident	Luna		
Heavy Lance	Six Dragons		
Obelisk	Cherry Blossom	Initiative	
Holy Lance	Dragon's Crest	Reis's Wind	
Kain's Lance	Dragon's Crest	Cherry Blossom	White Draw
Dragon's Hair	Dragon's Breath		
Cat's Claws	Chakra	Counter	
Poison Knuckles	Spare Change	Counter	
Mythril Claws	Curse	Counter	
Scissor Fang	Aura	Counter	
Dragon's Claw	No Mercy	Counter	
Tiger Fangs	Revive	Counter	
Avenger	Demi Shock	Counter	
Kaiser Knuckles	Countdown	Curse	Counter
Duel Claws	Aura	No Mercy	Counter
Rune Claws	Spare Change	Demi Shock	Revive

Item	Ability		
Air Racket	Scan	Panacea	
Multina Racket	Blind	Stona	Shell
Magic Racket	Berserk	Mini	Cure
Mythril Racket	Reflect	Shell	Protect
Priest's Racket	Silence	Might	
Tiger Racket	Dispel		
Rod	Cure	Panacea	Protect
Mythril Rod	Life	Silence	Shell
Stardust Rod	Ability Up	Reflect	Float
Healing Rod	Healer	Cura	Life
Asura's Rod	Mini	Confuse	Silence
Wizard Rod	Curaga	Protect	Shell
Whale Whisker	Curaga	Life	
Golem's Flute	Auto-Regen	Cura	Life
Lamia's Flute	Float	Stona	Silence
Fairy Flute	Esuna	Haste	Regen
Hamelin	Curaga	Might	Jewel
Siren's Flute	Full-Life	Dispel	Esuna
Angel Flute	Holy	Esuna	Curaga
Mage Staff	Fire		
Flame Staff	Fira	Sleep	
Ice Staff	Blizzara	Slow	
Lightning Staff	Thundara	Poison	
Oak Staff	Stop	Bio	Drain
Cypress Pile	Demi	Break	Comet
Octagon Rod	Firaga	Blizzaga	Thundaga
High Mage Staff	Meteor	Osmose	
Mace of Zeus	Doomsday		
Fork	High Tide		
Needle Fork	High Tide		
Mythril Fork	High Tide		
Silver Fork	High Tide		
Bistro Fork	High Tide		
Gastro Fork	High Tide		
Pinwheel	N/A		
Rising Sun	N/A		
Wing Edge	N/A		
Wrist	Flee-Gill		
Leather Wrist	Beast Killer	Blizzard	
Glass Armlet	Steal Gil	Antibody	
Bone Wrist	Add Status		
Mythril Armlet	Bug Killer		
Magic Armlet	Clear Headed	Silence	
Chimera Armlet	Mug	Add Status	
Egoist's Armlet	Beast Killer	Level Up	
N-Kai Armlet	Bandit	Undead Killer	Water
Jade Armlet	Body Temp	High Tide	
Thief Gloves	Master Thief		
Dragon Wrist	Jelly	Lancer	
Power Wrist	Accuracy+		
Bracer	Add Status	Power Throw	
Bronze Gloves	Antibody		
Silver Gloves	Undead Killer		
Mythril Gloves	Man Eater	Bug Killer	
Thunder Gloves	Devil Killer	Add Status	
Diamond Gloves	Ability Up	Jelly	
Venetia Shield	Auto-Float	Counter	

ITEM	ABILITY		
Defense Glove	HP+20%		
Genji Gloves	High Tide		
Aegis Gloves	Charge!		
Gauntlets	Cover		
Leather Hat	Fire		
Straw Hat	N/A		
Feather Hat	Bright Eyes	Add Status	
Steepled Hat	Protect		
Headgear	Undead Killer		
Magus Hat	Slow		
Bandana	Man Eater	Insomniac	
Mage's Hat	Loudmouth	Fira	
Lamia's Tiara	Clear Headed	Confuse	Float
Ritual Hat	Counter	Bright Eyes	Undead Killer
Twist Headband	Gamble Defense	Add Status	
Mantra Band	HP+20%	Antibody	
Dark Hat	High Tide	Jelly	
Green Beret	Ability Up	Clear Headed	
Black Hood	Accuracy+	Locomotion	Death
Red Hat	MP Attack	Cover	
Golden Hairpin	Auto-Regen	Loudmouth	
Coronet	Man Eater	Return Magic	
Flash Hat	Eye 4 Eye	Beast Killer	
Adaman Hat	HP+20%	Gamble Defense	
Thief Hat	Long Reach	Lucky Seven	Mug
Holy Miter	Insomniac	Body Temp	
Golden Skullcap	Power Up	Locomotion	
Circlet	Jelly	Clear Headed	
Rubber Helm	Minus Strike		
Bronze Helm	Bug Killer		
Iron Helm	Bright Eyes	Level Up	
Barbut	Alert	Dragon Killer	
Mythril Helm	Insomniac	Antibody	
Gold Helm	Mental Break	Reis's Wind	Clear Headed
Cross Helm	MP Attack	Devil Killer	
Diamond Helm	Accuracy+	Insomniac	
Platinum Helm	Restore HP	Stone Killer	
Kaiser Helm	Eye 4 Eye		
Genji Helmet	HP+20%		
Grand Helm	High Tide		
Aloha T-Shirt	N/A		
Leather Shirt	Protect Girls		
Silk Shirt	Cure	Thunder	
Leather Plate	Chakra		
Bronze Vest	Jelly		
Chain Plate	Devil Killer		
Mythril Vest	Auto-Potion		
Adaman Vest	Stone Killer	Bird Killer	
Magician Cloak	Insomniac	MP+10%	
Survival Vest	Locomotion	Antibody	Mug
Brigandine	Ability Up	Return Magic	
Judo Uniform	Distract	HP+10%	
Power Vest	Stone Killer	Gamble Defense	Counter
Gaia Gear	Insomniac	High Tide	Osmose
Demon's Vest	Devil Killer	Auto-Potion	Locomotion
Minerva's Plate	Restore HP	High Tide	
Ninja Gear	Alert	Locomotion	Eye 4 Eye

ITEM	ABILITY		
Dark Gear	Clear Headed	Jelly	
Rubber Suit	Eye 4 Eye	Esuna	
Brave Suit	Restore HP	Auto-Regen	
Cotton Robe	Chemist	Shell	
Silk Robe	Ability Up	Loudmouth	
Magician Robe	Auto-Potion	MP+10%	
Glutton's Robe	Antibody	Body Temp	Auto-Regen
White Robe	Loudmouth	Auto-Potion	Holy
Black Robe	MP+20%	Flare	Reflectx2
Light Robe	Half MP	Auto-Regen	Full-Life
Robe of Lords	Reflect Null	Concentrate	
Tin Armor	N/A		
Bronze Armor	Bird Killer		
Linen Cuirass	Cover		
Chain Mail	HP+10%	Bird Killer	
Mythril Armor	Jelly	Cover	
Plate Mail	Locomotion	Undead Killer	
Gold Armor	Stone Killer		
Shield Armor	Distract		
Demon's Mail	High Tide		
Diamond Armor	Ability Up		
Platina Armor	Beast Killer		
Carabini Mail	Auto-Regen		
Dragon Mail	High Jump		
Genji Armor	Body Temp	Accuracy+	
Maximillian	HP+20%		
Grand Armor	Chemist	Restore HP	
Desert Boots	Flee-Gil	Protect	Scan
Magician Shoes	MP+10%	Clear Headed	Blind
Germinas Boots	Alert	HP+10%	Flee
Sandals	N/A		
Feather Boots	Auto-Float	Float	Mini
Battle Boots	MP Attack	Initiative	HP+20%
Running Shoes	Auto-Haste	Auto-Potion	Haste
Anklet	Locomotion	Healer	Counter
Power Belt	MP Attack	Counter	Fira
Black Belt	HP+20%	Beast Killer	Demi
Glass Buckle	Antibody	Add Status	Thunder
Madain's Ring	Body Temp	Chemist	Guardian Mog
Rosetta Ring	Level Up	Concentrate	Reflectx2
Reflect Ring	Auto-Reflect	Distract	Reflect
Coral Ring	Insomniac	Man Eater	Lancer
Promist Ring	Restore HP	Absorb MP	Mag Elem Null
Rebirth Ring	Auto-Life	Life	Revive
Protect Ring	Long Reach	Mag Elem Null	Half MP
Pumice Piece	Boost		
Pumice	Ark		
Yellow Scarf	Bird Killer	Millionaire	Steal Gil
Gold Choker	Auto-Potion	Flee-Gil	Shell
Fairy Earrings	Level Up	Body Temp	Regen
Angel Earrings	Auto-Regen	MP+20%	Reis's Wind
Pearl Rouge	Level Up	Reflect-Null	Loudmouth
Pearl Armlet	N/A		
Cachusha	Bright Eyes	Ability Up	Life
Barette	Chemist	Gamble Defense	Cura
Extension	Auto-Potion	MP+10%	Level Up
Ribbon	Madeen	Ability Up	Guardian Mog

ITEM	ABILITY		
Maiden Prayer	Auto-Regen		
Ancient Aroma	Odin's Sword		
Garnet	Bahamut	Healer	
Amethyst	Atomos	Demi	
Aquamarine	Leviathan	HP+10%	
Diamond	Body Temp	Distract	
Emerald	Haste	MP+10%	White Draw
Moonstone	Shell	Beast Killer	
Ruby	Carbuncle	Reflect	
Peridot	Ramuh	Thundara	
Sapphire	Fenrir	High Tide	
Opal	Shiva	Blizzara	
Topaz	Ifrit	Fira	
Lapis Lazuli	Ability Up	Accuracy+	
Phoenix Pinion	Phoenix		
Dark Matter	Odin		

CHARACTER ABILITIES

The following section summarizes each of the main characters and their abilities.

PlayOnline.com KEYWORD: CHARABLT9 CHARACTER ABILITIES

Looking for a complete list of each character's abilities? Log on to PlayOnline!

ZIDANE TRIBAL

THIEVES' SKILLS

Name	Effect
Flee	Escape from battle with high probability
Detect	See the enemy's items
What's That!?	Allows back attack
Soul Blade	Draws out the hidden power of thief swords (inflicts status)
Annoy	Inflicts Trouble on the target
Sacrifice	Sacrifice yourself to restore HP and MP to the other party members
Lucky Seven	Deals physical damage by luck
Thievery	Deals physical damage to the target

DYNE SKILLS (TRANCE ONLY)

Name	Effect
Free Energy	Deals physical damage to the enemy
Tidal Flame	Deals physical damage to all enemies
Scoop Art	Deals physical damage to the enemy
Shift Break	Deals physical damage to all enemies
Stellar Circle 5	Deals physical damage to the enemy
Meo Twister	Deals physical damage to all enemies
Solution 9	Deals physical damage to the enemy
Grand Lethal	Deals physical damage to all enemies

ABILITIES

ZIDANE'S ABILITIES

Name	Learned From
Flee	Dagger, Mage Masher, Zorlin Shape, Ultima Weapon, Germinas Boots
Detect	Mage Masher, Orichalcon
What's That!?	Butterfly Sword
Soul Blade	The Ogre
Annoy	Gladius, Sargatanas
Sacrifice	Exploda, Masamune
Lucky Seven	Gladius, Exploda, Rune Tooth, The Tower, Thief Hat
Thievery	Angel Bless, The Tower
Auto-Reflect	Reflect Ring
Auto-Float	Feather Boots
Auto-Haste	Running Shoes
Auto-Regen	Golden Hairpin, Brave Suit
Auto-Life	Rebirth Ring
HP+20%	Mantra Band, Adaman Hat, Black Belt, Battle Boots
Accuracy+	Power Wrist, Black Hood, Lapis Lazuli
Distract	Judo Uniform, Reflect Ring, Diamond
Long Reach	Thief Hat, Protect Ring
MP Attack	Red Hat, Battle Boots, Power Belt
Bird Killer	Adaman Vest, Yellow Scarf
Bug Killer	Mythril Armlet
Stone Killer	Adaman Vest, Power Vest
Undead Killer	N-Kai Armlet, Headgear, Ritual Hat
Devil Killer	Chain Plate, Demon's Vest
Beast Killer	Leather Wrist, Egoist's Armlet, Flash Hat, Black Belt, Moonstone
Man Eater	Bandana, Coronet, Coral Ring
Master Thief	Thief Gloves
Steal Gil	Glass Armlet, Yellow Scarf
Add Status	Bone Wrist, Chimera Armlet, Bracer, Feather Hat, Twist Headband, Glass Buckle
Gamble Defense	Twist Headband, Adaman Hat, Power Vest
High Tide	Jade Armlet, Dark Hat, Gaia Gear, Sapphire
Counter	Ritual Hat, Power Vest, Power Belt
Protect Girls	Butterfly Sword, Leather Shirt
Eye 4 Eye	Flash Hat, Ninja Gear
Body Temp	Jade Armlet, Madain's Ring, Fairy Earrings, Diamond
Alert	Ninja Gear, Germinas Boots
Level Up	Egoist's Armlet, Rosetta Ring, Fairy Earrings
Ability Up	Green Beret, Brigandine, Ribbon, Lapis Lazuli
Flee-Gil	Wrist, Desert Boots, Gold Choker
Insomniac	Bandana, Gaia Gear, Coral Ring
Antibody	Glass Armlet, Mantra Band, Survival Vest, Glass Buckle
Bright Eyes	Feather Hat, Ritual Hat
Restore HP	Brave Suit, Promist Ring
Jelly	Dragon Wrist, Dark Hat, Circlet, Bronze Vest, Dark Gear
Auto-Potion	Mythril Vest, Demon's Vest, Running Shoes, Gold Choker
Locomotion	Black Hood, Golden Skullcap, Survival Vest, Demon's Vest, Ninja Gear
Clear Headed	Green Beret, Circlet, Dark Gear, Magician Shoes
Mug	Chimera Armlet, Thief Hat, Survival Vest
Bandit	Mythril Dagger, N-Kai Armlet

PRINCESS GARNET

GARNET'S SUMMONS

Eidolon	Effect
Shiva	Causes Ice damage to all enemies
Ifrit	Causes Fire damage to all enemies
Ramuh	Causes Thunder damage to all enemies
Atomos	Reduces all enemies' HP by a percentage
Odin	Causes KO to all enemies
Leviathan	Causes Water damage to all enemies
Bahamut	Causes non-elemental damage to all enemies
Ark	Causes Shadow damage to all enemies

WHITE MAGIC

Spell	Effect
Cure	Restores 300+ HP, single/multiple target
Cura	Restores 1500+ HP, single/multiple target
Curaga	Restores 4000+ HP, single/multiple target
Life	Recovers character from KO, restores some HP
Scan	Determines HP, MP, and weaknesses of enemy
Panacea	Cures Venom and Poison status
Stona	Cures Petrify and Gradual Petrify
Shell	Reduces damage from magic attacks
Protect	Reduces damage from physical attacks
Silence	Prevents single/multiple targets from casting magic
Mini	Shrinks, lowers defense and attack power
Reflect	Reflects magic attacks back onto caster
Confuse	Makes single/multiple targets erratic
Berserk	Raises attack strength, attacks uncontrollably
Blind	Causes Darkness, lowering physical attack accuracy
Float	Causes levitation, prevents earth damage

GARNET'S ABILITIES

Name	Learned From
Shiva	Opal
Ifrit	Topaz
Ramuh	Peridot
Atomos	Amethyst
Odin	Dark Matter
Leviathan	Aquamarine
Bahamut	Garnet
Ark	Pumice
Cure	Magic Racket, Rod, Silk Shirt
Cura	Healing Rod, Barette
Curaga	Wizard Rod, Whale Whisker
Life	Mythril Rod, Healing Rod, Whale Whisker, Rebirth Ring, Cachusha
Scan	Air Racket, Desert Boots
Panacea	Air Racket, Rod
Stona	Multina Racket
Shell	Multina Racket, Mythril Racket, Mythril Rod, Wizard Rod, Cotton Robe, Gold Choker, Moonstone
Protect	Mythril Racket, Rod, Wizard Rod, Steepled Hat, Desert Boots
Silence	Priest's Racket, Mythril Rod, Asura's Rod, Magic Armlet
Mini	Magic Racket, Asura's Rod, Feather Boots
Reflect	Mythril Racket, Stardust Rod, Reflect Ring, Ruby
Confuse	Asura's Rod, Lamia's Tiara

GARNET'S ABILITIES

Name	Learned From
Berserk	Magic Racket
Blind	Multina Racket, Magician Shoes
Float	Stardust Rod, Feather Boots
Auto-Reflect	Reflect Ring
Auto-Float	Feather Boots
Auto-Haste	Running Shoes
Auto-Regen	Golden Hairpin, Light Robe, Angel Earrings, Maiden Prayer
Auto-Life	Rebirth Ring
MP+20%	Angel Earrings
Healer	Healing Rod, Anklet, Garnet
Chemist	Cotton Robe, Madain's Ring, Barette
Reflect-Null	Robe of Lords, Pearl Rouge
Concentrate	Robe of Lords, Rosetta Ring
Half MP	Light Robe, Protect Ring
High Tide	Jade Armlet, Dark Hat, Gaia Gear, Minerva's Plate, Sapphire
Body Temp	Jade Armlet, Holy Miter, Madain's Ring, Fairy Earrings, Diamond
Level Up	Egoist's Armlet, Rosetta Ring, Fairy Earrings, Pearl Rouge, Extension
Ability Up	Stardust Rod, Green Beret, Silk Robe, Cachusha, Ribbon, Lapis Lazuli
Insomniac	Bandana, Holy Miter, Magician Cloak, Gaia Gear, Coral Ring
Antibody	Glass Armlet, Mantra Band, Survival Vest, Glass Buckle
Loudmouth	Mage's Hat, Golden Hairpin, Silk Robe, White Robe, Pearl Rouge
Jelly	Dragon Wrist, Circlet, Bronze Vest, Dark Gear
Auto-Potion	Mythril Vest, Demon's Vest, Magician's Robe, White Robe, Running Shoes, Gold Choker, Extension
Locomotion	Black Hood, Golden Skullcap, Survival Vest, Demon's Vest, Anklet
Clear Headed	Magic Armlet, Lamia's Tiara, Green Beret, Circlet, Dark Gear, Magician Shoes
Boost	Pumice Piece
Odin's Sword	Ancient Aroma

ADELBERT STEINER

SWORD ARTS

Name	Description
Darkside	Reduces HP to cause Shadow damage to the enemy
Minus Strike	Damages with difference between max HP and current HP
Iai Strike	KO's the target
Power Strike	Reduces the enemy's Attack Power
Armor Break	Reduces the enemy's Defense
Mental Break	Reduces the enemy's Magic Defense
Magic Break	Reduces the enemy's Magic
Charge!	Makes all Near Death party members 'Attack'
Thunder Slash	Causes Thunder damage to the enemy
Stock Break	Causes non-elemental damage to all enemies
Climhazzard	Causes non-elemental damage to all enemies
Shock	Deals physical damage to the enemy

Abilities

SWORD MAGIC

Spell	Effect
Fire	Strikes the enemy with Fire Sword
Fira	Strikes the enemy with Fira Sword
Firaga	Strikes the enemy with Firaga Sword
Blizzard	Strikes the enemy with Blizzard Sword
Blizzara	Strikes the enemy with Blizzara Sword
Blizzaga	Strikes the enemy with Blizzaga Sword
Thunder	Strikes the enemy with Thunder Sword
Thundara	Strikes the enemy with Thundara Sword
Thundaga	Strikes the enemy with Thundaga Sword
Bio	Strikes the enemy with Bio Sword
Water	Strikes the enemy with Water Sword
Flare	Strikes the enemy with Flare Sword
Doomsday	Strikes the enemy with Doomsday Sword

STEINER'S ABILITIES

Name	Learned From
Darkside	Blood Sword
Minus Strike	Iron Sword, Excalibur 2, Rubber Helm
Iai Strike	Rune Blade
Power Strike	Diamond Sword
Armor Break	Mythril Sword
Mental Break	Ice Brand, Gold Helm
Magic Break	Flame Saber
Charge!	Coral Sword, Aegis Gloves
Thunder Slash	Defender, Ragnarok
Stock Break	Ultima Sword, Excalibur 2
Climhazzard	Excalibur, Excalibur 2
Shock	Ragnarok
Auto-Reflect	Reflect Ring
Auto-Float	Venetia Shield, Feather Boots
Auto-Haste	Running Shoes
Auto-Regen	Carabini Mail
Auto-Life	Rebirth Ring
HP+10%	Chain Mail, Germinas Boots, Aquamarine
HP+20%	Defense Gloves, Genji Helmet, Maximillian, Black Belt
Accuracy+	Diamond Helm, Genji Armor, Lapis Lazuli
Distract	Shield Armor, Reflect Ring, Diamond
Long Reach	Protect Ring
MP Attack	Cross Helm, Battle Boots, Power Belt
Bird Killer	Bronze Armor, Chain Mail, Yellow Scarf
Bug Killer	Mythril Gloves, Bronze Helm
Stone Killer	Platinum Helm, Gold Armor
Undead Killer	Silver Gloves, Plate Mail
Devil Killer	Thunder Gloves, Cross Helm
Beast Killer	Broadsword, Platina Armor, Black Belt, Moonstone
Man Eater	Mythril Gloves, Coral Ring
Add Status	Thunder Gloves, Glass Buckle
Chemist	Grand Armor, Madain's Ring
High Tide	Genji Gloves, Grand Helm, Demon's Mail, Sapphire
Counter	Venetia Shield, Power Belt
Cover	Gauntlets, Linen Cuirass, Mythril Armor
Eye 4 Eye	Kaiser Helm
Body Temp	Genji Armor, Madain's Ring, Fairy Earrings, Diamond
Alert	Barbut, Germinas Boots

STEINER'S ABILITIES

Name	Learned From
Level Up	Iron Helm, Rosetta Ring, Fairy Earrings
Ability Up	Diamond Gloves, Diamond Armor, Ribbon, Lapis Lazuli
Insomniac	Mythril Helm, Diamond Helm, Coral Ring
Antibody	Bronze Gloves, Mythril Helm, Glass Buckle
Bright Eyes	Iron Helm
Restore HP	Platinum Helm, Grand Armor, Promist Ring
Jelly	Diamond Gloves, Mythril Armor
Auto-Potion	Running Shoes, Gold Choker
Locomotion	Plate Mail
Clear Headed	Gold Helm, Magician Shoes

VIVI ORUNITIA

BLACK MAGIC

Spell	Effect
Fire	Causes Fire damage to single/multiple targets
Fira	Causes a lot of Fire damage to single/multiple targets
Firaga	Causes big time Fire damage to single/multiple targets
Sleep	Puts single/multiple targets to sleep
Blizzard	Causes Ice damage to single/multiple targets
Blizzara	Causes a lot of Ice damage to single multiple targets
Blizzaga	Causes big time Ice damage to single/multiple targets
Slow	Slows down ATB Gauge
Thunder	Causes Thunder damage to single/multiple targets
Thundara	Causes a lot of Thunder damage to single/multiple targets
Thundaga	Causes big time Thunder damage to single/multiple targets
Stop	Stops targets from taking any action
Poison	Causes Poison to single/multiple targets
Bio	Causes non-elemental damage and Poison to single/multiple targets
Osmose	Absorbs MP from the target and transfers it to the spell caster
Drain	Drains HP from the target and transfers it to the spell caster
Demi	Amount of damage depends on the target's HP
Comet	Causes non-elemental damage
Death	KO's the target
Break	Causes Petrify
Water	Causes Water damage to single/multiple targets
Meteor	Causes non-elemental damage to all enemies
Flare	Causes non-elemental damage
Doomsday	Causes Shadow damage to all targets

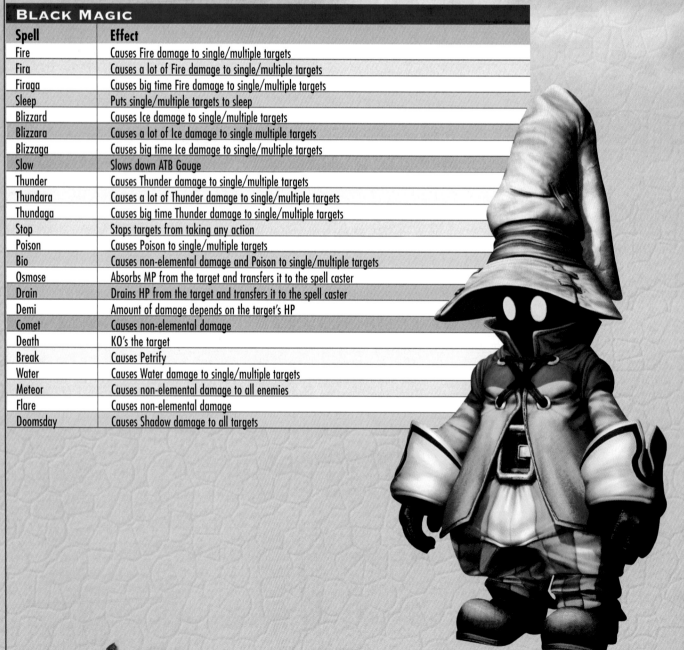

VIVI'S ABILITIES

Name	Learned From
Fire	Mage Staff, Leather Hat
Fira	Flame Staff, Mage's Hat, Power Belt, Topaz
Firaga	Octagon Rod
Sleep	Flame Staff
Blizzard	Leather Wrist
Blizzara	Ice Staff, Opal
Blizzaga	Octagon Rod
Slow	Ice Staff, Magus Hat
Thunder	Silk Shirt, Glass Buckle
Thundara	Lightning Staff, Peridot
Thundaga	Octagon Rod
Stop	Oak Staff
Poison	Lightning Staff
Bio	Oak Staff
Osmose	High Mage Staff, Gaia Gear
Drain	Oak Staff
Demi	Cypress Pile, Black Belt, Amethyst
Comet	Cypress Pile
Death	Black Hood
Break	Cypress Pile
Water	N-Kai Armlet
Meteor	High Mage Staff
Flare	Black Robe
Doomsday	Mace of Zeus
Auto-Reflect	Reflect Ring
Auto-Float	Feather Boots
Auto-Haste	Running Shoes
Auto-Regen	Golden Hairpin, Light Robe
Auto-Life	Rebirth Ring
MP+20%	Black Robe
Healer	Garnet
Add Status	Bone Wrist, Chimera Armlet, Bracer, Feather Hat, Twist Headband, Glass Buckle
Reflect-Null	Robe of Lords
Reflectx2	Black Robe, Rosetta Ring
Mag Elem Null	Promist Ring, Protect Ring
Half MP	Light Robe, Protect Ring
High Tide	Jade Armlet, Dark Hat, Gaia Gear, Sapphire
Body Temp	Jade Armlet, Holy Miter, Madain's Ring, Fairy Earrings, Diamond
Level Up	Egoist's Armlet, Rosetta Ring, Fairy Earrings
Ability Up	Green Beret, Silk Robe, Ribbon, Lapis Lazuli
Insomniac	Bandana, Holy Miter, Magician Cloak, Gaia Gear, Coral Ring
Antibody	Glass Armlet, Mantra Band, Survival Vest, Glass Buckle
Loudmouth	Mage's Hat, Golden Hairpin, Silk Robe
Jelly	Dragon Wrist, Dark Hat, Circlet, Bronze Vest, Dark Gear
Return Magic	Coronet
Auto-Potion	Mythril Vest, Demon's Vest, Magician Robe, Running Shoes, Gold Choker
Locomotion	Black Hood, Golden Skullcap, Survival Vest, Demon's Vest
Clear Headed	Magic Armlet, Green Beret, Circlet, Dark Gear, Magician Shoes

FREYA CRESCENT

DRAGON KNIGHT SKILLS

Skill	Effect
Lancer	Reduces the enemy's HP and MP
Reis's Wind	Casts Regen on entire party
Dragon Breath	Reduces HP of all enemies
White Draw	Restores MP of all party members
Luna	Causes Berserk to all targets
Six Dragons	Draws HP and MP from two characters to revitalize the other two
Cherry Blossom	Causes non-elemental damage to all enemies
Dragon Crest	Deals physical damage to the enemy

FREYA'S ABILITIES

Name	Learned From
Lancer	Partisan, Dragon Wrist, Coral Ring
Reis's Wind	Mythril Spear, Holy Lance, Gold Helm, Angel Earrings
Dragon Breath	Dragon's Hair
White Draw	Ice Lance, Kain's Lance, Emerald
Luna	Trident
Six Dragons	Heavy Lance
Cherry Blossom	Obelisk, Kain's Lance
Dragon Crest	Holy Lance, Kain's Lance
Auto-Reflect	Reflect Ring
Auto-Float	Venetia Shield, Feather Boots
Auto-Haste	Running Shoes
Auto-Regen	Carabini Mail, Angel Earrings, Maiden Prayer
Auto-Life	Rebirth Ring
HP+10%	Chain Mail, Germinas Boots, Aquamarine
HP+20%	Defense Gloves, Genji Helmet, Black Belt
MP+10%	Magician Shoes, Extension, Emerald
Accuracy+	Diamond Helm, Genji Armor, Black Belt
Distract	Shield Armor, Reflect Ring, Diamond
Long Reach	Protect Ring
MP Attack	Cross Helm, Battle Boots, Power Belt
Bird Killer	Bronze Armor, Chain Mail, Yellow Scarf
Bug Killer	Mythril Gloves, Bronze Helm
Stone Killer	Platinum Helm, Gold Armor
Undead Killer	Silver Gloves, Plate Mail
Dragon Killer	Javelin, Barbut
Devil Killer	Thunder Gloves, Cross Helm
Beast Killer	Platina Armor, Black Belt, Moonstone
Man Eater	Mythril Gloves, Coral Ring
High Jump	Dragon Mail
Add Status	Thunder Gloves, Glass Buckle
Gamble Defense	Barette
Chemist	Grand Armor, Madain's Ring, Barette
High Tide	Partisan, Genji Gloves, Grand Helm, Minerva's Plate, Demon's Mail, Sapphire
Counter	Venetia Shield, Anklet, Power Belt
Cover	Gauntlets, Linen Cuirass, Mythril Armor
Eye 4 Eye	Kaiser Helm, Rubber Suit
Body Temp	Genji Armor, Madain's Ring, Fairy Earrings, Diamond
Initiative	Obelisk, Battle Boots

FREYA'S ABILITIES

Name	Learned From
Level Up	Iron Helm, Rosetta Ring, Fairy Earrings, Pearl Rouge, Extension
Ability Up	Diamond Gloves, Diamond Armor, Cachusha, Ribbon, Lapis Lazuli
Insomniac	Mythril Helm, Diamond Helm, Coral Ring
Antibody	Bronze Gloves, Mythril Helm, Glass Buckle
Bright Eyes	Iron Helm, Cachusha
Restore HP	Platinum Helm, Minerva's Plate, Grand Armor, Promist Ring
Jelly	Dragon Wrist, Diamond Gloves, Mythril Armor
Auto-Potion	Running Shoes, Gold Choker, Extension
Locomotion	Plate Mail, Anklet
Clear Headed	Lamia's Tiara, Gold Helm, Magician Shoes

QUINA QUEN

BLUE MAGIC

Spell	Effect
Goblin Punch	Causes non-elemental damage to enemy
Lv5 Death	KO's all enemies whose Levels are multiples of 5
Lv4 Holy	Causes Holy damage to enemies whose Levels are multiples of 4
Lv3 Def-less	Reduces defense of enemies whose Levels are multiples of 3
Doom	Target's life ends after a 10 count
Roulette	Randomly KO's a target
Aqua Breath	Causes Water damage to all enemies
Mighty Guard	Casts Shell and Protect on all party members
Matra Magic	Reduces the target's HP to 1
Bad Breath	Causes Confuse, Darkness, Poison, Slow, and Mini to the enemy
Limit Glove	Causes non-elemental damage to the target when your HP is 1
1,000 Needles	Reduces the enemy's HP by 1,000
Pumpkin Head	Damages with the difference between your max HP and current HP
Night	Causes Sleep to all targets
Twister	Causes Wind damage to all enemies
Earth Shake	Causes Earth damage to all enemies
Angel's Snack	Uses Remedy on all party members
Frog Drop	Amount of damage depends on the number of frogs you have caught
White Wind	Restores HP of all party members
Vanish	Makes a party member disappear
Frost	Causes Freeze to the enemy
Mustard Bomb	Causes Heat to the enemy
Magic Hammer	Reduces the enemy's MP
Auto-Life	Casts Life when KO'ed

Quina's Abilities

Name	Learned From
Goblin Punch	Goblin, Goblin Mage
Lv5 Death	Stroper, Dracozombie, Whale Zombie, Lich
Lv4 Holy	Feather Circle, Torama, Amdusias
Lv3 Def-less	Carve Spider, Lamia, Lizard Man, Sand Scorpion, Ochu, Grand Dragon
Doom	Veteran, Ash
Roulette	Ghost, Zombie, Hecteyes
Aqua Breath	Clipper, Axolotl, Sahagin, Vepal
Mighty Guard	Serpion, Myconid, Gigan Octopus, Antlion, Gargoyle
Matra Magic	Trick Sparrow, Dragonfly, Zaghnol, Ogre, Land Worm, Armstrong, Ogre
Bad Breath	Anemone, Worm Hydra, Malboro
Limit Glove	Mu, Axe Beak, Mandragora, Blazer Beetle, Jabberwock, Catoblepas
1,000 Needles	Cactuar
Pumpkin Head	Python, Hedgehog Pie, Ladybug, Skeleton, Yeti, Basilisk, Bandersnatch
Night	Nymph, Abomination, Seeker Bat, Grimlock
Twister	Red Dragon, Abadon, Tiamat
Earth Shake	Adamantoise, Earth Guardian, Shell Dragon
Angel's Snack	Ironite, Mistodon, Epitaph, Behemoth
Frog Drop	Gigan Toad
White Wind	Zuu, Griffin, Zemzelett, Garuda
Vanish	Vice, Hornet, Gnoll, Troll, Drakan
Frost	Wraith, Chimera, Kraken
Mustard Bomb	Bomb, Red Vepal, Grenade, Wraith, Maliris
Magic Hammer	Magic Vice, Ring Leader
Auto-Life	Carrion Worm, Gimme Cat, Cerberus, Yan, Stilva
Auto-Reflect	Reflect Ring
Auto-Float	Feather Boots
Auto-Haste	Running Shoes
Auto-Regen	Golden Hairpin, Glutton's Robe, Light Robe
Auto-Life	Rebirth Ring
MP+10%	Magician Cloak, Magician Robe, Magician Shoes, Emerald
Healer	Garnet
Add Status	Bone Wrist, Chimera Armlet, Bracer, Feather Hat, Twist Headband, Glass Buckle
Gamble Defense	Twist Headband, Adaman Hat, Power Vest
Half MP	Light Robe, Protect Ring
High Tide	Fork, Needle Fork, Mythril Fork, Silver Fork, Bistro Fork, Gastro Fork, Jade Armlet, Dark Hat, Gaia Gear, Sapphire
Counter	Ritual Hat, Power Vest, Power Belt
Body Temp	Jade Armlet, Holy Miter, Glutton's Robe, Madain's Ring, Fairy Earring, Diamond
Level Up	Egoist's Armlet, Rosetta Ring, Fairy Earrings
Ability Up	Green Beret, Silk Robe, Ribbon, Lapis Lazuli
Millionaire	Yellow Scarf
Insomniac	Bandana, Holy Miter, Magician Cloak, Gaia Gear, Coral Ring
Antibody	Glass Armlet, Mantra Band, Survival Vest, Glutton's Robe, Glass Buckle
Loudmouth	Mage's Hat, Golden Hairpin, Silk Robe
Jelly	Dragon Wrist, Dark Hat, Circlet, Bronze Vest, Dark Gear
Absorb MP	Promist Ring
Auto-Potion	Mythril Vest, Demon's Vest, Magician Robe, Running Shoes, Gold Choker
Locomotion	Black Hood, Golden Skullcap, Survival Vest, Demon's Vest
Clear Headed	Magic Armlet, Lamia's Tiara, Green Beret, Circlet, Dark Gear, Magician Shoes

EIKO CAROL

EIKO'S SUMMONS

Eidolon	Effect
Carbuncle	Casts Reflect, Haste, Protect, or Vanish on all party members*
Fenrir	Causes Earth or Wind damage to all enemies*
Phoenix	Causes Fire damage to all enemies, and all party members recover from KO
Madeen	Causes Holy damage to all enemies

Depending on Add-on gem equipped while summoning.

ALTERNATE SUMMONS

Eidolon	Item Equipped	Spell Name	Effect
Carbuncle	None	Ruby Light	Casts Reflect on entire party
	Emerald	Emerald Light	Casts Haste on entire party
	Moonstone	Pearl Light	Casts Protect on entire party
	Diamond	Diamond Light	Casts Vanish on entire party
Fenrir	None	Terrestrial Rage	Causes Earth damage to all enemies
	Maiden Prayer	Millennial Decay	Causes Wind damage to all enemies

WHITE MAGIC

Spell	Effect
Cure	Restores 300+ HP, single/multiple target
Cura	Restores 1500+ HP, single/multiple target
Curaga	Restores 4000+ HP, single/multiple target
Regen	Gradually restores HP
Life	Recovers character from KO, restores some HP
Full-Life	Recover from KO with full HP
Panacea	Cures Venom and Poison status
Stona	Cures Petrify and Gradual Petrify
Esuna	Removes various abnormal status effects
Shell	Reduces damage from magic attacks
Protect	Reduces damage from physical attacks
Haste	Speeds up ATB Gauge
Silence	Prevents single/multiple targets from casting magic
Mini	Shrinks, lowers defense and attack power
Reflect	Reflects magic attacks back onto caster
Float	Causes levitation, prevents Earth damage
Dispel	Removes abnormal status caused by magic attacks
Might	Raises physical attack power
Jewel	Extracts Ore from a target
Holy	Causes Holy damage

EIKO'S ABILITIES

Name	Learned From
Carbuncle	Ruby
Fenrir	Sapphire
Phoenix	Phoenix Pinion
Madeen	Ribbon
Cure	Magic Racket, Silk Shirt
Cura	Golem's Flute, Barette
Curaga	Hamelin, Angel Flute
Regen	Fairy Flute, Fairy Earrings
Life	Golem's Flute, Rebirth Ring, Cachusha
Full-Life	Recover from KO with full HP
Panacea	Air Racket
Stona	Multina Racket, Lamia's Flute
Esuna	Fairy Flute, Siren's Flute, Angel Flute, Rubber Suit
Shell	Multina Racket, Mythril Racket, Cotton Robe, Gold Choker, Moonstone
Protect	Mythril Racket, Steepled Hat, Desert Boots
Haste	Fairy Flute, Running Shoes, Emerald
Silence	Priest's Racket, Lamia's Flute, Magic Armlet
Mini	Magic Racket, Feather Boots
Reflect	Mythril Racket, Reflect Ring, Ruby
Float	Lamia's Flute, Feather Boots
Dispel	Tiger Racket, Siren's Flute
Might	Priest's Racket, Hamelin
Jewel	Hamelin
Holy	Angel Flute, White Robe
Auto-Reflect	Reflect Ring
Auto-Float	Feather Boots
Auto-Haste	Running Shoes
Auto-Regen	Golem's Flute, Golden Hairpin, Light Robe, Angel Earrings, Maiden Prayer
Auto-Life	Rebirth Ring
MP+10%	Magician Cloak, Magician Robe, Magician Shoes, Extension, Emerald
MP+20%	Angel Earrings
Healer	Anklet, Garnet
Reflect-Null	Robe of Lords, Pearl Rouge
Concentrate	Robe of Lords, Rosetta Ring
Half MP	Light Robe, Protect Ring
High Tide	Jade Armlet, Dark Hat, Gaia Gear, Minerva's Plate, Sapphire
Body Temp	Jade Armlet, Holy Miter, Madain's Ring, Fairy Earrings, Diamond
Level Up	Egoist's Armlet, Rosetta Ring, Fairy Earrings, Pearl Rouge, Extension
Ability Up	Green Beret, Silk Robe, Cachusha, Ribbon, Lapis Lazuli
Guardian Mog	Madain's Ring, Ribbon
Insomniac	Bandana, Holy Miter, Magician Cloak, Gaia Gear, Coral Ring
Antibody	Glass Armlet, Mantra Band, Survival Vest, Glass Buckle
Loudmouth	Mage's Hat, Golden Hairpin, Silk Robe, White Robe, Pearl Rouge
Jelly	Dragon Wrist, Dark Hat, Circlet, Bronze Vest, Dark Gear
Auto-Potion	Mythril Vest, Demon's Vest, Magician's Robe, White Robe, Running Shoes, Gold Choker, Extension
Locomotion	Black Hood, Golden Skullcap, Survival Vest, Demon's Vest, Anklet
Clear Headed	Magic Armlet, Lamia's Tiara, Green Beret, Circlet, Dark Gear, Magician Shoes
Boost	Pumice Piece

AMARANT CORAL

AMARANT'S FLAIR

Skill	Effect
Chakra	Restores HP and MP of one party member
Spare Change	Causes non-elemental damage to the enemy by using Gil
No Mercy	Causes non-elemental damage to the enemy
Aura	Casts Auto-Life and Regen on one party member
Curse	Makes the enemy weak against some elemental property
Revive	Recover from KO
Demi Shock	Amount of damage depends on the enemy's HP
Countdown	Casts Doom on the enemy

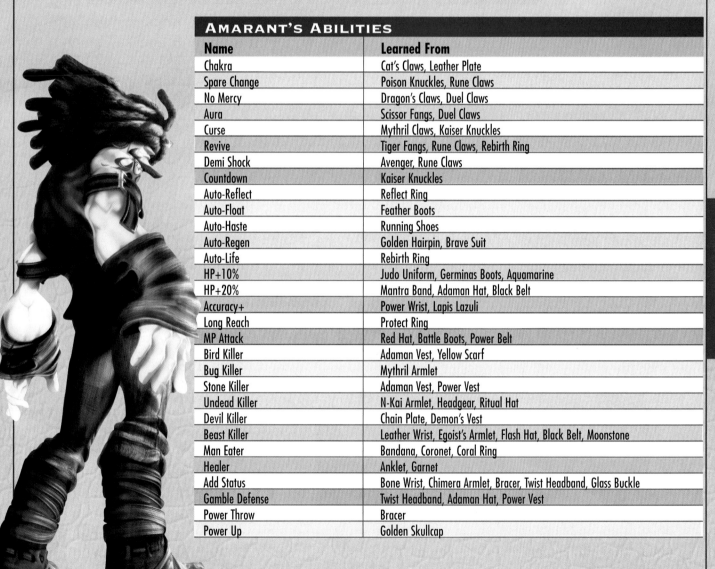

AMARANT'S ABILITIES

Name	Learned From
Chakra	Cat's Claws, Leather Plate
Spare Change	Poison Knuckles, Rune Claws
No Mercy	Dragon's Claws, Duel Claws
Aura	Scissor Fangs, Duel Claws
Curse	Mythril Claws, Kaiser Knuckles
Revive	Tiger Fangs, Rune Claws, Rebirth Ring
Demi Shock	Avenger, Rune Claws
Countdown	Kaiser Knuckles
Auto-Reflect	Reflect Ring
Auto-Float	Feather Boots
Auto-Haste	Running Shoes
Auto-Regen	Golden Hairpin, Brave Suit
Auto-Life	Rebirth Ring
HP+10%	Judo Uniform, Germinas Boots, Aquamarine
HP+20%	Mantra Band, Adaman Hat, Black Belt
Accuracy+	Power Wrist, Lapis Lazuli
Long Reach	Protect Ring
MP Attack	Red Hat, Battle Boots, Power Belt
Bird Killer	Adaman Vest, Yellow Scarf
Bug Killer	Mythril Armlet
Stone Killer	Adaman Vest, Power Vest
Undead Killer	N-Kai Armlet, Headgear, Ritual Hat
Devil Killer	Chain Plate, Demon's Vest
Beast Killer	Leather Wrist, Egoist's Armlet, Flash Hat, Black Belt, Moonstone
Man Eater	Bandana, Coronet, Coral Ring
Healer	Anklet, Garnet
Add Status	Bone Wrist, Chimera Armlet, Bracer, Twist Headband, Glass Buckle
Gamble Defense	Twist Headband, Adaman Hat, Power Vest
Power Throw	Bracer
Power Up	Golden Skullcap

AMARANT'S ABILITIES

Name	Learned From
High Tide	Jade Armlet, Dark Hat, Gaia Gear, Sapphire
Counter	Cat's Claws, Poison Knuckles, Mythril Claws, Scissor Fangs, Dragon's Claws, Tiger Fangs, Avenger, Kaiser Knuckles, Duel Claws, Ritual Hat, Power Vest, Anklet, Power Belt
Cover	Red Hat
Eye 4 Eye	Flash Hat, Ninja Gear
Body Temp	Jade Armlet, Madain's Ring, Fairy Earrings, Diamond
Alert	Ninja Gear, Germinas Boots
Level Up	Egoist's Armlet, Rosetta Ring, Fairy Earrings
Ability Up	Green Beret, Brigandine, Ribbon, Lapis Lazuli
Flee-Gil	Wrist, Desert Boots, Gold Choker
Insomniac	Bandana, Gaia Gear, Coral Ring
Antibody	Glass Armlet, Mantra Band, Survival Vest, Glass Buckle
Bright Eyes	Ritual Hat
Restore HP	Brave Suit, Promist Ring
Jelly	Dragon Wrist, Dark Hat, Circlet, Bronze Vest, Dark Gear
Return Magic	Coronet, Brigandine
Auto-Potion	Mythril Vest, Demon's Vest, Running Shoes, Gold Choker
Locomotion	Golden Skullcap, Survival Vest, Demon's Vest, Ninja Gear, Anklet
Clear Headed	Green Beret, Circlet, Dark Gear, Magician Shoes

Abilities

WEAPONS

Each character has a weapon equipped at all times. Not only is the weapon a way of inflicting physical damage, but it also determines the spells or skills the character is capable of learning.

Some weapons can inflict status effects on enemies if the Add Status ability is equipped. The enemy's Defense reduces your chance to inflict the status effect, however.

The following information provides a key to the tables in this section.

NOTE	DEFINITION
Buy	Cost to purchase at a shop.
Sell	Resale value.
Attack Power	Strength of weapon.
Notes	Description of weapon.
Add ST	Status Effect inflicted by weapon when Add Status ability is effective.
Elem-Atk	Special elemental property of attack.
Elem-Def	Special defense against elemental attacks.
Abilities	Skills that you can learn from a weapon.
(##)	AP required to learn skill or ability.
A	Action ability usable during combat.
S	Support ability to be equipped.

DON'T FORGET...
Some items may not be available at all points during the game.

KEYWORD: WEPNS7

WEAPON LOCATIONS

Having trouble finding a specific weapon? PlayOnline tells you where you can find or buy it!

THIEF SWORDS

Used by: Zidane

DAGGER

BUY	SELL	ATTACK POWER	NOTES	ADD ST	ABILITIES
320	160	12	Weapon used by thieves.	None	Flee (40)A

MAGE MASHER

BUY	SELL	ATTACK POWER	NOTES	ADD ST	ABILITIES
500	250	14	Weapon originally used for combating mages.	Silence	Flee (40)A, Detect (40)A

MYTHRIL DAGGER

BUY	SELL	ATTACK POWER	NOTES	ADD ST	ABILITIES
950	475	18	Thief's dagger made of mythril	None	Bandit (40)S

BUTTERFLY SWORD

BUY	SELL	ATTACK POWER	NOTES	ADD ST	ABILITIES
300	850	21	Standard thief's sword.	Silence	What's That!? (30)A, Protect Girls (35)S

THE OGRE

BUY	SELL	ATTACK POWER	NOTES	ADD ST	ABILITIES
700	650	24	Standard thief's sword.	Darkness	Soul Blade (35)A

GLADIUS

BUY	SELL	ATTACK POWER	NOTES	ADD ST	ABILITIES
2300	1150	30	Light dagger that is easy to handle.	Slow	Annoy (50)A, Lucky Seven (85)A

EXPLODA

BUY	SELL	ATTACK POWER	NOTES	ADD ST	ABILITIES
1000	1400	31	Sword made by processing trouble knife.	Trouble	Sacrifice (55)A, Lucky Seven (85)A

RUNE TOOTH

BUY	SELL	ATTACK POWER	NOTES	ADD ST	ABILITIES
2000	1900	37	Also known as 'The Viper.'	Poison	Lucky Seven (85)A

ZORLIN SHAPE

BUY	SELL	ATTACK POWER	NOTES	ADD ST	ABILITIES
6000	3000	42	Popular weapon among thieves.	None	Flee (40)A

ANGEL BLESS

BUY	SELL	ATTACK POWER	NOTES	ADD ST	ABILITIES
9000	3500	44	Weapon with an angel's spirit dwelling inside.	Confuse	Thievery (100)A

SARGATANAS

BUY	SELL	ATTACK POWER	NOTES	ADD ST	ABILITIES
12000	4750	53	Sword made by processing 'Epitaph's Fragment.'	Petrify	Annoy (50)A

MASAMUNE

BUY	SELL	ATTACK POWER	NOTES	ADD ST	ABILITIES
16000	6500	62	Sword from a foreign land.	Doom	Sacrifice (55)A

ORICHALCON

BUY	SELL	ATTACK POWER	NOTES	ADD ST	ABILITIES
17000	8500	71	The most powerful thief's dagger.	None	Detect (40)A

THE TOWER

BUY	SELL	ATTACK POWER	NOTES	ADD ST	ABILITIES
N/A	15000	86	Weapon that defines a great thief.	Mini	Lucky Seven (85)A, Thievery (100)A

ULTIMA WEAPON

BUY	SELL	ATTACK POWER	NOTES	ADD ST	ABILITIES
N/A	20000	100	Considered the most powerful weapon in the world.	Sleep	Flee (40)A

RODS

Used by: Dagger

ROD

BUY	SELL	ATTACK POWER	NOTES	ADD ST	ABILITIES
260	130	11	Combat Rod.	None	Cure (55)A, Panacea (15)A, Protect (30)A

MYTHRIL ROD

BUY	SELL	ATTACK POWER	NOTES	ADD ST	ABILITIES
760	280	14	Rod made of mythril	None	Life (30)A, Silence (30)A, Shell (35)A

STARDUST ROD

BUY	SELL	ATTACK POWER	NOTES	ELEM-DEF	ABILITIES
760	380	16	Rod adorned with beautiful stars.	Shadow damage reduced by 50%.	Ability Up (60)S, Reflect (20)A, Float (20)A

HEALING ROD

BUY	SELL	ATTACK POWER	NOTES	ADD ST	ABILITIES
1770	885	23	Weapon that can restore target's HP.	None	Healer (30)S, Cura (50)A, Life (30)A

ASURA'S ROD

BUY	SELL	ATTACK POWER	NOTES	ELEM-ATK	ABILITIES
3180	1590	27	Holy Rod.	Holy	Mini (40)A, Confuse (35)A, Silence (30)A

WIZARD ROD

BUY	SELL	ATTACK POWER	NOTES	ADD ST	ABILITIES
4000	1995	31	Rod used by mages.	None	Curaga (155)A, Protect (30)A, Shell (35)A

WHALE WHISKER

BUY	SELL	ATTACK POWER	NOTES	ADD ST	ABILITIES
N/A	5140	36	Legendary weapon that holds powerful magic.	None	Curaga (155)A, Life (30)A Break (35)A

RACKETS

Used by: Dagger, Eiko

AIR RACKET

BUY	SELL	ATTACK POWER	NOTES	ELEM-ATK	ABILITIES
400	200	13	Long-range combat racket.	Wind	Scan (25)A, Panacea (15)A

MULTINA RACKET

BUY	SELL	ATTACK POWER	NOTES	ELEM-ATK	ABILITIES
750	375	17	Long-range weapon that holds mysterious powers.	Wind	Blind (40)A, Stona (25)A, Shell (35)A

MAGIC RACKET

BUY	SELL	ATTACK POWER	NOTES	ELEM-ATK	ABILITIES
1350	675	23	Long-range weapon that holds magic powers.	Wind, raises Holy Elem-Atk	Berserk (30)A, Mini (40)A, Cure (30)A

MYTHRIL RACKET

BUY	SELL	ATTACK POWER	NOTES	ADD ST	ABILITIES
2250	1125	27	Long-range weapon made of mythril.	Wind	Reflect (20)A, Shell (35)A, Protect (30)A

PRIEST'S RACKET

BUY	SELL	ATTACK POWER	NOTES	ELEM-ATK	ABILITIES
11000	4000	35	Long-range holy racket.	Wind	Silence (30)A, Might (25)A

TIGER RACKET

BUY	SELL	ATTACK POWER	NOTES	ELEM-ATK	ABILITIES
N/A	2900	45	The most powerful long-range racket.	Wind	Dispel (25)A

FLUTES

Used by: Eiko

GOLEM'S FLUTE

BUY	SELL	ATTACK POWER	NOTES	ADD ST	ABILITIES
2700	1350	17	Flute with a golem's power dwelling inside.	None	Auto-Regen (35)S, Cura (40)A, Life (35)A

LAMIA'S FLUTE

BUY	SELL	ATTACK POWER	NOTES	ADD ST	ABILITIES
3800	1900	21	Flute with Lamia's power dwelling inside.	None	Float (25)A, Stona (25)A, Silence (25)A

FAIRY FLUTE

BUY	SELL	ATTACK POWER	NOTES	ADD ST	ABILITIES
4500	2250	24	Flute with an angel's power dwelling inside.	None	Esuna (80)A, Haste (30)A, Regen (25)A

HAMELIN

BUY	SELL	ATTACK POWER	NOTES	ADD ST	ABILITIES
5700	2850	27	Flute that holds magic powers.	None	Curaga (80)A, Might (25)A, Jewel (50)A

SIREN'S FLUTE

BUY	SELL	ATTACK POWER	NOTES	ADD ST	ABILITIES
7000	3500	30	Flute with a siren's power dwelling inside.	None	Full-Life (90)A, Dispel (25)A, Esuna (80)A

ANGEL FLUTE

BUY	SELL	ATTACK POWER	NOTES	ADD ST	ABILITIES
N/A	4150	33	Legendary flute that is said to enchant anyone who hears its tune.	None	Holy (110)A, Esuna (80)A, Curaga (80)A

SWORDS

Used by: Steiner

BROADSWORD

BUY	SELL	ATTACK POWER	NOTES	ADD ST	ABILITIES
330	165	12	Ordinary sword used in combat.	None	Beast Killer (55)S

IRON SWORD

BUY	SELL	ATTACK POWER	NOTES	ADD ST	ABILITIES
660	330	16	Sword made of iron.	None	Minus Strike (35)A

MYTHRIL SWORD

BUY	SELL	ATTACK POWER	NOTES	ADD ST	ABILITIES
1300	650	20	Sword made out of mythril.	None	Armor Break (30)A

BLOOD SWORD

BUY	SELL	ATTACK POWER	NOTES	ADD ST	ABILITIES
N/A	950	24	Sword varnished with blood.	None	Darkside (30)A

ICE BRAND

BUY	SELL	ATTACK POWER	NOTES	ADD ST	ELEM-ATK	ABILITIES
3780	1890	35	Weapon with an ice spirit dwelling inside.	Freeze	Ice	Mental Break (45)A

CORAL SWORD

BUY	SELL	ATTACK POWER	NOTES	ELEM-ATK	ABILITIES
4000	2000	38	Sword made of coral.	Thunder	Charge! (30)A

DIAMOND SWORD

BUY	SELL	ATTACK POWER	NOTES	ADD ST	ABILITIES
4700	2350	42	Sword made of diamond.	None	Power Break (40)A

FLAME SABER

BUY	SELL	ATTACK POWER	NOTES	ADD ST	ELEM-ATK	ABILITIES
5190	2595	46	Weapon with a fire spirit dwelling inside.	Heat	Fire	Magic Break (25)A

RUNE BLADE

BUY	SELL	ATTACK POWER	NOTES	ADD ST	ABILITIES
N/A	4450	57	Weapon that has Rune inscriptions.	Darkness	Iai Strike (40)A

DEFENDER

BUY	SELL	ATTACK POWER	NOTES	ELEM-DEF	ABILITIES
9340	4670	65	Sword possessing a guardian angel.	Ice/Thunder damage reduced by 50%.	Thunder Slash (30)A

ULTIMA SWORD

BUY	SELL	ATTACK POWER	NOTES	ADD ST	ABILITIES
14000	7000	74	Sword that can only be used by chosen knights.	Sleep	Stock Break (35)A

EXCALIBUR

BUY	SELL	ATTACK POWER	NOTES	ADD ST	ABILITIES
N/A	9500	77	Light sword used by holy knights.	Holy	Climhazzard (70)A

RAGNAROK

BUY	SELL	ATTACK POWER	NOTES	ADD ST	ABILITIES
N/A	14500	87	Knight sword bearing divine inscriptions.	Slow	Shock (60)A, Thunder Slash (30)A

EXCALIBUR 2

BUY	SELL	ATTACK POWER	NOTES	ADD ST	ABILITIES
N/A	19500	108	N/A	None	Minus Strike (35)A, Climhazzard (70)A, Stock

Weapons

STAVES

Used by: Vivi

MAGE STAFF

BUY	SELL	ATTACK POWER	NOTES	ADD ST	ABILITIES
320	160	12	Staff used by black mages.	None	Fire (25)A

FLAME STAFF

BUY	SELL	ATTACK POWER	NOTES	ELEM-ATK	ABILITIES
1100	550	16	Staff with a divine fire power dwelling inside.	Fire	Fire (50)A, Sleep (20)A

ICE STAFF

BUY	SELL	ATTACK POWER	NOTES	ELEM-ATK	ABILITIES
980	490	16	Staff with a divine ice power dwelling inside.	Ice	Blizzara (50)A, Slow (20)A

LIGHTNING STAFF

BUY	SELL	ATTACK POWER	NOTES	ELEM-ATK	ABILITIES
1200	600	16	Staff with a divine thunder power dwelling inside.	Thunder	Thundara (50)A, Poison (35)A

OAK STAFF

BUY	SELL	ATTACK POWER	NOTES	ADD ST	ABILITIES
2400	1200	23	Staff made from a legendary tree.	Slow	Stop (25)A, Bio (40)A, Drain (60)A

CYPRESS PILE

BUY	SELL	ATTACK POWER	NOTES	ADD ST	ABILITIES
3200	1600	27	Weapon that radiates a mysterious light.	Confuse	Demi (30)A, Break (30)A, Comet (55)A

OCTAGON ROD

BUY	SELL	ATTACK POWER	NOTES	ADD ST	ELEM-ATK	ABILITIES
4500	2250	29	Staff with water god dwelling inside.	Absorbs Water/Wind Elem-Atk	Trouble/raises Water Elem-Atk	Firaga (75)A, Blizzaga (85)A, Thundaga (80)A

HIGH MAGE STAFF

BUY	SELL	ATTACK POWER	NOTES	ADD ST	ABILITIES
6000	3000	32	Staff that holds powerful magic.	Silence	Meteor (95)A, Osmose (70)A

MACE OF ZEUS

BUY	SELL	ATTACK POWER	NOTES	ADD ST	ABILITIES
N/A	5000	35	Legendary staff that once belonged to a grand magician.	Mini	Doomsday (150)A

POLEARMS

Used by: Freya

JAVELIN

BUY	SELL	ATTACK POWER	NOTES	ADD ST	ABILITIES
880	440	18	Spear used by dragon knights.	None	Dragon Killer (70)S

MYTHRIL SPEAR

BUY	SELL	ATTACK POWER	NOTES	ADD ST	ABILITIES
1100	550	20	Spear made of mythril.	None	Reis's Wind (40)A

PARTISAN

BUY	SELL	ATTACK POWER	NOTES	ADD ST	ABILITIES
1600	800	25	Spear adorned with brilliant gems.	None	Lancer (20)A, High Tide (20)S

ICE LANCE

BUY	SELL	ATTACK POWER	NOTES	ELEM-ATK	ADD ST	ABILITIES
2430	1215	31	Spear made of ice.	Ice	Freeze	White Draw (90)A

TRIDENT

BUY	SELL	ATTACK POWER	NOTES	ADD ST	ABILITIES
3580	1790	37	Also known as the 'Spear of Enchantment.'	Darkness	Luna (30)A

HEAVY LANCE

BUY	SELL	ATTACK POWER	NOTES	ADD ST	ABILITIES
4700	2350	42	Heavy weapon that can deal massive damage.	Stop	Six Dragons (25)A

OBELISK

BUY	SELL	ATTACK POWER	NOTES	ADD ST	ABILITIES
N/A	3000	52	Spear made from magic stone.	Petrify	Cherry Blossom (40)A, Initiative (95)S

HOLY LANCE

BUY	SELL	ATTACK POWER	NOTES	ELEM-ATK	ABILITIES
11000	5500	62	Holy spear.	Holy	Dragon's Crest (45)A, Reis's Wind (40)A

KAIN'S LANCE

BUY	SELL	ATTACK POWER	NOTES	ADD ST	ABILITIES
N/A	7500	71	Spear from the distant past.	Confuse	Dragon's Crest (45)A, Cherry Blossom (40)A, White Draw (90)A

DRAGON'S HAIR

BUY	SELL	ATTACK POWER	NOTES	ADD ST	ABILITIES
N/A	11750	77	Legendary spear made from dragon king's hair.	None	Dragon Breath (205)A

FORKS

Used by: Quina

FORK

BUY	SELL	ATTACK POWER	NOTES	ADD ST	ABILITIES
1100	550	21	Combat fork used by the Qu Clan.	None	High Tide (250)S

NEEDLE FORK

BUY	SELL	ATTACK POWER	NOTES	ADD ST	ABILITIES
3100	1550	34	Mysterious fork that causes the opposite effect of "Soft."	Petrify	High Tide (250)S

MYTHRIL FORK

BUY	SELL	ATTACK POWER	NOTES	ADD ST	ABILITIES
4700	2350	42	Fork made of mythril.	None	High Tide (250)S

SILVER FORK

BUY	SELL	ATTACK POWER	NOTES	ADD ST	ABILITIES
7400	3700	53	Fork made of silver.	Slow	High Tide (250)S

BISTRO FORK

BUY	SELL	ATTACK POWER	NOTES	ADD ST	ABILITIES
10300	5150	68	Popular fork among gourmands.	Sleep	High Tide (250)S

GASTRO FORK

BUY	SELL	ATTACK POWER	NOTES	ADD ST	ABILITIES
N/A	6650	77	Legendary fork known for its ability to crush anything.	Stop	High Tide (250)S

FIST WEAPONS

Used by: Amarant

CAT'S CLAWS

BUY	SELL	ATTACK POWER	NOTES	ADD ST	ABILITIES
4000	2000	23	Ordinary claws used for combat.	None	Chakra (30)A, Counter (240)S

POISON KNUCKLES

BUY	SELL	ATTACK POWER	NOTES	ADD ST	ABILITIES
5000	2500	33	Combat knuckles.	Poison	Spare Change (90)A, Counter (240)S

MYTHRIL CLAWS

BUY	SELL	ATTACK POWER	NOTES	ADD ST	ABILITIES
6500	3250	39	Claws made of mythril.	None	Curse (20)A, Counter (240)S

SCISSOR FANGS

BUY	SELL	ATTACK POWER	NOTES	ADD ST	ABILITIES
8000	4000	45	Weapon with deadly venom on the tip.	Venom	Aura (25)A, Counter (240)S

DRAGON'S CLAWS

BUY	SELL	ATTACK POWER	NOTES	ELEM-ATK	ABILITIES
N/A	5180	53	Weapon made from a dragon's claw.	Water	No Mercy (25)A, Counter (240)S

TIGER FANGS

BUY	SELL	ATTACK POWER	NOTES	ADD ST	ABILITIES
13500	6750	62	Long, sharp claws.	None	Revive(35)A, Counter (240)S

AVENGER

BUY	SELL	ATTACK POWER	NOTES	ADD ST	ABILITIES
16000	8000	70	Powerful claws that can kill opponents with one hit.	Death Blow	Demi Shock (50)A, Counter (240)S

KAISER KNUCKLES

BUY	SELL	ATTACK POWER	NOTES	ELEM-ATK	ADD ST	ABILITIES
18000	9000	75	Claws with a wind spirit dwelling inside.	Wind	Trouble	Countdown (40)A, Curse (20)A, Counter (240)S

DUEL CLAWS

BUY	SELL	ATTACK POWER	NOTES	ADD ST	ABILITIES
16000	9000	75	Weapon once used by a legendary hero.	Berserk	Aura (25)A, No Mercy (25)A, Counter (240)S

RUNE CLAWS

BUY	SELL	ATTACK POWER	NOTES	ADD ST	ABILITIES
N/A	14400	83	Legendary combat claws that use the power of darkness to unleash a destructive force beyond imagination.	Darkness	Spare Change (90)A, Demi Shock (50)A, Revive (35)A

HEAD GEAR

KEYWORD: HEDGER8

ABILITIES

You can learn abilities by equipping Head Gear. More details at PlayOnline.

Item	Buy	Sell	Stat Bonuses	Description
Straw Hat	N/A	750	None	Provides a southern, tropical feel.
Leather Hat	150	75	Magic Def +6	Not a suitable item to wear in combat.
Feather Hat	200	100	Spirit +1, Magic Def +7	Hat that raises Spirit. Raises Wind Elem-Atk.
Steepled Hat	260	130	Strength +1, Magic Def +9	Hats worn by mages.
Magus Hat	400	200	Magic Def +10	Hat suited for mages. Raises Ice Elem-Atk.
Bandana	500	250	Speed +1, Spirit +1, Evade +2, Magic Def +12	Mysterious bandana that makes you light-footed.
Mage's Hat	600	300	Magic +1, Magic Def +14	Hat that holds magic powers. Raises Holy/Shadow Elem-Atk.
Ritual Hat	1000	500	Strength +1, Defense +1, Magic Def +16	Hat worn for ceremonies and festivals in Conde Petie.
Lamia's Tiara	800	400	Magic +1, Spirit +1, Magic Def +17	Tiara worn by Lamia. Elem-Def: Wind damage reduced by 50%.
Twist Headband	1200	600	Strength +1, Magic Def +17	Headband that raises Strength. Raises Earth Elem-Atk.
Mantra Band	1500	750	Magic +1, Spirit +1, Defense +1, Magic Def +19	Draws on hidden strength.
Dark Hat	1800	900	Magic Def +21	Old hat, steeped in legend. Elem-Def: Ice damage reduced by 100%.
Green Beret	2180	1090	Speed +1, Strength +1, Magic Def +23	Improves movement.
Red Hat	3000	1500	Defense +1, Magic Def +26	Dark-red hat. Raises Fire Elem-Atk.
Black Hood	2550	1275	Magic Def +27	Hood from a foreign land. Elem-Def: Fire/Thunder/Water damage reduced by 50%.
Adaman Hat	6100	3050	Defense +3, Magic Def +33	Extremely durable hat. Elem-Def: Thunder damage reduced by 100%.
Coronet	4400	2200	Defense +1, Magic Def +35	Coronet that radiates a mysterious light. Elem-Def: Wind damage reduced by 100%.
Flash Hat	5200	2600	Speed +1, Evade +2, Magic Def +37	Holy hat. Raises Thunder/Holy Elem-Atk.
Holy Miter	8300	4150	Magic +1, Spirit +2, Magic Def +39	Holy hat.
Golden Skullcap	15000	6000	Defense +2, Magic Def +47	Known for providing great defense. Elem-Def: Earth damage reduced by 50%. Raises Water Elem-Atk.
Circlet	20000	6500	Magic Def +51	Circlet protected by magic. Elem-Def: Earth damage reduced by 100%.
Rubber Helm	250	125	Magic Def +5	Helm worn by soldier trainees. Elem-Def: Thunder damage reduced by 50%.
Bronze Helm	330	165	Magic Def +6	Helm made of bronze. Elem-Def: Water damage reduced by 50%.
Iron Helm	450	225	Spirit +1, Magic Def +7	Helm made of iron.
Mythril Helm	1000	500	Spirit +1, Magic Def +11	Helm made of mythril. Raises Holy Elem-Atk.
Gold Helm	1800	900	Magic +1, Magic Def +13	Helm made of gold.
Diamond Helm	3000	1500	Spirit +1, Magic Def +20	Helm made of diamond.
Platinum Helm	4600	2300	Magic Def +23	Helm made of platinum. Elem-Def: Ice damage reduced by 50%.
Kaiser Helm	7120	3560	Strength +1, Magic +1, Magic Def +26	Helm that raises Strength and magic.
Genji Helmet	N/A	1	Magic +2, Defense +2, Magic Def +29	Very famous brand of helmet.
Grand Helm	20000	7000	Speed +1, Magic Def +33	The greatest helmet.
Headgear	330	165	None	Wearing it will make you popular. Elem-Def: Water damage reduced by 50%.
Golden Hairpin	3700	1850	Magic +1, Magic Def +32, Magic Eva +2	Hairpin that holds magic powers. Raises Water Elem-Atk.
Barbut	600	300	Spirit +1, Magic Def +9	Headgear that raises spirit.
Cross Helm	2200	1100	Strength +1, Magic +16	Helm that raises strength.
Thief Hat	7100	3550	Speed +2, Evade +3, Magic Def +38	Hat for theives.

ARMOR

Item	Buy	Sell	Stat Bonuses	Description
Aloha T-Shirt	N/A	9500	None	Provides a southern, tropical feel.
Leather Shirt	270	135	Defense +6	Clothes made of leather.
Silk Shirt	400	200	Defense +7	Silk burns easily. Elem-Def: Thunder damage reduced by 50%.
Leather Plate	530	265	Defense +8	Plate worn for combat. Elem-Def: Ice damage reduced by 50%.
Bronze Vest	670	335	Spirit +1, Defense +9, Magic Def +1	Plate made of bronze.
Chain Plate	810	405	Strength +1, Defense +10	Plate that provides brimming strength.
Cotton Robe	1000	2000	Strength +1, Magic +1, Defense +10, Magic Def +2	Ordinary robe.
Mythril Vest	1180	590	Defense +12	Vest braided with mythril. Elem-Def: Water damage reduced by 50%.
Adaman Vest	1600	800	Defense +14, Magic Def +2	Very durable vest. Elem-Def: Fire damage reduced by 50%.
Magician Cloak	1850	925	Magic +1, Defense +15, Magic Def +2	Cloak that holds magic powers. Raises Ice Elem-Atk.
Silk Robe	2000	2900	Strength +1, Magic +1, Defense +16, Magic Def +2	Robe made of silk.
Survival Vest	2900	1450	Spirit +2, Defense +17	Vest that raises Spirit.
Brigandine	4300	2150	Strength +1, Defense +20	Clothes that raise Strength.
Magician Robe	3000	4000	Magic +2, Defense +21, Magic Def +3	Robe made for mages.
Judo Uniform	5000	2500	Strength +1, Spirit +1, Defense +23	Clothes from a foreign land.
Gaia Gear	8700	4350	Defense +25, Magic Def +2	Robe blessed by the earth god. Absorbs Earth Elem-Atk. Raises Earth Elem-Atk.
Power Vest	7200	3600	Strength +2, Defense +27	Raises Strength.
Demon's Vest	10250	3600	Magic +1, Defense +31	Supposedly, a vest that belonged to a demon. Elem-Def: Shadow damage reduced by 50%.
Ninja Gear	14000	7000	Speed +1, Defense +35	Gear that makes you light-footed. Absorbs Shadow Elem-Atk.
Dark Gear	16300	8150	Spirit +3, Defense +37	Gear that raises Spirit.
Rubber Suit	20000	10000	Defense +39, Evade +2, Magic Eva +3, Magic Def +1	Suit worn by women. Elem-Def: Thunder damage reduced by 100%.
Light Robe	20000	20000	Strength +1, Magic +1, Spirit +1, Defense +41, Magic Def +6	Robe possessed by the spirit of light. Raises Holy/Shadow Elem-Atk.
Glutton's Robe	6000	8000	Strength +1, Magic +1, Defense +41, Magic Def +4	Robe worn by Qus.
White Robe	8000	14500	Magic +2, Defense +42, Magic Def +4	Robe made for white mages. Raises Holy Elem-Atk.

KEYWORD: ARMR2

ABILITIES

What can you learn by equipping these different types of Armor? PlayOnline has all the answers.

PlayOnline.com

Item	Buy	Sell	Stat Bonuses	Description
Black Robe	8000	14500	Magic +2, Defense +43, Magic Def +4	Robe made for black mages. Raises Shadow Elem-Atk.
Robe of Lords	30000	26000	Speed +1, Strength +1, Magic +1, Spirit +1, Defense +46, Magic Def +5	The greatest robe. Elem-Def: Wind damage reduced by 100%.
Bronze Armor	650	325	Defense +9	Armor made of bronze. Elem-Def: Wind damage reduced by 50%.
Linen Cuirass	800	400	Magic +1, Defense +10	Armor packed with magic.
Chain Mail	1200	600	Defense +12	Armor made with chains. Elem-Def: Earth damage reduced by 50%.
Plate Mail	2320	1160	Spirit +1, Defense +17, Magic Def +1	Armor that raises Spirit.
Gold Armor	2950	1475	Magic +1, Defense +19	Armor made of gold.
Shield Armor	4300	2150	Defense +23, Magic Def +5	Armor that provides excellent protection. Elem-Def: Fire/Ice/Thunder damage reduced by 50%.
Demon's Mail	5900	2950	Defense +27	Armor made in the dark world. Absorbs Shadow Elem-Atk. Raises Shadow Elem-Atk.
Diamond Armor	8800	4400	Strength +1, Magic +1, Defense +33, Magic Def +2	Armor made of diamond.
Minerva's Plate	12200	6100	Strength +1, Magic +2, Defense +34, Magic Def +1	Plate worn by women.
Platina Armor	10500	5250	Defense +36	Armor made of platinum. Elem-Def: Ice damage reduced by 100%.
Carabini Mail	12300	6150	Speed +1, Spirit +1, Defense +39, Magic Def +1	Armor protected by extraordinary powers.
Dragon Mail	14000	7000	Strength +1, Magic +1, Defense +42	Armor made from a dragon's scales.
Genji Armor	N/A	1	Magic +2, Defense +45, Magic Def +1	Very famous brand of armor.
Maximillian	N/A	11300	Spirit +3, Defense +54	Armor worn exclusively by knights.
Grand Armor	45000	14000	Strength +1, Defense +59	The greatest armor. Elem-Def: Shadow damage reduced by 50%.
Tin Armor	50000	10	Defense +62, Evade +32, Magic Def +27, Magic Evd +17	Tin armor that looks like a toy.
Brave Suit	26000	11250	Spirit +1, Defense +42	Extremely durable suit. Raises Fire Elem-Atk.
Mythril Armor	1830	915	Defense +15	Armor made of mythril. Elem-Def: Water damage reduced by 50%.

ARM GEAR

Item	Buy	Sell	Stat Bonuses	Description
Pearl Armlet	N/A	490	None	Provides a southern, tropical feel.
Wrist	130	65	Evade +5, Magic Eva +3	Regular wristlet.
Leather Wrist	200	100	Spirit +1, Evade +7, Magic Eva +5	Wristlet that raises Spirit when equipped.
Glass Armlet	250	125	Evade +10, Magic Eva +7	Armlet made of glass. Elem-Def: Water damage reduced by 50%.
Bone Wrist	330	165	Strength +1, Evade +13, Magic Eva +9	Wristlet made from bones. Raises Earth Elem-Atk.
Mythril Armlet	500	250	Spirit +1, Evade +17, Magic Eva +11	Armlet made of mythril.
N-Kai Armlet	3000	1500	Spirit +2, Defense +2, Evade +27	Armlet formerly worn by a ninja.
Jade Armlet	3400	1700	Magic Def +2, Magic Eva +27	Armlet made of jade. Raises Holy Elem-Atk.
Magic Armlet	1000	500	Magic +2, Evade +16, Magic Def +1, Magic Eva +16	Armlet packed with magic.
Chimera Armlet	1200	600	Evade +22, Magic Eva +14	Armlet adorned with Chimera wings. Elem-Def: Holy damage reduced by 100%.
Egoist's Armlet	2000	1000	Evade +20, Magic Eva +20	Armlet made in the dark world. Elem-Def: Shadow damage reduced by 100%.
Dragon Wrist	4800	2400	Spirit +1, Evade +28, Magic Def +1, Magic Eva +12	Wristlet made from dragon bones. Elem-Def: Shadow damage reduced by 50%.
Thief Gloves	50000	25000	Speed +1, Evade +26, Magic Eva +13	Gloves used by thieves.
Power Wrist	5100	2550	Strength +2, Evade +30, Magic Eva +10	Wristlet guard that raises Strength when equipped.
Bronze Gloves	480	240	Spirit +1, Evade +8, Magic Eva +2	Gloves made of bronze.
Mythril Gloves	980	490	Spirit +1, Evade +13, Magic Eva +7	Gloves made of mythril.
Thunder Gloves	1200	600	Evade +16, Magic Eva +10	Gloves with a thunder god's power dwelling inside. Elem-Def: Thunder damage reduced by 50%. Raises Thunder Elem-Atk.
Diamond Gloves	2000	1000	Evade +19, Magic Eva +13	Gloves made of diamond. Elem-Def: Water damage reduced by 100%.

PlayOnline.com

KEYWORD: ARMGR9

ABILITIES

What can your characters learn from this equipment? Go to PlayOnline for all the details.

ARM GEAR

Item	Buy	Sell	Stat Bonuses	Description
Aegis Gloves	7000	3500	Defense +1, Evade +30, Magic Eva +10	Gloves worn exclusively by knights. Nulls Fire damage.
Genji Gloves	N/A	1	Magic +2, Evade +27, Magic Eva +17	Very famous brand of gloves.
Gauntlets	8000	4400	Speed +1, Evade +36, Magic Eva +7	Gloves worn by swordsmen. Elem-Def: Fire/Earth/Water/Wind damage reduced by 50%.
Defense Gloves	6000	3000	Defense +1, Evade +25, Magic Def +1, Magic Eva +20	Protects you from various attacks. Elem-Def: Fire/Ice/Thunder damage reduced by 50%.
Venetia Shield	2800	1400	Strength +1, Magic +1, Evade +17, Magic Def +1, Magic Eva +26	Popular shield among soldiers.
Bracer	24000	4000	Strength +1, Evade +35, Magic Eva +18	Bracer used by gamblers. Raises Wind Elem-Atk.
Silver Gloves	720	360	Evade +10, Magic Eva +5	Combat gloves. Elem-Def: Ice damage reduced by 50%.

ADD-ONS

Item	Buy	Sell	Stat Bonuses	Description
Desert Boots	300	750	Magic +1, Spirit +1, Evade +2	Boots with good traction. Elem-Def: Earth damage reduced by 50%.
Magician Shoes	1500	3750	Magic +2, Magic Eva +6	Shoes packed with magic.
Germinas Boots	900	2000	Strength +1, Evade +2	Boots that raise Strength. Raises Earth Elem-Atk.
Sandals	N/A	600	None	Provides a southern, tropical feel.
Feather Boots	4000	3000	Evade +3	Boots that are light as a feather. Absorbs Earth Elem-Atk.
Battle Boots	6500	10500	Strength +2, Defense +2, Magic Def +1	Combat boots.
Running Shoes	12000	16500	Speed +2, Evade +4, Magic Eva +4	Shoes that enable you to walk with light steps.
Anklet	4000	1600	Magic +3, Spirit +1, Evade +5	Anklet adorned with a four-leaf clover that raises spirit.
Power Belt	2000	3500	Defense +2, Strength +3	Belt that raises Strength.
Black Belt	4000	5500	Strength +2, Spirit +2, Defense +1	Belt that raises Strength. Raises Wind Elem-Atk.
Glass Buckle	500	800	Magic Eva +5, Strength +1, Magic +1, Spirit +2	Buckle protected by mysterious powers.
Madain's Ring	3000	3750	Spirit +2, Magic Def +2	Ring used as a charm since ancient times. Absorbs Ice Elem-Atk.
Rosetta Ring	24000	18000	Defense +1, Evade +2, Magic +1, Magic Def +3, Magic Eva +2	Ring with a fire god's spirit dwelling inside. Absorbs Fire Elem-Atk.
Reflect Ring	7000	3500	Spirit +1, Strength +1, Magic Def +1	Ring enchanted with the spell 'Reflect.'
Coral Ring	1200	2000	Spirit +2, Magic Eva +3	Ring adorned by corals. Absorbs Thunder Elem-Atk.
Promist Ring	6000	4500	Strength +2, Evade +3	Ring that raises Strength.
Rebirth Ring	7000	5000	Spirit +4, Magic Def +2	Ring with a phoenix's power dwelling inside. Raises Holy Elem-Atk.
Protect Ring	40000	20000	Spirit +1, Defense +2, Evade +4, Magic Def +3, Magic Eva +6	Protects you from various attacks. Elem-Def: All elemental damage reduced by 50%.
Pumice Piece	25000	1	Evade +5, Magic +2, Magic Def +1, Strength +2	'Put it together with the other piece.' Absorbs Holy/Shadow Elem-Atk.
Pumice	50000	1	Speed +1, Magic +1, Defense +1, Magic Def +2	'Summon the beast from the dark.'
Yellow Scarf	400	900	Strength +2, Magic Def +1	Scarf that raises Strength.
Gold Choker	1300	2000	Evade +2, Magic +2, Magic Def +1	Magic choker. Elem-Def: Wind damage reduced by 50%. Raises Shadow Elem-Atk.
Fairy Earrings	3200	3000	Evade +4, Magic Eva +2, Spirit +2	Earrings that raise Spirit. Raises Wind Elem-Atk.

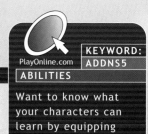

PlayOnline.com

KEYWORD: ADDNS5

ABILITIES

Want to know what your characters can learn by equipping these Add-ons? Log on to PlayOnline for the scoop.

ADD-ONS

Item	Buy	Sell	Stat Bonuses	Description
Angel Earrings	8000	10000	Strength +2, Defense +2	Holy earrings worn by women. Raises Holy Elem-Atk.
Pearl Rouge	5000	2000	Magic Eva +4, Spirit +4, Magic +2	Rouge used by women that draws out Holy power. Elem-Def: Holy damage reduced by 50%. Raises Water Elem-Atk.
Cachusha	1000	1500	Speed +1, Magic +2, Spirit +1, Magic Def +1	Hair ornament enchanted with various powers, worn by women. Raises Fire Elem-Atk.
Barette	1800	3500	Strength +3, Magic +1, Spirit +1, Magic Def +1	Hair ornament enchanted with various powers, worn by women. Raises Ice Elem-Atk.
Extension	3500	5000	Strength +1, Spirit +1, Defense +1, Magic +2, Magic Def +1	Hair ornament enchanted with various powers, worn by women. Raises Thunder Elem-Atk.
Ribbon	N/A	1	Strength +1, Spirit +1, Defense +1, Evade +5, Magic +3, Magic Def +1, Magic Eva +4	Item that always keeps Mog beside you. Absorbs Water/Wind Elem-Atk. Elem-Def: Fire/Ice/Thunder/Holy damage reduced by 50%.
Maiden Prayer	N/A	1	Magic +1, Magic Def +1, Magic Eva +3	Item that has a nice fragrance. Raises Holy Elem-Atk.
Ancient Aroma	N/A	1	Strength +2, Evade +4	Item that radiates a mysterious light. Raises Shadow Elem-Atk.
Garnet	350	1	None	Restores HP. It cannot be used in the field. Equip as an Add-on.
Amethyst	200	1	None	Restores HP. It cannot be used in the field. Equip as an Add-on.
Aquamarine	N/A	1	None	Restores HP. It cannot be used in the field. Equip as an Add-on.
Diamond	N/A	1	None	Restores HP. It cannot be used in the field. Equip as an Add-on.
Emerald	N/A	1	None	Restores HP. It cannot be used in the field. Equip as an Add-on.
Moonstone	N/A	1	None	Restores HP. It cannot be used in the field. Equip as an Add-on.
Ruby	N/A	1	None	Restores HP. It cannot be used in the field. Equip as an Add-on.
Peridot	100	1	None	Restores HP. It cannot be used in the field. Equip as an Add-on.
Sapphire	200	1	None	Restores HP. It cannot be used in the field. Equip as an Add-on.
Opal	100	1	None	Restores HP. It cannot be used in the field. Equip as an Add-on.
Topaz	100	1	None	Restores HP. It cannot be used in the field. Equip as an Add-on.
Lapis Lazuli	400	1	None	Restores HP. It cannot be used in the field. Equip as an Add-on.
Phoenix Pinion	300	1000	None	Cures KO. It cannot be used in the field.
Dark Matter	N/A	1	Strength +3, Magic +2	Deals damage to the target. Equip as an Add-on.

TETRA MASTER

The official name of the card game is Tetra Master. Many people all over the world play Tetra Master. The only way to find out who plays is by challenging them. Tetra Master players never back down from a challenge. To challenge people, walk up to them and press the Square button. If you challenge a person who isn't a player, he or she will probably just talk to you.

You need to know how to play the card game to finish *FINAL FANTASY IX*, since you must compete and become a finalist in the Treno Card Tournament event. You can find cards in hidden treasure chests throughout the game, and you receive them after defeating monsters. Not all monsters will yield their own card after a battle; some monsters drop the card of another monster after a battle.

CARD BASICS

Describing Tetra Master is actually more complicated than playing it! When the card game begins, you must select five cards to play. You can't play the game unless you have at least five cards. You should choose cards based on the number of arrows they have, and by the statistics shown on the card. Both features of cards are explained later.

After selecting five cards, a 4x4 grid appears. Anywhere from 0 to 6 tiles on the game table can be blocked off, preventing you and your opponent from placing a card there. A coin toss determines whether you or your opponent goes first.

PlayOnline.com

KEYWORD: TETRMST5

CARD GAME BASICS

Tetra Master can be a bit tricky to learn. If you need some help, PlayOnline has it covered.

CARD STATISTICS

Each card has a combination of four letters and numbers on it. These numbers and letters display the strength of the card, and determine which card wins in a card battle.

- The first number is the card's attack power in hexadecimal, from 0 to E, with E being the highest.
- The second statistic is the card's attack type. P is Physical, M is Magical, X attacks the lowest defense number, and A attacks the lowest number on the card.
- The third number is the card's physical defense in hexadecimal. The fourth number is the card's magical defense in hexadecimal.

When two cards battle, the newly-placed card attacks using the attack number (the first stat on the card) and the attack type (the second stat on the card). The newly-placed card's attack number is compared to the corresponding defense number on the enemy card. The card with the highest number usually wins, although there is a small chance that a weaker card can still beat a stronger card.

You can raise the statistics on some cards by playing with the same cards over and over and winning numerous Tetra Master games with them.

CARD INVENTORY

You can view your catalog of cards at any time by selecting the Card option from the Main Menu. You can never carry more than 100 cards. You should always discard weaker cards in the hopes of finding stronger or "rare" cards. A weaker card is one that has few arrows and low stats.

If you end up with more than 100 cards after a game of cards, you must throw away cards of your choice until you have 100. If you want to collect all 100 unique cards, you can only carry one of each card.

RARE CARDS

KEYWORD: NAMWAY7
RARE CARD
Want to find a rare card? Go to PlayOnline to find out where it's located.

There are some very rare cards you can only obtain by searching certain areas of the game. If you pass up these opportunities, then you may not be able to collect all 100 cards.

You can find rare cards in other ways, such as by uncovering treasure chests during the Chocograph side quest.

KEYWORD: CRDMST2
CARD MASTERS
Looking for the elusive Card Masters? PlayOnline will point you in the right direction.

There are also rare cards to obtain for various weapons, towns, airships, for most of the Eidolons, and for several of the Boss monsters and the rare items.

COLLECTOR'S RANK

As you collect cards, you gain prestige as a Tetra Master player. This is measured by your Collector's Rank, a number between 0-1700 that is viewable in the Card menu.

KEYWORD: CARDTPS3
CARD TIPS
Looking for a few good card tips? PlayOnline has the answers you're looking for!

To get the maximum number of collector's points, you must collect or capture one of every card type, and each card must have a unique arrow arrangement. You must also play with each card enough times until they all level up to attack type A.

CARD LISTING

The following section summarizes all of the cards in Tetra Master. For convenience, we've listed them by the columns in which they appear on the card sub-screen.

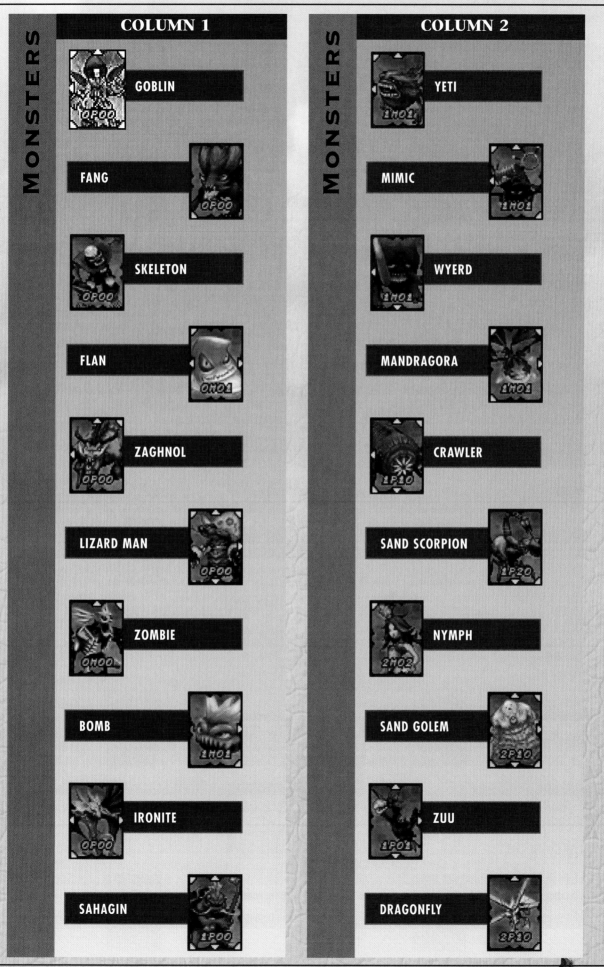

MONSTERS

COLUMN 1

GOBLIN

FANG

SKELETON

FLAN

ZAGHNOL

LIZARD MAN

ZOMBIE

BOMB

IRONITE

SAHAGIN

MONSTERS

COLUMN 2

YETI

MIMIC

WYERD

MANDRAGORA

CRAWLER

SAND SCORPION

NYMPH

SAND GOLEM

ZUU

DRAGONFLY

COLUMN 3

 CARRION WORM

CERBERUS

 ANTLION

CACTUAR

 GIMME CAT

RAGTIMER

 HEDGEHOG PIE

RALVUIMAHGO

 OCHU

TROLL

COLUMN 4

 BLAZER BEETLE

ABOMINATION

 ZEMZELETT

STROPER

 TANTARIAN

GRAND DRAGON

 FEATHER CIRCLE

HECTEYES

 OGRE

ARMSTRONG

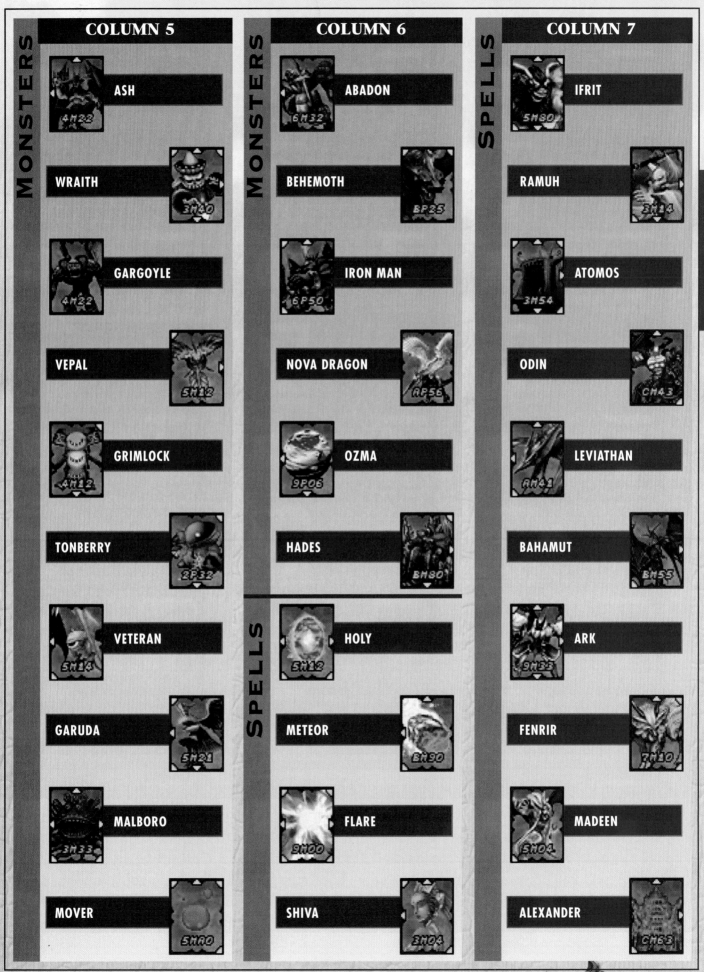

COLUMN 5

MONSTERS

ASH — 4M22

WRAITH — 3M40

GARGOYLE — 4M22

VEPAL — 5M12

GRIMLOCK — 4M12

TONBERRY — 2P32

VETERAN — 5M14

GARUDA — 5M21

MALBORO — 3M33

MOVER — 5M00

COLUMN 6

MONSTERS

ABADON — 6M32

BEHEMOTH — 8P25

IRON MAN — 6P50

NOVA DRAGON — 8P56

OZMA — 9P05

HADES — 8M80

SPELLS

HOLY — 5M12

METEOR — 8M90

FLARE — 8M00

SHIVA — 3M04

COLUMN 7

SPELLS

IFRIT — 5M80

RAMUH — 3M14

ATOMOS — 3M54

ODIN — CM43

LEVIATHAN — AM41

BAHAMUT — BM55

ARK — 8M33

FENRIR — 7M10

MADEEN — 5M04

ALEXANDER — CM63

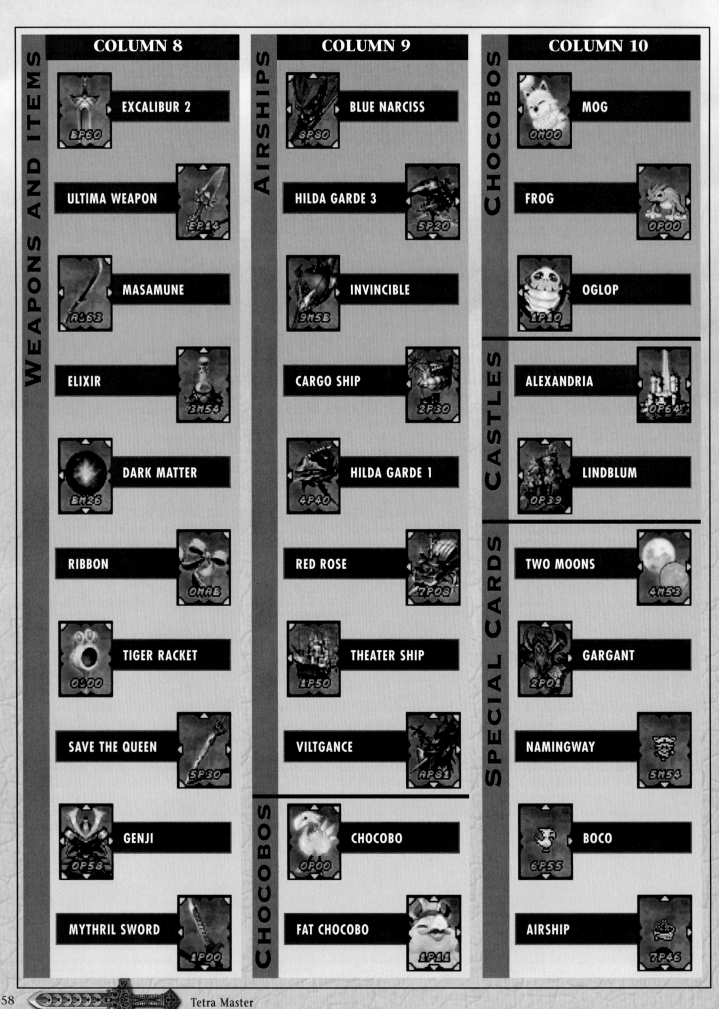

WEAPONS AND ITEMS

COLUMN 8	
EXCALIBUR 2	8P60
ULTIMA WEAPON	EP14
MASAMUNE	8M63
ELIXIR	3M54
DARK MATTER	8M26
RIBBON	0MAB
TIGER RACKET	0800
SAVE THE QUEEN	8P30
GENJI	0P58
MYTHRIL SWORD	1P00

AIRSHIPS

COLUMN 9	
BLUE NARCISS	8P30
HILDA GARDE 3	8P20
INVINCIBLE	9M5B
CARGO SHIP	2P30
HILDA GARDE 1	4P40
RED ROSE	7P08
THEATER SHIP	1P50
VILTGANCE	AP81

CHOCOBOS

CHOCOBO	0P00
FAT CHOCOBO	1P11

CHOCOBOS

COLUMN 10	
MOG	0M00
FROG	0P00
OGLOP	1P10

CASTLES

ALEXANDRIA	0P64
LINDBLUM	0P39

SPECIAL CARDS

TWO MOONS	4M53
GARGANT	2P01
NAMINGWAY	5M54
BOCO	6P55
AIRSHIP	7P46

WALKTHROUGH

Walkthrough

PRIMA VISTA AIRSHIP

ENEMIES:
BAKU

ITEMS:
POTION

CARDS:
NONE

OBJECTIVES

Defeat Baku in the Dragon's mask

BAKU'S CREW

As the Prima Vista soars over the city of Alexandria preparing to land, our hero Zidane enters the lower cabin. After striking a match, walk around the cabin and explore the surroundings to find some goodies. When you're finished, light the candle on the table.

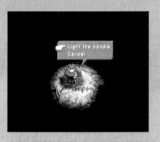

When Baku leaps at his crew in a Dragon mask, you will command a party of four characters. Order each of them to attack, with the exception of Cinna. Make Cinna steal from Baku instead.

KEYWORD:
RUBY1

SECRET

Wonder what would happen if you answer Baku's question incorrectly? PlayOnline will explain everything.

ALEXANDRIA

KEY ITEMS:
TICKET

ITEMS:
POTION (X7), PHOENIX PINION, ETHER, EYE DROPS, TENT, REMEDY

CARDS:
FANG (X3), ZOMBIE, LIZARD MAN, SAHAGIN, GOBLIN (X3), FLAN, SKELETON, IRONITE, BOMB

OBJECTIVES

Show Vivi's ticket at the booth

Help steal Dante's ladder

Give the crowd a good show

Impress the Queen with your stunts

A Little Lost...

The young black mage named Vivi seems a little lost in Alexandria. You'll need a few tips to get your bearings, and you can greatly boost your inventory in no time at all by searching every nook and cranny.

This town is full of all kinds of items and extra Gil, so explore the area fully and leave no stone unturned. (Refer to the Items list at the beginning of this section for a complete list of the items available in this area.) Make sure you scour the landscape, and don't forget to go indoors to visit the locals. There may be a few items to pick up there as well.

When you're done exploring, travel back the way Vivi came into Memorial Square. Search around the outer perimeter to find a **Zombie Card**, a **Lizard Man Card**, and a **Sahagin Card**. Return to Vivi's path and continue upward through the streets.

In the areas where the nobles are marching off, search in the grass close to the screen to uncover a **Goblin Card**. Then duck inside the Morning Star Bar and search for a **Flan Card** and some additional stuff for your inventory.

Continuing into the next section, talk to Mick about Vivi's **Ticket**. Also, pay a visit to Doug's Item Shop. You can purchase items for your inventory if Vivi's stock isn't up to par.

The ticket booth is in the center of Alexandria's Main Square. This is where Vivi learns that his ticket is a fake. The Ticketmaster feels bad and gives Vivi **Goblin**, **Fang**, and **Skeleton Cards** in return. You also learn about a person named "Alleyway Jack," who knows a great deal about cards.

The building on the far right side of Alexandria Square is a Synthesist. You can't create any new weapons at this time but make sure you thoroughly search the area before leaving. The weapons smiths are in the connecting room, but they don't seem to be selling to Vivi either.

Mischief Afoot

While running down the alley, Vivi suddenly trips and falls causing a nearby handyman to quit for the day. When the rat-boy Puck offers to get Vivi in to see the show, you have a choice of accompanying him as his "slave" or refusing him. If you feel that you've explored the town enough and have found all of the items, accept his offer. Once you agree to be his slave, Puck then steals the ladder, and leads Vivi to an old bell tower.

KEYWORD: JUMPRP1
PlayOnline.com
MINI-GAME

Those girls look like they're having fun jumping rope. You might receive a reward for exceptional jumping skills. Refer to PlayOnline for all the details.

KEYWORD: HIPCDS1
PlayOnline.com
SPECIAL ITEM

If you decide to refuse Puck, you'll be treated to a little secret, courtesy of Hippaul. To find out what it's all about, the details are listed at PlayOnline.

MUGGER, ...OR CARD GURU?!

*Don't remain in the alley too long after Puck runs off; you could get mugged and lose some Gil. However, if you speak to this person before he mugs you, you'll find that you've discovered "Alleyway Jack"! A brief tutorial follows, where the card game "Tetra Master" is explained. This game is also explored in the **Tetra Master** section of this book. Alleyway Jack also lets you play him, and your chances to defeat him and gain a strong card are extremely good.*

As you head for the bell tower, make sure you go inside each area and explore. You don't want to pass up any extra items or Gil and you'll definitely find some in this area.

Inside the bell tower, Puck and Vivi bump into the friendly moogles named Kupo and Stiltzkin. The moogles found throughout the game enable you to save your game or use Tents to rest up and restore your HP and MP. Kupo also has a letter that needs to be delivered to Monty. Offer to deliver letters for the Mognet, and purchase items from Stiltzkin whenever he appears. After exploring the area, join Puck at the top of the tower.

Puck leads Vivi across the rooftops of Alexandria. Don't rush to catch up, but instead take the time to search the chimneys off the path to find a few stashes of Gil. As Vivi and Puck make it inside the castle, the play begins!

KEYWORD: MITTEN1
SPECIAL ITEM
PlayOnline.com
There is a boy at the docks who has lost his pet. PlayOnline can show you how the search can be worth your while.

PERFORMANCE OF A LIFETIME

During Tantalus' performance, Zidane and the gang fight Baku and the others. They come equipped with Special Effects (SFX) to liven up the event, although these amazing pyrotechnics cause no damage. Eliminate the two guards immediately. Baku proves to be a bit tougher, though.

Next up, Blank and Zidane begin a choreographed stage fight. You must follow Blank's lead by pushing the buttons he tells you to push—very quickly. Accuracy and speed are both factors in how well things go.

After the stage fight, the audience approval is tallied. The number of nobles impressed by the stage fight dictates whether or not the Queen is impressed as well. Luckily, you can try this event over and over until you are satisfied with your score. It's definitely a good idea to do your best on your first try though.

KEYWORD: QUEENS1
SPECIAL ITEM
PlayOnline.com
Wowing the crowd has a second effect that Steiner may benefit from. Check PlayOnline for the details.

ALEXANDRIA CASTLE

ENEMIES:
STEINER

ITEMS:
PHOENIX DOWN (x2),
ELIXIR, PHOENIX PINION

CARDS:
NONE

OBJECTIVES

Find the Princess

Search for the
Knights of Pluto

Join forces to stop Steiner

THE ELUSIVE PRINCESS

Kidnapping Princess Garnet is the goal of the next segment, but the little lady is more than a handful! To locate her, run straight up the steps.

When the Queen learns of Garnet's disappearance, Captain Steiner of the Knights of Pluto is ordered to find the Princess. As Steiner, the objective is to rally the guards under him and search for Garnet. However, the Knights of Pluto aren't exactly a tip-top outfit, so as Steiner you must be forceful to get things going! Check the registry on the wall in the Guardhouse to learn the names of all of the Knights of Pluto. Then, conduct a thorough search of Alexandria Castle to locate each of the knights.

PlayOnline.com

KEYWORD:
KOPS1

SPECIAL ITEM

The personality traits of the various knights will come into play later. Find out where at PlayOnline.

THE QUEEN'S TEMPER

At the top of the tower, Steiner spots Zidane chasing the Princess. Now, controlling Zidane, you must pursue Garnet through the Prima Vista.

Lead the princess through the hold and back up to the stage. After a stunning stage show, Garnet's true identity is revealed to all by an unfortunate act.

STEINER

BOSS FIGHT

HP	169, 162, 167, 1867	AP	N/A	Weak vs.	N/A
Steal Items	Leather Hat, Silk Shirt			**Spoils**	None

This fight consists of three separate confrontations, resulting in an explosive finish. This fight really isn't that difficult, so to make it through unscathed follow these suggestions.

BATTLE TACTICS #1 (ON PRIMA VISTA):

- Have Zidane and Blank concentrate on attacking
- Make Cinna steal on every round

BATTLE TACTICS #2 (ON STAGE):

- Focus Zidane and Marcus on attacking Steiner every round
- Use Vivi's magic ability
- When necessary, have Garnet act as the party's medic

BATTLE TACTICS #3 (ON STAGE):

- Follow the same tactics as described for Battle Tactics #2 (use Zidane and Marcus to attack; cast Vivi's Fire ability; use Garnet to heal)

PlayOnline.com

KEYWORD: BOMBOS1

BOSS FIGHT TIPS

If you're still having trouble with this Boss, check out PlayOnline for further details.

EVIL FOREST

ENEMIES:	ITEMS:	ITEMS:	CARDS:
FANG, GOBLIN, PRISON CAGE, DENDROBIUM, PLANT BRAIN (BOSS), PLANT SPIDER	PHOENIX DOWN, BRONZE GLOVES, ETHER (X3), LEATHER HAT, RUBBER HELM, POTION, WRIST	BLANK'S MEDICINE, CONTINENTAL MAP	NONE

OBJECTIVES

1 Search for the missing princess

2 Save Garnet and Vivi from the Prison Cage

3 Reassure Vivi

4 Quit Tantalus

5 Match blows with Baku

6 Recruit Steiner and Vivi

7 Find the master of the Evil Forest

8 Escape the petrifying woods

RISING FROM THE WRECKAGE

The Prima Vista crash-lands in a rather nasty region called Evil Forest. After Zidane rejoins the troupe, you can't re-enter the ship, so make sure you search everywhere outside the ship. Because of the violent nature of the wreck, some items may have be thrown outside. Now it's time to search for the missing characters by equipping Zidane with the best armor pieces available.

ATE, Kupo!

Mosco the moogle introduces the concept of the "Active Time Event." This is a new feature in the FINAL FANTASY® series, whereby you view scenes occurring in other locales involving characters that are not currently in your party. When the words "ACTIVE TIME EVENT" flash in the bottom-left corner of the screen, press the SELECT button to watch the event(s). If there is more than one ATE, you can view them in whatever order you want. Some ATEs are optional, as indicated by flashing blue words, but you must view some ATEs to advance the game.

THE DANGEROUS WOODS

When you're ready to search the Evil Forest, head through the hollow tree. Zidane will most likely encounter some Fangs and Goblins on his own, but they won't pose much of a threat to the powerful Zidane. If your inventory is rather thin, make sure you steal from each enemy.

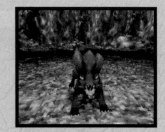

Not far into the woods, Zidane finds Vivi and Steiner watching as Garnet gets attacked by some strange forest monster. The two rivals will team up to take on the wretched plant.

PlayOnline.com
KEYWORD: PRISCG1
BOSS FIGHT TIPS

Can't seem to crack this Boss's fighting techniques? PlayOnline has all the answers.

PRISON CAGE

BOSS FIGHT

HP 513, 533		AP 3		Weak vs. Fire
Steal Items	Leather Wrist, Broadsword		**Spoils**	Phoenix Down, Eye Drops, Goblin Card

This battle consists of two fights, the first of which takes place with Zidane and Steiner.

BATTLE TACTICS #1:

- Once Zidane goes into Trance, use his ability

- With Garnet held captive, this Boss drains her HP so hit it with everything you have

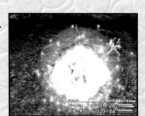

BATTLE TACTICS #2:

- During the second part of the fight, Vivi is held captive by the Prison Cage. Vivi casts Fire each round against the Boss

- Use Steiner to attack the Boss, and have Zidane focus on stealing items

QUITTING THE CREW

Back onboard the wrecked Prima Vista, Zidane decides to go looking for the Princess. However, Baku won't let Zidane go that easily. After the captain finishes lecturing, scour the bridge of the ship looking for items.

After Blank emerges from Vivi's room, go in and speak to the mage. Outside Vivi's room, Zidane must decide whether to quit Tantalus and go searching for Garnet. Whichever option you choose, Zidane will search for her, but it's fun to see how the two different choices affect the dialogue.

Go down into the hold into the meeting room, where Baku will accept Zidane's dismissal. However, Zidane must face Baku in one-on-one combat before he can leave!

BOSS FIGHT

BAKU

HP	150	AP	N/A	Weak vs.	N/A
Steal Items	Hi-Potion, Iron Sword			**Spoils**	None

BATTLE TACTICS:

- Make sure you attempt to steal items from Baku
- Alternate attacks with attempts at thievery
- Use Potions if Zidane's HP gets too low

PlayOnline.com
KEYWORD:
BAKUFI1
BOSS FIGHT TIPS

You can find more extensive coverage of the Baku Boss fight at PlayOnline.

AN UNEASY ALLIANCE

Now that Zidane is free to go, return to the room in which Steiner is being held. Steiner joins your party, albeit hesitantly. Then make sure you fully equip Steiner with good items that will let him learn some abilities. Also, make sure he has a powerful weapon. If you were adept at stealing during the Baku Boss fight, you will have a nice addition to add to Steiner's arsenal.

When Vivi joins your party, equip the mage with a Leather Wrist and a Silk Shirt if you have them. By doing so, Vivi can add to his somewhat thin magic casting abilities. On your way out of the hold, Blank gives Zidane **Blank's Medicine** to use on the Princess when you rescue her. Before leaving, however, make sure you thoroughly search the room for any spare items.

If your inventory is low, make a few purchases from Cinna, but otherwise make sure you save your game before traveling through the forest.

Eventually, the party enters a small clearing where a crystal-clear pond will fully restore HP and MP. Also, Monty the moogle is hiding in a hollow tree stump nearby, so give him the letter from Kupo and save your game if desired.

KEYWORD:
PLNTBR1

BOSS FIGHT TIPS

This is one tough Boss fight, but additional fighting techniques await you at PlayOnline.

PLANT BRAIN

BOSS FIGHT

HP 916	AP 20	Weak vs. Fire
Steal Items Iron Helm, Eye Drops		**Spoils** Phoenix Down

Not far after the save point is the cavern of Plant Brain, which holds the unconscious Princess Garnet captive. This is by far the most difficult Boss fight at this point in the game, so come prepared!

BOSS PREPARATIONS:

- Equip Steiner with the Iron Sword (if available)
- Equip Vivi with a Leather Wrist and a Silk Shirt (if available)

BATTLE TACTICS:

- Have Steiner and Vivi use their strongest attacks; use all of his MP to perform the Fire Sword magic attack
- Keep your party's HP up
- Alternate Zidane between attacking and stealing
- When the Plant Brain performs its Pollen attack, have the unaffected party member, if any, use Eye Drops to cure the Darkness status

A DESPERATE ESCAPE

While the heroes attempt to flee the forest, they will encounter some Plant Spiders on occasion. They don't pose much of a threat, so dispose of them quickly.

Blank saves the rest of the party, and throws the **Continental Map** to Zidane. This item will allow the party to mark important locations on the World Map, so that travel in the large areas beyond will be easier. You can view the Continental Map while the party is on the World Map by pressing the SELECT button.

GUNITAS BASIN/MELDA PLAINS

ENEMIES:	KEY ITEMS:	ITEMS:	CARDS:
GOBLIN, PYTHON, MU	NONE	POTION, EYE DROPS	NONE

OBJECTIVES

1 Learn Abilities while roaming the plains

2 Visit the east side of North Gate

3 Prepare to enter the Ice Cavern

FREE ROAMING

After a brief tutorial given by some friendly moogles, your party is ready to cross an open area called the Gunitas Basin in search of the legendary Ice Cavern. This is an easy trip, because the Ice Cavern is almost directly south of the petrified Evil Forest.

However, rather than proceeding directly to the Ice Cavern, you should explore the area around the basin. As you explore, you'll randomly encounter monsters and when this occurs make sure you have Zidane try to steal some items to add to your inventory. This will help you improve your inventory, learn Abilities, and level up your party members so that they can handle the creatures in the Ice Cavern. When you feel your party's strength is sufficient, save your game before you enter.

WORLD MAP NAVIGATION

Button	What It Does
X	Enter buildings/area; ride a vehicle
Square	Calls a moogle
SELECT	Toggles navigation map
L1, R1	Camera control
L2	Locks/unlocks camera rotation
R2	Switches perspective

THE NORTH GATE

The eastern side of the North Gate is to the far west of the Ice Cavern's entrance. Upon entering the area, approach the door and an icon should appear over Zidane's head.

You can select from the following options: "Listen close/Call out to someone inside/Buy some medicine from her." Also, make sure you explore the area completely. It's important to visit all the gates in the world so you can pick up free items, even if there's not much going on there.

ICE CAVERN

ENEMIES:
FANG, WYERD, CAVE IMP, FLAN, BLACK WALTZ No.1 (BOSS), SEALION (BOSS)

KEY ITEMS:
NONE

ITEMS:
POTION (X2), TENT, ETHER, ELIXIR, LEATHER WRIST, PHOENIX DOWN, MAGE MASHER

CARDS:
NONE

OBJECTIVES

Thaw the frozen treasure chests

Defrost the moogle

Fight a supernatural enemy... alone.

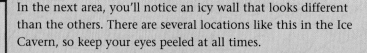

WINTER WONDERLAND

Great dangers lurk within this winter wonderland. Follow the frozen path upward into an area with a fork in the path.

In the next area, you'll notice an icy wall that looks different than the others. There are several locations like this in the Ice Cavern, so keep your eyes peeled at all times.

MONSTERS OF THE ICE

All of the creatures in the Ice Cavern are extremely sensitive to fire. Use Vivi's Fire spell and Steiner's Fire SWD MAG to quicken battles before your enemies gain the upper hand. The monsters have powerful abilities that drastically reduce your characters' HP and can even put them to sleep. They won't hesitate to use these abilities if you're not swift and merciless in your battles.

In the next chamber, explore everything and make sure you pick up all of the items in the treasure chests. When you're finished exploring, follow the path into the next area.

KEYWORD:
PlayOnline.com **ICECAV1**
SPECIAL ITEM

Vivi will be helpful in expanding your inventory in this area. PlayOnline can tell you how.

Disc One

Pick up the goodies in the next area, and then head onward until you reach a fork in the road. By all means, head to the left first because this takes you to a frozen moogle named Mois. Save your game and use a Tent if needed, because a difficult trial is up ahead.

This time take the right path. After the group is mysteriously put to sleep, follow the sound of the ringing bell to reach the source of the sudden blizzard at the top of the slope.

BOSS FIGHT

BLACK WALTZ No.1/SEALION

HP	229, 472		AP	5		Weak vs.	Fire (both)

Steal Items	Black Waltz No.1: Silk Shirt, Remedy	Spoils	Hi-Potion, Phoenix Down, Fang Card

Sealion: Mythril Dagger, Ether

The insidious Black Waltz immediately summons the titanic Sealion into battle. The enemies cast Fire and Blizzard spells at Zidane, so take Potions whenever his HP gets around 100 or so. If Zidane dies, the Game Over screen appears as your only reward.

BATTLE TACTICS:

- Make sure Zidane has his best weapon and armor equipped

- When Zidane goes into Trance, hit the Sealion with Tidal Flame to cause big damage

KEYWORD:
BWALTZ1
BOSS FIGHT TIPS
You can find additional Boss strategy at PlayOnline.

NORLICH HEIGHTS

ENEMIES:
CARVE SPIDER, PYTHON

KEY ITEMS:
MINI-PRIMA VISTA

ITEMS:
HI-POTION

CARDS:
NONE

OBJECTIVES

1

Fight your way across the highlands

2

Visit the nice folks at South Gate

3

Introduce yourself to Morrid

4

Head to Dali for some R&R

HIGH ABOVE THE MIST

The neighboring village to the Ice Cavern is called Dali, but it's not as close as it looks. Your party must cross a treacherous area full of monsters and random battles. It's at this point in the game that Garnet decides to use a different name.

THE SOUTH GATE

After speaking with the guard, you learn that you can't pass through without the Gate Pass, a Key Item that you won't find until later on. If you go through all of the guard's options at least once, even if you cancel an option, then Part-time Worker Mary appears and offers to sell your crew medicines.

KEYWORD: MORRID1
SIDE QUESTS

Keep Morrid in mind as you continue the game, and bring back what he asks for later in the game. Check out PlayOnline for all the information.

THE OLD MAN AND THE TOWER

Before heading into the village, check out the strange mountain close to the edge of the plain and find the old fellow named Morrid. He offers you a sweet deal for some rare coffees.

VILLAGE OF DALI

ENEMIES:	KEY ITEMS:	ITEMS:	CARDS:
GHOST, VICE, BLACK WALTZ NO.2 (BOSS)	ARIES STELLAZZIO	POTION (X4), ANTIDOTE, EYE DROPS, ETHER, IRON HELM, LEATHER WRIST, PHOENIX DOWN, PHOENIX PINION	NONE

OBJECTIVES

1 Spend the night at the Dali Inn

2 Meet Vivi in the morning

3 Find Dagger at the shop

4 Return to the Inn to wait for the others.

5 Search for Vivi

6 Find the underground hatch

7

8

9

Rescue Vivi from confinement

Follow the trail of eggs

Protect the Princess from the floating evil

SUSPICIOUS ACTIVITY

After spending the night at the Dali Inn, Zidane wakes up to find that everyone else has wandered off. Explore the room for some items, and then head out to find everyone.

Although Dali is rather small, there are all kinds of different places to visit. Make sure you stock up on items at the shops, and search everywhere for other hidden items or useful bits of information.

As you explore the town, you come to realize that something isn't quite right in this town. Dagger's at Eve's shop now; talk to her and return to the Inn after the encounter.

Q PlayOnline.com
KEYWORD: STELLA1
SPECIAL ITEM

If you've been collecting the various Stellazzios in the game, you can find another one in Dali. For the exact location, please refer to PlayOnline.

Return to the Inn to speak with Dagger again. Now it's time to look for the missing Vivi. Leave the Inn and head toward the windmill, where you discover that Vivi is underground. Enter the windmill and open the hatch to go down below.

DARK BUSINESS

Take the lift down and proceed up the passage until Zidane and Dagger overhear two men talking about Vivi. As they lead the little mage off, search everywhere because there are plenty of things to add to your inventory.

Follow Vivi's captors through a corridor, and then search the barrel to speak with Kumop the moogle. Take a moment to save your game, because things are going to get a little tricky ahead!

In the room with a strange machine, Dagger and Zidane discover that Vivi has been stored in a coffin-like box. Before continuing, go ahead and enter the door to the top.

Q PlayOnline.com
KEYWORD: MISTMA1
SPECIAL ITEM

There are some really good items to retrieve in this area. To find out where, check out PlayOnline.

After some mishaps and blunders, the three party members find themselves bound for shipping on a Cargo Airship. Luckily, Steiner is poking around and his nose leads him to the rescue just in time! However, the heroes aren't out of the woods yet; another Black Waltz appears, threatening to destroy the crew and kidnap the Princess!

BLACK WALTZ NO.2

BOSS FIGHT

HP 1030		**AP** 5		**Weak vs.** Fire
Steal Items	Steepled Hat, Leather Plate		**Spoils**	Ether, Zaghnol Card

The evil one's goal is to knock out your entire party and hypnotize the Princess. It's crucial that you come to this battle properly prepared. Take a look at the following Battle Preparation for some help:

BOSS PREPARATIONS:

- Equip Vivi with the Leather Wrist

BATTLE TACTICS:

- Use Vivi's Blizzard magic or Steiner's Blizzard Sword
- Have Dagger serve as your medic by casting Cure and Protect when necessary
- Black Waltz No. 2 will retaliate against types of magic other than Blizzard

Following the battle, take Dagger's advice and go rest at the Inn. The Airship will still be there when you're ready to continue. If you move onwards now, you will proceed directly to another Boss fight without collecting any new items or healing your party.

KEYWORD: BWALTZ2

PlayOnline.com

BOSS FIGHT TIPS

For additional Boss fight tactics, refer to PlayOnline.

DALI VILLAGE SHOP INVENTORY

EVE'S ITEM SHOP	
Item	Gil
Dagger	320
Mage Masher	500
Broadsword	330
Iron Sword	660
Rod	260
Mage Staff	320
Wrist	130
Leather Wrist	200
Bronze Gloves	480
Leather Hat	150
Feather Hat	200
Rubber Helm	250
Bronze Helm	330
Leather Shirt	270
Silk Shirt	400
Bronze Armor	650

TAVERN MEDICINE SHOP	
Item	Gil
Potion	50
Phoenix Down	150
Antidote	50
Eye Drops	50
Tent	800

CARGO AIRSHIP

ENEMIES:	KEY ITEMS:	ITEMS:	CARDS:
BLACK WALTZ NO.3 (BOSS)	NONE	NONE	NONE

OBJECTIVES

Board the Cargo
Airship

Head for the Bridge

Dance with the
final Black Waltz

IT'S GONNA BE A BUMPY RIDE...

Return to the airfield and board the vessel, and lead Zidane up to the ladder at the front of the engine room. Then go up to the deck to find Steiner.

When you enter the ship's bridge, Zidane takes over and turns the ship around. Looks like the rest of this adventure should be smooth sailing—but that's hardly the case. As the Cargo Ship heads toward Lindblum, the ship is tracked by the most powerful of the black mages.

KEYWORD: BWALTZ3

PlayOnline.com

BOSS FIGHT TIPS

For more Boss fight strategy, check out PlayOnline.

BLACK WALTZ NO.3

BOSS FIGHT

HP	1128	AP	???	Weak vs.	Thunder
Steal Items	Steepled Hat, Linen Cuirass, Silver Gloves			**Spoils**	None

BATTLE TACTICS:

- When Vivi Trances, cast two consecutive magic spells
- Use Steiner's Thunder Sword
- When Black Waltz No. 3 floats, have Zidane concentrate on stealing and curing the party.

LINDBLUM GRAND CASTLE

ENEMIES:
Fang, Mu, Zaghnol

KEY ITEMS:
Kupo Nut, Mini-Burmecia, Autograph, Moogle Suit

ITEMS:
Glass Armlet, Ether, Hi-Potion, Echo Screen, Tent (x2), Leather Plate, Silver Gloves, Ore, Leather Wrist, Bronze Vest, Steepled Hat

CARDS:
Mimic, Wyerd

OBJECTIVES

1
Follow Minister Artania into the castle

2
Appeal to Regent Cid

3
Catch up on old times with Freya

4
Explore the city's shops and find freebies

5
Synthesize necessary weapons

6
Check in at the Tantalus theatre

7
Join Lowell's fan club... momentarily

8
Search for Dagger at the castle

9
Take the sleepy guard's uniform

10
Ride the lift to the Upper Level

11
Find Dagger at the overlook

12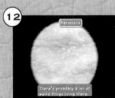
Use the telescope to mark locations

13
Win the Festival of the Hunt

14
Prepare to depart for Burmecia

THE CASTLE CITY

After disembarking the Cargo Airship, follow Minister Artania through the castle's lobby to the lift. Pay close attention to Artania, so you can grasp something about the layout of this awesome city. You're then escorted into the chambers of Regent Cid.

While lunch is served, Zidane heads into the Industrial District and runs into Freya, an old comrade in arms hailing from the nearby kingdom of Burmecia.

Later, Zidane wakes up the next day at the Business District Inn. Head into the next room to speak to the moogle Moodon, who has a letter from Ruby. Also, make sure you explore the Inn thoroughly. Maybe one of the Inn's former guests may have lost something.

Although Zidane's goal is to head to the Theater District to visit the Tantalus hideout, there are some great benefits in fully searching the rest of the city beforehand. A brief description of those areas is detailed in the following section.

Directly across from the Inn is the air cab terminal, where cars wait to take you to Lindblum Castle, the Industrial District, or the Theater District. At the bottom of the screen is the Hunter's Gate, but if you head the other way down the street, past the Inn and the air cab terminal, you'll reach the market square.

Positioned around the market are several vendors, including an action figure stand. The door next to Ivan's Fish Shack leads upstairs into Card Freak Gon's house. He's very sharp, so only take him on if you've been playing the card game rather

regularly up to this point. Take a moment to check out the various volumes on his bookshelves. Different ones are on display at different points in the game.

The church is down the street beyond Gon's house. Don't forget to explore the area before returning to the market square. Upon returning to the market square, take the right-hand street to keep exploring.

KEYWORD: TORRES1
PlayOnline.com
POWERFUL WEAPON

You'll have a chance to upgrade your armor and weaponry here. Find out where and how at PlayOnline.

The second street from the market square leads to a mall with a large sundial fountain. On the right side is the Dragoos Armory, where you can buy a variety of new and familiar weapons, armor, and accessories. (For a complete inventory list, see the end of this section.) The store at the top of the mall is Alice's Item Shop, where Vivi acquires a **Kupo Nut**.

THE INDUSTRIAL DISTRICT

This smaller area of Lindblum is where most of the city's airship engineers dwell. Some businesses once existed here, but they all pulled out and moved into the more lucrative Business District, such as Dragoos' Shop.

There are various items scattered about the area, so before you go too far, make sure you scour the area. Don't forget to speak to Marolo, who's behind the statue of Cid VIII. This guy enjoys to debate, so take part in the fun and take his side for now to make him happy.

Head up the stairs into the next section, where you'll come across Bobo's familiar dive. There's a house in the back of this neighborhood, wherein Ludruff the engineer is working on

a prototype steam engine. There's not much else to do in the Industrial District; it's really just a cozy neighborhood. Return to the air cab and ride to the Theater District now.

THE THEATER DISTRICT

There's a boy in the Theater District named Tim who knows that most of the people in the Theater District play cards. So, brush the dust off your deck and challenge a few folks, because there are some rare cards to win.

Continue down the steps to a building marked with a clock. This is the Tantalus troupe's playhouse, but no one's home. Zidane will park it and wait for a bit. After resting up, Zidane has a brief discussion with the kids Lucella and Bunce, who suggest that he search for the princess. Now that we know where she is, that's not too much of a problem. Since you're familiar with Tantalus, ransack the place for items before leaving. Leave the Tantalus playhouse and head down the steps.

DAGGER IN DESPAIR

Take an air cab to Lindblum Castle. In the lobby, take the red-carpeted stairs up to the right, and then go through the doorway on the balcony to reach the guest room where Dagger was seen previously. This is where Zidane reunites with "Rusty," who's throwing another fit about the princess. Once Steiner leaves, thoroughly search the room on the upper balcony.

As you return to the lobby, Zidane hears Dagger's sweet and melancholy voice. However, the guard at the lift isn't letting a miscreant like Zidane get past. Go back up the steps toward the guest room, but then head down the next set of steps and wake up the sleeping soldier. Zidane takes the guard out of sight and pounds him, taking the uniform as a disguise. Now return to the lobby, and you'll have no problem getting past the guard. Operate the control on the left side of the lift to reach the Upper Level.

Zidane switches back to street clothes on the ride up, so that Dagger will immediately recognize him. However, you must stay away from the guards as well to avoid detection. Take the stairs to the left up through an engine room to the top of the tower.

There's a telescope nearby, and while looking through it you can spot six locations before the scene moves on (a Marshland, the Aerbis Mountains, South Gate, the mountain between Lindblum and Alexandria, the Chocobo Forest, and the Ceebell River). Viewing them marks them on the World Map for later use.

THE FESTIVAL OF THE HUNT

Inside the guest room, the rules of the festival are explained. You receive points for each monster killed within the time limit. As you fight, your score is displayed in the bottom-right corner of the screen. The top score and whom it belongs to is displayed on top.

The winner of the Festival of the Hunt receives the **Master Hunter** award. Each character also specifies an additional prize that they want: if Vivi wins, you receive a **Theater Ship Card**; if Freya wins, you get a **Coral Ring**; and if Zidane wins, you'll get **5000 Gil**.

To begin the contest, equip Zidane with the strongest weapon and armor available. Also, equip the Beast Killer ability to help. Then take the air cab to the Theater District.

GRAVE MESSENGER

Following the Festival, the Master Hunter trophy is awarded to one of the three heroes who participated. In addition, they receive the prize of their choice. The celebration is aborted, however, when a wounded soldier from Burmecia drops dead after delivering a shocking message. Afterward, Dagger and Steiner flee from Lindblum, leaving Zidane and Vivi to go with Freya to Burmecia. Make sure your party is completely stocked up before leaving.

When your crew is ready to resume the adventure, take the Lindblum Castle lift to the lower level. The left trolley goes only to the Dragon's Gate, from which you need to depart, but the right trolley takes you to the Serpent's Gate first. Then you can go straight from there to the Dragon's Gate.

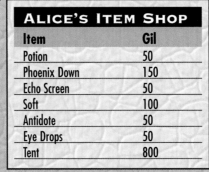

At this exit, you'll meet Moonte the moogle, who just received a letter from Stiltzkin. It's recommended that you save your game before leaving. There's also a Merchant nearby, who sells items for decent prices.

KEYWORD: FESTIV1

SPECIAL ITEM

Do you want to know how to win the Festival of the Hunt? For complete details, visit PlayOnline.

ALICE'S ITEM SHOP

Item	Gil
Potion	50
Phoenix Down	150
Echo Screen	50
Soft	100
Antidote	50
Eye Drops	50
Tent	800

TORRES' SYNTHESIS SHOP

Item	Gil	Required Items
Butterfly Sword	300	Dagger, Mage Masher
The Ogre	700	2 Mage Mashers
Cotton Robe	1000	Wrist, Steepled Hat
Desert Boots	300	Leather Hat, Leather Shirt
Yellow Scarf	400	Feather Hat, Steepled Hat
Glass Buckle	500	Glass Armlet, Leather Wrist

DRAGOOS' ARMORY

Item	Gil
Dagger	320
Mage Masher	500
Mythril Dagger	950
Iron Sword	660
Javelin	880
Rod	260
Fork	1100
Leather Wrist	200
Glass Armlet	250
Bronze Gloves	480
Silver Gloves	720
Steepled Hat	260
Headgear	330
Iron Helm	450
Leather Plate	530
Linen Cuirass	800

EUNORUS PLAINS/KING ED PLAINS

ENEMIES:
SERPION, LADYBUG, IRONITE,
VICE, HEDGEHOG PIE

KEY ITEMS:
MOCCHA
COFFEE

ITEMS:
ETHER

CARDS:
NONE

OBJECTIVES

1

Cross the plains

2

Enter areas of interest

3

Find the South Gate

THE FLATLANDS

Leaving from the Dragon's Gate, your main destination is a cavern in the mountains directly to the north called Gizamaluke's Grotto. The world is a bit foggier throughout the plains, making overland travel difficult.

Visiting a few other areas will make your travel across the plains easier as well. Between Dragon's Gate and the Grotto is Qu's Marsh, where you can recruit a new character to strengthen your party. The other area of extreme interest is the Chocobo's Forest, where you will gain the ability to call a Chocobo. Riding a Chocobo prevents random battles from occurring while travelling on the World Map.

As with the previous wide-open area, you should spend some time fighting lots of enemies in random battles, leveling up and learning Abilities from items before replacing them with better ones. It's best to wander and fight in the area close to the South Gate's south end.

KEYWORD:
CHOCO1

SIDE QUESTS

The ever-popular Chocobo returns with his own mini-game called Chocobo Hot and Cold! PlayOnline has the story covered.

REFILLING STATION

Another area to visit is the other end of the South Gate, which you can find at the far east end of the King Ed Plains. Upon entering the area, move across the tree roots to the right, where you'll find a spring that completely restores HP and MP. You can return here as often as you like to restore your party after several hard and draining battles. With this option available, you can continue to level up without having to use a lot of valuable Potions or Tents. Don't forget to explore the area near the spring to find some useful items.

QU'S MARSH

ENEMIES:	KEY ITEMS:	ITEMS:	CARDS:
AXOLOTL, GIGAN TOAD	NONE	NONE	NONE

OBJECTIVES

Catch a frog for Quina

Let Quina join your party

Practice catching frogs

INTRODUCING THE QU'S

The marsh area should be marked on your Continental Map if you noted it using the telescope in Lindblum. After crossing the planks into the marsh, you should run across the moogle tutors. You can review or catch up on any tutorials you skipped or didn't understand at this point.

Next, proceed into the high grass. You'll lose sight of Zidane completely, but just hold up on the directional button to get through. Regardless of where you enter the tall grass, you should arrive at a pond area where a jolly creature called a Qu is trying to catch frogs.

S/he isn't having much luck, so run around the area and press the X button to catch a frog. Then speak to the Qu to learn that its name is Quina. Another creature named Quale emerges, and escorts everyone back to its hut. Here you are offered the option of having Quina join your party. It's a definite benefit to have four party members at a time.

Quina has the ability to "Eat" enemies and learn their special powers. This will come in quite handy in more than a few Boss fights.

Any time you return to the pond area, Quina will want to catch frogs. The number of frogs Quina catches is cumulative, so even if you catch some frogs and then leave the marsh, the number you caught before is remembered. The number of frogs Quina catches determines the items s/he receives from the marsh master.

KEYWORD: QUFROG1
SIDE QUESTS
Frog catching for fun and profit. Details at PlayOnline.

QUINA & "FROG DROP"
The number of frogs s/he catches determines how much damage the "Frog Drop" attack causes. More on frog catching is detailed at PlayOnline.

GIZAMALUKE'S GROTTO

ENEMIES:
BLACK MAGE, HORNET, SKELETON, LAMIA, GIZAMALUKE (BOSS)

KEY ITEMS:
GIZAMALUKE BELL, HOLY BELL

ITEMS:
BRONZE VEST, MYTHRIL GLOVES, MAGUS HAT

CARDS:
NONE

OBJECTIVES

1 Take the Gizamaluke Bell from the Burmecian soldier

2 Ring the bells to open the doors

3 Annihilate the Black Mages

4 Reunite the honeymooning moogles

5 Stand your ground against Master Gizamaluke

ASK NOT FOR WHOM THE BELL TOLLS...

The mountain underpass to Burmecia, called Gizamaluke's Grotto, has already been laid to waste. As Freya recoils from the atrocities in evidence, run inside the Grotto and head to the right. A Burmecian soldier hands you a **Gizamaluke Bell** before passing on.

Go to the door at the back and ring the bell to unlock it. The bell will shatter upon use, meaning you must find another bell to use on the next door.

Inside the next large cavern, Thorn and Zorn unleash a set of Black Mages on your party. These creatures use powerful magic, mostly aimed at Vivi. Protect the little fellow by having a character such as Quina use Potions on him.

After the first battle, cross under the bridge and attack the next Black Mage. Upon completion of this fight, you receive another **Gizamaluke Bell**. Run up the steps at the rear, and use the bell on the left door. This path leads around to another wounded soldier. Pick up a **Bronze Vest** along the way, and then tend to the wounded man to get another bell.

Return to the main area and use the bell on the lower-right door. A staircase encircles the next area. You may encounter a tough monster called a Lamia that casts Might every round to increase its attack power. Dispose of these things quickly, and have Quina eat it if possible to learn the Lv3 Def-less ability. As you ascend the stairs, make sure you look closely for any wastefully dropped items on the path.

These stairs round into the central area in which a large bell has fallen, trapping the moogle Moguta. His bride, Mogmi, sniffs out the Kupo Nut on Vivi, and asks to have it. Give it to her and Moguta will summon super strength to free himself. The couple then runs into the right-hand room. Take the **Gizamaluke Bell** from the treasure chest, and then follow them inside.

Talk to Mogmi to save your game or use a Tent, which isn't a bad idea right now because you're about to enter a major Boss fight. She also has a letter from Moodon.

If you climb up the vine, you'll enter a mountain plain area where the monsters (Grand Dragons) are way too tough to fight at this point in the game. So avoid climbing the vine, and talk to Moguta instead. Tell him you love Kupo Nuts too, and when you're returning to the bell room he'll give you the **Holy Bell** hidden in a statue.

Run back around the overturned bell and unlock the other bell door in the room. Beyond here, the group enters the actual grotto chamber, where fallen Burmecian soldiers warn that something is wrong with Master Gizamaluke. The warning comes too late, however, as a large and terrifying shape slithers out of an aqueduct and challenges the party to a tough battle.

BOSS FIGHT

GIZAMALUKE

HP	3175	AP	5	Weak vs.	Thunder
Steal Items	Ice Staff, Magus Hat, Elixir			Spoils	Tent

BATTLE TACTICS:

- Use Zidane's Soul Blade ability (using The Ogre) to blind the Boss
- Have Vivi cast Thunder, while Freya should Jump
- Use Quina for healing purposes

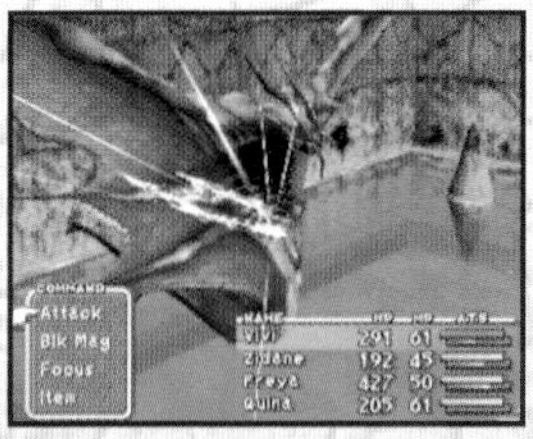

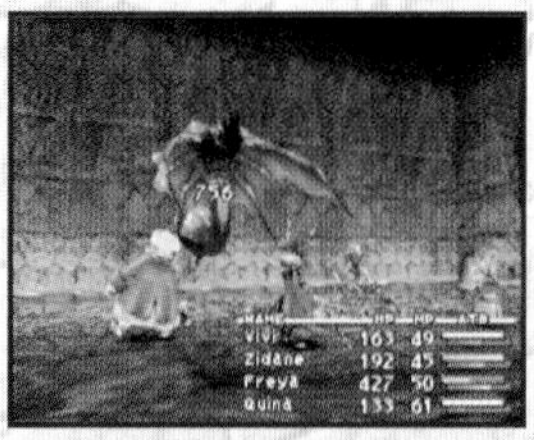

PlayOnline.com KEYWORD: GIZMAL1

BOSS FIGHT TIPS

For more detailed Boss strategy, check out PlayOnline.

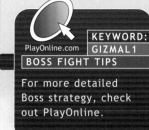

GRAND CITADEL SOUTH GATE

ENEMIES:	KEY ITEMS:	ITEMS:	CARDS:
NONE	GATE PASS	MULTINA RACKET, POTION	NONE

OBJECTIVES

1

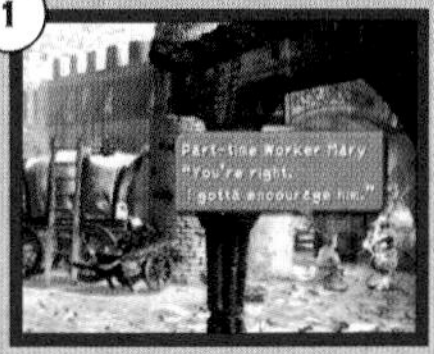

Move the two people away from the alley

2

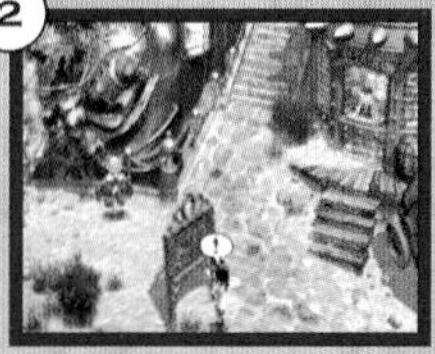

Search the area outside the cable car

3

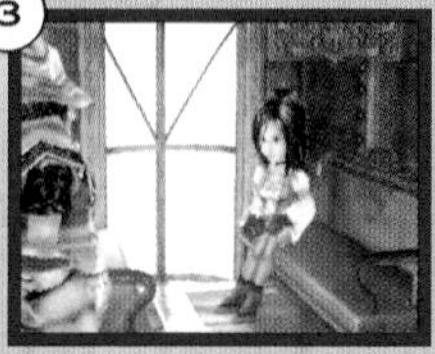

Board the cable car to Treno

THE PRINCESS'S CROSSING

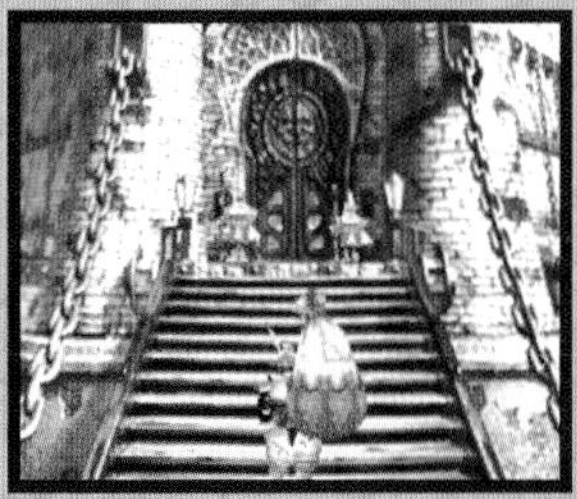

Now the game takes a break from the hectic struggle of the fighters to reach Burmecia. Steiner is attempting to enter South Gate with a bag of smelly gysahl pickles. The secret is that Dagger is hidden in the bag! Making it inside is easy, but now Steiner must find a spot to set the Princess free. A nearby alleyway seems ideal, but you must convince the people loitering there to move.

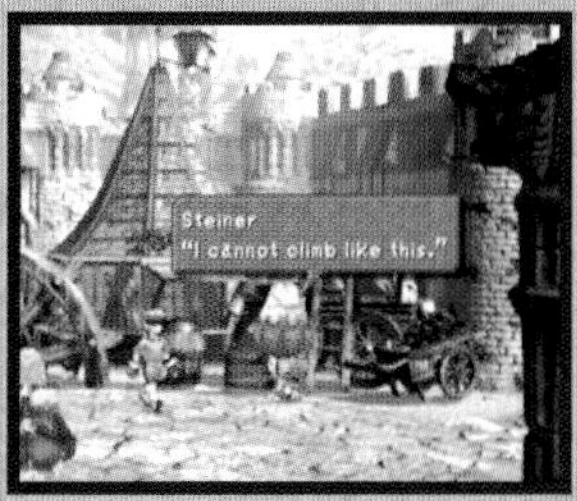

With the bag slung over his shoulder, Steiner will be unable to climb the ladder to the chest on top the wagon. Circumstances later will prevent it as well, so you must return at a later point in the game to retrieve it.

PlayOnline.com KEYWORD: STEINE1

POWERFUL WEAPON

Someone is due for a weapon upgrade. Find out who at PlayOnline.

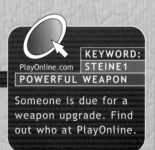

Part-time Worker Mary is easy to move; simply console her and she will move away. The Earnest Young Man is only slightly more difficult, depending on which option you choose. You can either remain silent or say that you're here to work. Tell him that you're here to work, and then move to the far left to speak to the Worker. It seems the Worker is actually slacking off, and is naive enough to admit it to Steiner. Return to the Earnest Young Man and inform the worker, and the Earnest young man will go scold him.

This clears the alley of witnesses, but the Short Guard stops Steiner dead in his tracks. It seems that they forgot to give Steiner a **Gate Pass** upon his entry. Now that you have it, you can access any of the gates in the world at any time.

In the alleyway, Dagger gets out of the pickle bag and takes over. The cable car to the summit is in the next area, and won't depart until you're ready to board.

Before boarding the cable car, save your game by talking to Grimo the moogle. It's important that you take this opportunity to equip Dagger with the Multina Racket, and make sure that Steiner has the best equipment possible too. A Boss fight will suddenly occur during the trip, so make sure you equip Steiner and Dagger at the Summit Station. Once you're properly prepared, board the cable car to the Aerbis Peak Station.

Bohden Station Medicine Shop	
Item	Gil
Potion	50
Phoenix Down	150
Echo Screen	50
Soft	100
Antidote	50
Eye Drops	50
Tent	800

BURMECIAN PLAINS

ENEMIES:
LIZARD MAN, YETI, SKELETON, NYMPH

KEY ITEMS:
NONE

ITEMS:
HI-POTION, TENT

CARDS:
NONE

OBJECTIVES

Examine the North Gate   Cross the plains to Burmecia

THE MURKY PLAINS

After Zidane's group leaves Gizamaluke's Grotto, head for the Burmecian capital to the north. To the east of the Grotto is the North Gate. When you investigate here, Freya will go through a range of emotions while Quina looks for good food.

There's a whirling sandstorm to the southwest of Burmecia, but you can't enter this area right now. However, beyond the desert and through a short valley is the Healing Shore, where you can find Chocobo tracks.

BURMECIA

ENEMIES:
MAGIC VICE, BLACK MAGE, IRONITE, MIMIC, BASILISK, BEATRIX (BOSS)

KEY ITEMS:
CANCER STELLAZZIO, PROTECTION BELL, KUPO NUT

ITEMS:
POTION, SOFT (X2), GERMINAS BOOTS, ETHER, TENT, PHOENIX DOWN, MYTHRIL SPEAR, LIGHTNING STAFF

CARDS:
NONE

OBJECTIVES

Bridge the gap with the platform

Hop balconies to the bedroom

Ring the bell to open the door

Rescue the trapped citizens

Inherit the Mythril Spear

Spy on the enemy

Challenge an Alexandrian General

City of Perpetual Rain

The rainy Burmecian Kingdom stands in ruins, the populace having fled in fear of the Black Mage Army. The dead or dying litter the streets, with nothing to offer but their eternal silence. Quickly move the group through the rainy area toward the back of the kingdom, searching for items along the way. Random encounters will be numerous and frequent, so be quick to keep your party from getting worn out before the finish.

Proceed through the arch at the back. Zorn and Thorn are just steps ahead of you it seems. Once again, your group gets attacked by Black Mages, so hit them with each character's strongest attacks. When the jester twins retreat, head up the stairs to the left door.

In the next area, there are numerous treasure chests. However, some are filled with items, while others contain a Mimic enemy. You can avoid these fights by not encountering the chests, but you receive Ethers for defeating them. During the fights, make sure you kill the Magic Vice it calls before it steals any of your inventory.

Proceed past the locked bell door to the western foyer. As you run toward the treasure chest on the left, a section of balcony drops below, bridging a gap.

Run back through the other foyer and go outside. Cross under the balconies to the right-hand door. Continue up the stairs and head through the doorway on the second floor balcony.

Angle your way through the next room and hop balconies to the bedroom. A dying Burmecian soldier points out that you can find the **Protection Bell** by searching behind the bed. With the bell in hand, return to the bell door on the third level, and ring it to enter.

Running up a magnificent staircase, the party encounters fleeing soldiers who mistake Vivi for the enemy. Freya smoothes things over with Burmecian Soldier Dan so that you can proceed up the stairs to the temple area.

Go in the central bottom door to rescue some Burmecians who invite you to visit them in Lind-blum. Keep that in mind for later in the game. Then exit and take the right stairs, crossing the balcony in front to the left doorway.

In the courtyard under the royal castle, there are doors to the left and right. Enter the left one first, where Freya will claim the **Mythril Spear** held by the statue. Equip this weapon immediately, so Freya can cast Regen on all the party members at once. The right-hand door from the courtyard leads to a similar treasure room,

where you can find a **Lightning Staff** for Vivi in the chest behind Atla the Moogle. Atla will let you use a Tent and Save (both are recommended), and he sells a variety of good items too in a new feature called Mogshop. (A complete inventory is listed at the end of this section.)

MORE LETTERS FOR MOGNET
If you have a letter to give Atla from Mogki, then the moogle will give you a **Kupo Nut**. *Atla also needs you to deliver a letter to Monev.*

THE EVIL REVEALED

On the outside of the castle walls, Zidane has some choices about approaching Freya. Choose to leave her alone. The Dragon Knight then leaps up to the top of the castle walls, and leads the heroes inside. There, Zidane and Freya overhear a conversation between the Queen and a mysterious new villain. When a Burmecian soldier foolishly risks his life, Freya and Zidane intervene. As the Queen escapes, the superhuman General Beatrix threatens to end the adventures of our heroes.

Beatrix puts up quite a fight. If you're still having trouble with this Boss, refer to PlayOnline for more extensive Boss strategies.

BOSS FIGHT

GENERAL BEATRIX

HP 3630	AP ???	Weak vs. None
Steal Items Chain Plate, Mythril Sword, Phoenix Down		**Spoils** None

BOSS PREPARATIONS:

- Equip Zidane and Quina with their strongest weapons
- Equip Freya with the Mythril Spear and give Vivi the Lightning Staff and a Magus Hat
- Equip Zidane with the Bandit ability

BATTLE TACTICS:

- Have Vivi cast Slow
- Cast Freya's Reis's Wind during the first round
- Have Vivi hit Beatrix with Thundara and Blizzara
- Use Quina's Mighty Guard ability (if available)

ATLA'S MOGSHOP	
Item	**Gil**
Needle Fork	3100
Glass Armlet	250
Mythril Gloves	980
Steepled Hat	260
Headgear	330
Magus Hat	400
Barbut	600
Bronze Vest	670
Linen Cuirass	800
Potion	50
Phoenix Down	150
Echo Screen	50
Soft	100
Antidote	50
Eye Drops	50
Tent	800

SUMMIT STATION

ENEMIES:
BLACK WALTZ
NO. 3 (BOSS)

KEY ITEMS:
NONE

ITEMS:
PHOENIX DOWN

CARDS:
NONE

OBJECTIVES

1

2

3

Relax in Summit Station

Speak with the Attendant

Spot Cinna and Marcus at the station

4

5

6

Make Steiner settle down

Board the train to Treno

Finish off Black Waltz No. 3

MOUNTAIN RENDEZVOUS

Summit Station is a good place to keep playing while you take a deep breath and relax after all the recent excitement. The Cable Car Enthusiast will tell you what this mode of travel is all about. You'll have to wait for the car going to Alexandria to arrive. Head across the walkway into the station.

The rest area is full of people, so make sure you talk to them. It's always important to talk to everyone, because you never know what you might learn or find. When you're done exploring, speak to the Attendant to get the game rolling again. Two voices heard from outside should coax you into peeking out to see what's going on.

Entering the station from the Alexandria train are the recognizable bandits, Cinna and Marcus. Follow them into the station, where Steiner is giving them some grief. You must tell Steiner to be silent before you can fully speak with the two Tantalus members. When the car to Alexandria arrives, the Princess should follow Marcus onboard.

KEYWORD: BWALTZ4

PlayOnline.com

BOSS FIGHT TIPS

For more strategy on the Black Waltz No. 3 fight, go to PlayOnline.

BOSS FIGHT

BLACK WALTZ NO. 3

HP	1292	AP	5	Weak vs.	None

Steal Items	Lightning Staff, Steepled Hat	Spoils	None

BATTLE TACTICS:

- Have Steiner use his physical attacks
- Let Marcus alternate between stealing and attacking
- Using Dagger, cast Protect on the group and cure the party when needed

SUMMIT STATION SHOP

Item	Gil
Air Racket	400
Mythril Rod	560
Glass Armlet	250
Silver Gloves	720
Mythril Gloves	980
Steepled Hat	260
Headgear	330
Magus Hat	400
Rubber Helm	250
Iron Helm	450
Barbut	600
Bronze Vest	670
Linen Cuirass	800
Potion	50
Phoenix Down	150
Echo Screen	50
Soft	100
Antidote	50
Eye Drops	50
Tent	800

SOUTH GATE, NORTH STATION

ENEMIES:	KEY ITEMS:	ITEMS:	CARDS:
NONE	NONE	ELIXIR	NONE

OBJECTIVES

1

2

Read the road signs

Use the Gate Pass to head for Treno

A QUIET LITTLE AREA

The cable car deposits the trio in the quiet little area protected by the well-guarded barricades of the South Gate Area. Part-time Worker Mary will immediately open up the Item Shop VEGA, where you can refill your inventory. Proceed upward to a fork in the path, where the right direction continues onward toward your current destination of Treno. The left path takes you back to Dali.

Don't miss the large engraving at the fork in the path, extolling the benevolence between the two nations of Lindblum and Alexandria. Travel along the path to the gate facing Treno, and show the guards your Gate Pass. Then head across the Bentini Heights toward Treno, the city of never-ending night.

ITEM SHOP VEGA	
Item	**Gil**
Potion	50
Phoenix Down	150
Antidote	50
Eye Drops	50
Tent	800

BENTINI HEIGHTS

ENEMIES:	KEY ITEMS:	ITEMS:	CARDS:
GHOST, MANDRAGORA, CARVE SPIDER, TRICK SPARROW	SCORPIO STELLAZZIO	ETHER (X3)	NONE

OBJECTIVES

1

2

3

Explore the mountain high plateau

Check out Quan's Dwelling behind the forest

Enter the Dark City Treno

SHADOWS IN THE MOUNTAINS

Crossing the Bentini Heights area, you're very likely to come across Treno immediately. However, if you proceed past Treno for the time being and push through the expansive forest to the east, you can enter Quan's Dwelling and pick up some additional items.

PlayOnline.com

KEYWORD:
APUP1
CHARACTER BOOST

There's one particular enemy that can supply lots of AP. To find out what it is and what you need to do, go to PlayOnline.

Quan's Dwelling

This cavern is behind a long and dangerous stretch of forest to the southeast of Treno. You'll encounter some creatures called Mandragoras along the way, and you should fight them with everything you've got. This cave holds a few items and a few points of interest, and it's a great resting spot for parties seeking to level up in the surrounding area.

Explore the area thoroughly, looking for items. Take note of the spring pond, which you can use to restore HP and MP. While leveling up by fighting monsters outside, you can return here and refresh your party as often as you like.

Return to the top portion and enter the darker cave at the back. Climb the ladder, and check the wall on the right to find a note about Vivi. Out on the ledge overlooking the ocean, a clock seems to hold some interest for Dagger but contains no items… for now, anyway.

Q PlayOnline.com

KEYWORD: STELLA2

SPECIAL ITEM

Your search isn't complete in this area until you find another Stellazzio. PlayOnline has the complete details.

DARK CITY TRENO

ENEMIES:
GRIFFIN (DISC 2), CATOBLEPAS (DISC 3; FIRST HALF), AMDUSIAS (DISC 3; SECOND HALF), BEHEMOTH (DISC 4)

OBJECTIVES

KEY ITEMS:
GEMINI STELLAZZIO, TAURUS STELLAZZIO, SUPERSOFT

ITEMS:
MYTHRIL DAGGER, POWER BELT, TONBERRY CARD (DEFEAT GRIFFIN), 15,000 GIL (DEFEAT CATOBLEPAS), RUNNING SHOES (DEFEAT CATOBLEPAS OR AMDUSIAS), CIRCLET (DEFEAT BEHEMOTH)

CARDS:
YETI CARD

1 Follow Dagger around the city

2 Find Dagger at the auction

3 Catch up with Marcus at the Inn

4 Attempt to steal Supersoft

5 Return to the tower to meet Dr. Tot

THE CITY OF NOBLES

Just inside the gates, the trio is understandably dazzled by the spectacle of Treno. Dagger and Marcus then run off, leaving Steiner to fend for himself. A series of ATEs become available immediately, and you should watch them all. During the scene entitled "Treno Tradition," Dagger loses 1000 Gil from a pickpocket.

 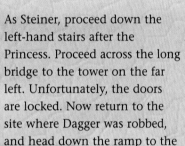

As Steiner, proceed down the left-hand stairs after the Princess. Proceed across the long bridge to the tower on the far left. Unfortunately, the doors are locked. Now return to the site where Dagger was robbed, and head down the ramp to the ground level. The nobles of Treno will proudly snub Steiner, so head to the door just above the Café. Along the carpeted hall, Steiner meets the four-armed man that lifted Dagger's Gil. There's a Synthesis Shop at the far end of the open corridor; the inventory of forgeable items appears at the end of this section.

STELLAZZIO COLLECTOR
The Queen of Treno accepts the Stellazzios you've been collecting. To find her, exit the red-carpeted hallway and continue upward.

FUN AND GAMES IN TRENO

If Steiner exits below the Café Carta, he will discover the Card Stadium. There's not an event going on right now, but the Usher will explain more about the card game than has been revealed thus far. You can challenge the boy and his father nearby, but they're strong players.

PlayOnline.com
KEYWORD: ATES1
SECRET
You can view multiple ATEs in this section. To find out what you must do to watch them all, go to PlayOnline.

PlayOnline.com
KEYWORD: SAVGIL1
SECRET
Wanna save some Gil? Then visit PlayOnline for the scoop.

PlayOnline.com
KEYWORD: STELLA3
SPECIAL ITEM
If you're collecting the Stellazzios, you can get another one in this area. To find out what to do, visit PlayOnline.

PlayOnline.com
KEYWORD: PWRBLT1
SPECIAL ITEM
There's a nice reward for meeting the Four-armed Man. PlayOnline has it covered.

PlayOnline.com
KEYWORD: STELLA4
SPECIAL ITEM
Are you curious as to what the Queen of Treno gives you for the astrological coins you've found? PlayOnline has it covered.

KEYWORD:
PlayOnline.com   **GRIFF1**
BOSS FIGHT TIPS

This can be a difficult fight. PlayOnline provides the tips you'll need.

Continuing to the right past the Card Stadium, you pass the Weapons and Armor Shop. Also, Mogrich the moogle is trying not to get eaten by a dog; talk to her, because she may have a letter from Stiltzkin. There's a monster in the pit under the grate that serves as a floor. If you're feeling confident, you can request to fight the monster. However, this is only recommended for characters who go properly prepared into battle. A full inventory of items sold in this area appears at the end of this section.

KEYWORD:
PlayOnline.com   **AUCTN1**
SPECIAL ITEM

The items you can sell or give to people are listed at PlayOnline.

The entrance to the Treno Auction is above the Weapons Shop. Steiner finally catches up to Dagger here, and she resumes control of the party. You can return to Treno later and bid on rare items that are auctioned here, but for now, Dagger is haunted by the appearance of a familiar figure… You don't have to bid on items, but some of the items up for auction can be sold or given to certain individuals in exchange for Gil or other items.

The Quest for the Supersoft!

KEYWORD:
PlayOnline.com   **STELLA7**
SPECIAL ITEM

The Stellazzio search continues! Additional details at PlayOnline.

Head down past the Weapons Shop, where you'll find the poorer part of Treno. Descend the ladder on the left to find another Item Shop. The shop's inventory is detailed at the end of this section.

You can pay the grouchy Innkeeper 100 Gil to stay the night, if Dagger and "Rusty" are in poor spirits. You'll be fighting a few enemies shortly, so it's not a bad idea to rest up. At the bottom of the Inn's stairs, Marcus has been patiently waiting for Dagger's arrival. The Tantalus troupe is ready to steal the rare **Supersoft** item, needed to revive their petrified comrade.

When you're ready, you must ignore a whining Steiner while walking through a series of platforms until Dagger meets Baku face to face. The head thief boats everyone to a location where you can steal the rare Supersoft.

During the attempted robbery, Dagger has a chance encounter with her old teacher, Doctor Tot. The Doc offers to get the Supersoft for the Princess, and says to meet him at the locked tower to the left of the entrance of Treno. After Tantalus returns to the Treno Inn, head back to the tower and the door will now be open.

After Tot allows Marcus to have the Supersoft, have Dagger talk to the Doctor some more and a flashback will occur. Then climb up the ladders and go down the open manhole into the Gargan Roo.

TRENO WEAPONS & ARMOR SHOP

Item	Gil
Dagger	320
Mage Masher	500
Mythril Dagger	950
Mythril Sword	1300
Mythril Spear	1100
Air Racket	400
Mythril Rod	560
Flame Staff	1100
Ice Staff	980
Lightning Staff	1200
Fork	1100
Needle Fork	3100
Leather Wrist	200
Glass Armlet	250
Bone Wrist	330
Mythril Gloves	980
Magus Hat	400
Bandana	500
Barbut	600
Silk Shirt	400
Leather Plate	530
Bronze Vest	670
Chain Plate	810
Linen Cuirass	800
Chain Mail	1200

TRENO ITEM SHOP

Item	Gil
Potion	50
Phoenix Down	150
Echo Screen	50
Soft	100
Antidote	50
Eye Drops	50
Tent	800

TRENO SYNTHESIS SHOP

Item	Gil	Required Items
Butterfly Sword	300	Dagger, Mage Masher
The Ogre	700	2 Mage Mashers
Cotton Robe	1000	Wrist, Steepled Hat
Desert Boots	300	Leather Hat, Leather Shirt
Yellow Scarf	400	Feather Hat, Steepled Hat
Glass Buckle	500	Glass Armlet, Leather Wrist
Germinas Boots	900	Desert Boots, Fork
Cachusha	1000	Magus Hat, Rubber Helm
Coral Ring	1200	Lightning Staff, Rod
Gold Choker	1300	Linen Cuirass, Soft

GARGAN ROO

ENEMIES:
DRAGONFLY, CRAWLER,
RALVURAHVA (BOSS)

KEY ITEMS:
NONE

ITEMS:
CHAIN PLATE,
PHOENIX DOWN

CARDS:
NONE

OBJECTIVES

1. Pull the sequence activator lever

2. Find the gargant call lever

3. Feed the gargant to hitch a ride

4. Scare off the big bad worm

THE SPEEDY INSECT

Doctor Tot says that the first thing to look for is a sequence activator. Head to the left from the circular area. Mochos the moogle remains in the first area if you decide to save your game. Hit the lever and return to the circular area. Go down the steps to the right this time.

The lever to the left in the next chamber is clearly marked "feed," but you must call the gargant first. To do that, go to the right and Doctor Tot will join Dagger to explain further. Pull the lever at the end, and the massive gargant will run by. Now return to the feed lever

and use it. The trio gets onboard the gargant's carriage and heads toward Alexandria. However, the journey is only just beginning...

PlayOnline.com
KEYWORD:
RALV1
BOSS FIGHT TIPS

For more tactics against this Boss, check out PlayOnline.

BOSS FIGHT → **RALVURAHVA**

HP	2296	AP	0	Weak vs.	None

Steal Items	Bone Wrist, Mythril Fork	Spoils	None

BOSS PREPARATIONS:

↓ Equip the Antibody ability on both Dagger and Steiner

BATTLE TACTICS:

↓ Make Dagger cast Protect, and act as a medic for the party

↓ Have both Marcus and Steiner concentrate on attacking

↓ Make sure you steal on occasion using Marcus

CLEYRA'S TRUNK

ENEMIES:
DRAGONFLY,
SAND GOLEM,
CARRION WORM,
ZUU

KEY ITEMS:
NONE

ITEMS:
PHOENIX DOWN, ICE STAFF,
FLAME STAFF, MAGICIAN
SHOES, ETHER, TENT,
NEEDLE FORK, KUPO NUT,
DESERT BOOTS, REMEDY,
MYTHRIL VEST, MYTHRIL
GLOVES, POTION, ELIXIR,
HI-POTION, GYSAHL GREENS

CARDS:
NONE

OBJECTIVES

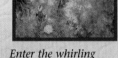

①
Enter the whirling sandstorm

②
Raise the sand floor of the chamber

③
Close the upper sand gate

④
Navigate between whirling sink holes

THE SANDY TREEHOUSE

The story finally returns to Zidane's party, where they were last seen languishing in Burmecia. Upon leaving the fallen kingdom, head west to the whirling sandstorm protecting Cleyra. Most of the citizens from Burmecia have fled the area, so you can visit there now. However, the trip won't be easy as you attempt to climb up the massive trunk full of flooding sand, swirling traps, and dangerous monsters. Reorganize your party so that everyone has the best equipment possible.

KEYWORD:
KUPNUT1
PlayOnline.com
SPECIAL ITEM
Remember the significance of Gizamaluke's Grotto and Kupo Nuts? If not, check out PlayOnline for the details.

Upon entering the sandstorm, the characters uncover the path leading up the trunk. At the entrance, pull the lever to the right to open the seal. Just inside, head to the right and then continue up the path to a sand-filled room. There are some partially hidden chests in here, so don't leave until you've collected everything. The main reason to get these items now is because you're about to flood this room with sand, and you won't be able to get all of the items afterward.

TRUNK ENEMY NOTES
You're bound to encounter the Dragonflies and the Sand Golems while navigating the Trunk. You can defeat the Dragonflies if Vivi casts Blizzard on them. To eliminate the Sand Golem, attack it until it melts and then attack the red core. If you attack the Sand Golem's core at any other time, it responds with a brutal physical counterattack. The red center is extremely weak against Ice spells, so equip the Ice Staff on Vivi.

Run up the slope outside the tree, all the way to the top. Now put Zidane's hand into the hole just below the last chest and trigger the switch; this causes sand to pour into the room

 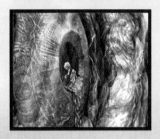

below. This cuts off the lower access, so return to the outside of the tree and climb the vines into the large ornate entrance.

Cross the sand-flooded room to the opposite hole, and search for a weapon at the base of a tall slope. You'll find Monev the moogle on the midlevel. You may have a letter for Monev from Atla. Monev will give you another **Kupo Nut** for delivery of the letter!

KEYWORD:
ITMS1

PlayOnline.com

SPECIAL ITEM

There are LOTS of items in this area to find, some of which are hidden. For all the locations, go to PlayOnline.

Continue up the rise and take the left stairs in the next area. Then cross a plank bridge into a cavern with three caves at the back. Going through the center tunnel takes you to the center portion of the back of the cave. Now head through the cave in the very center of the back three.

Head through the cave in the very back. Press the switch on the pulley at the end of this path to make a chest available in another area. Upon doing this, return to the main cavern and exit through the far-left passage.

Veer up the right branch. Return to the path and continue to the left, where Zidane nearly runs into a whirling sink hole. If he gets caught in one of these holes, continuously press the X button to avoid being sucked in. At the end of the path, there's a ladder leading up to the settlement.

UNDERSTANDING THE SINK HOLES

When you're caught in a sink hole mashing the X button to get out, press the directional buttons or analog stick in the direction opposite the target area where you want to land. This ensures that you'll end up where you desire upon leaping from the sink hole. However, if you release the analog stick as soon as Zidane jumps out, you may go right back into the hole! Also, use the directional buttons and walk around the sink holes, don't run! This increases your chances of avoiding the whirling traps.

CLEYRA SETTLEMENT

ENEMIES:
ANTLION (BOSS),
TYPE B,
ALEXANDRIAN
SOLDIER,
BEATRIX (BOSS)

KEY ITEMS:
NONE

ITEMS:
PHOENIX PINION (x3),
REMEDY (x2), ETHER
(x2), ORE, THUNDER
GLOVES, MYTHRIL
VEST, GYSAHL GREENS,
ECHO SCREEN,
YELLOW SCARF,
ELIXIR, PHOENIX
DOWN, EMERALD

CARDS:
NYMPH CARD,
ZUU CARD

OBJECTIVES

1 Take the Cleyra tour

2 Explore the town

3 Talk to the guards at the cathedral

4 Find Dan at the Inn

5 Save Puck from the Antlion

6 Fight invaders in the trunk

7 Rescue as many villagers as possible

8 Fight Beatrix for the village jewel

9 Stow onboard the Queen's airship

LIFE AMONGST THE BRANCHES

Upon entering the Cleyra tree settlement, Freya will run off to confer with the King of Burmecia. One of the Oracles offers to take you on a tour of Cleyra. This is a great way to get acquainted with the town. All of the branches are connected by similar rope bridges, and it's difficult to remember which bridge leads to which branch. You must become very familiar with the layout of Cleyra in a short amount of time.

The conclusion of the tour brings Zidane back to the front gate. Return to the front and head up the stairs. Continue up either set of stairs to continue searching for items. Meanwhile, a series of ATEs will show you what kind of mischief your buddies are up to.

CLEYRA INN

There are several items to find in the large area that houses several buildings. In front of the Inn is Dan, the soldier you saved in Burmecia. Although he doesn't treat Vivi very well, Dan will sell you weapons and armor. His inventory is listed at the end of this section.

You will find a depressed Vivi at the Inn. He is inconsolable, so take a moment to thoroughly explore the Inn. It's full of items. When you're done searching, talk to the moogle Mopli, who may have a letter for Zidane from Ruby.

> **LOOK EVERYWHERE!**
> *For such a small place, the Inn is packed full of goodies. Make sure you explore EVERYWHERE before continuing.*

WATERFALLS

Two Burmecian soldiers lament the fall of their kingdom near the life-giving falls. Also, Moon Maiden Claire is happy to discuss the magic that keeps the sandstorm in place around the settlement.

THE CLEYRA CATHEDRAL

KEYWORD: ITMS3
PlayOnline.com
SPECIAL ITEM
You can pick up a couple of items before triggering the Boss fight. To find out what you must do, go to PlayOnline.

At the very top of the tree is the Cathedral, wherein the citizens of Cleyra perform their magic ritual to maintain the whirling sandstorm protecting their home. Enter the Cathedral. The guards barring access further into the chapel have a message from Freya to wait for her at the Inn.

PESTILENCE OF THE SETTLEMENT

After speaking to the guards at the cathedral and returning to the Inn, Burmecian Soldier Dan reports that a giant creature is attacking a child near the entrance of the settlement. Follow him down the stairs, and then proceed to the right into the area with the large sinkhole. The Antlion has arisen from the sands, and has Vivi's old friend Puck in its grasp.

KEYWORD: ANTL1
BOSS FIGHT TIPS

Need more help with this Boss? Go to PlayOnline for additional strategy.

KEYWORD: FREYA1
SPECIAL ITEM

Freya can learn a new ability at this point of the game. If you're curious, check out PlayOnline for the details.

BOSS FIGHT — ANTLION

HP 2938	AP 5	Weak vs. Wind
Steal Items Gold Helm, Mythril Vest, Annoyntment		**Spoils** Ether, Annoyntment

BOSS PREPARATIONS:
- Equip Desert Boots on some characters

BATTLE TACTICS:
- When your party's HP gets low, cast Freya's Reis's Wind
- Have Vivi cast Blizzara
- Concentrate on using magic and abilities

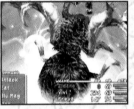

THE INVASION OF CLEYRA

After the Antlion battle, you'll control Freya for a short time. Meet the party at the entrance and get prepared to fight before climbing back down the trunk.

The chamber with the sink holes is now dormant following the cessation of the sand storm. This is the first place where the heroes get attacked by Alexandrian Soldiers. The feminine warriors attack in duets, but are extremely easy to overcome.

Proceed down the trunk, taking as few side paths as possible, until the party reaches the plank bridge and suspects a trap. Puck calls the entire party back to the village, where the real battle is currently underway!

At the town's entrance, you must protect the Shrine Maidens from a Black Mage and then a trio of Alexandrian Soldiers. This time, it's a no-holds barred fight where the enemies cast the powerful Blizzara and Fira spells over and over. Then more Black Mages appear, and the party retreats up the stairs. You can win these battles with ease by using straightforward fighting tactics.

To the right of the town's entrance, you can find the moogles Stiltzkin and Mopli. Stiltzkin will have another "value deal" available to you at a low cost, and Mopli will give you a letter intended for Serino. Make sure you save your game at this point.

KEYWORD:
ITMS4
SPECIAL ITEM

Need help with the directions, or curious about the items you receive from the survivors? Check out PlayOnline.

Up the steps, Zidane encounters the Oracles, who are fleeing from enemies. A decision must be made to either go up the steps or flee to the right. The next couple of decisions you make determine whether or not some of the citizens of Cleyra survive. Each surviving townsperson will thank you by giving you an item.

Outside the Inn, Burmecian Soldier Dan's family is looking for him. Choose a direction and hope for the best. In the meantime, you must fend off a combined Black Mage/Alexandrian Soldier party.

Zidane follows the family to the waterfall. You get to choose which direction you proceed. Another vicious battle ensues, and then the survivors all meet at the overlook area.

After the group sorts things out inside the Cathedral, General Beatrix commits an act of thievery. Follow her out to the lobby, where all the survivors are gathered. Talk to each one to receive a prize for rescuing them. Mopli the moogle is also in the lobby, and would like you to deliver a letter to Serino.

Because you're about to face the warrior who decimated your group previously, this is a good time to save your game. Then prepare your party well and proceed outside to face off against the powerful General once again.

GENERAL BEATRIX (REMATCH)

BOSS FIGHT

HP	4736	AP	N/A	Weak vs.	Ice

Steal Items	Ice Brand, Thunder Gloves, Phoenix Down	Spoils	None

BATTLE TACTICS:

- Have Vivi cast Slow on Beatrix immediately
- If available, use Quina's Mighty Guard
- Attack and steal with Zidane
- Use Freya's Reis's Wind when needed

KEYWORD: BEATRX2
PlayOnline.com
BOSS FIGHT TIPS

More strategy is available for the General Beatrix Boss fight at PlayOnline.

STOWAWAYS

The heroes escape Cleyra in the nick of time, finding their way miraculously onto the Queen's hovering airship. Follow Beatrix to the forefront of the ship, where you'll overhear Brahne's savage plans for the Princess. It's up to you to save her!

As you head back to the launch pods, Serino the moogle will make an appearance. Your party should be back to full health, so don't waste a Tent. But you should have a letter for Serino from Mopli, and it won't hurt to save your game again. Then return to the pods and use them to reach Alexandria, where the others are being held captive.

BURMECIAN SOLDIER DAN'S WEAPONS & ARMOR SHOP

Item	Gil
Partisan	1600
Multina Racket	750
Mythril Rod	560
Flame Staff	1100
Ice Staff	980
Needle Fork	3100
Bone Wrist	330
Mythril Armlet	500
Mythril Gloves	980
Thunder Gloves	1200
Magus Hat	400
Bandana	500
Mage's Hat	600
Mythril Helm	1000
Chain Plate	810
Mythril Vest	1180
Chain Mail	1200
Mythril Armor	1830

STAR MAIDEN NINA'S MEDICINE SHOP

Item	Gil
Potion	50
Phoenix Down	150
Echo Screen	50
Soft	100
Antidote	50
Eye Drops	50
Annoyntment	150
Tent	800

RESCUE IN ALEXANDRIA

ENEMIES:

ALEXANDRIAN SOLDIER, ZORN AND THORN (BOSSES), BEATRIX (BOSS), BANDERSNATCH, BLACK MAGE, RALVUIMAGO (BOSS)

KEY ITEMS:

NONE

ITEMS:

ICE BRAND, TENT

CARDS:

NONE

OBJECTIVES

1. Rock the cage to make an escape

2. Rejoin the returning heroes

3. Fight your way into the Queen's chambers

4. Find the secret passage

5. Descend the pit to the Ceremonial Chamber

6. Topple the Jester twins

7. Settle the score with Beatrix

8. Join forces to escape the castle

9. Ride the gargant out of Alexandria

10. Stop the Ralvuimago in its tracks

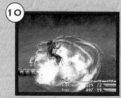

BIRDS OF A FEATHER

Steiner is still trapped in a cage suspended high in the air. He and Marcus must escape by rocking the cage back and forth until it crashes into the right balcony. Using the basic princi-

ples of momentum, rock the cage to one side, and then power the swing to the other side by rocking in that direction. Marcus will help you learn the timing of rocking the cage by telling you whether you're moving right or wrong.

Once freed, equip Steiner and Marcus with the strongest blades in your inventory. Also, give Steiner a Mythril Vest and equip the Auto-Potion ability. Two or three teams of Alexandrian soldiers will give chase, so you can either try to avoid or fight them.

After your encounter with the soldiers, run to the other side of the balcony and climb up the ladder. When you reach the top of the ladder, you'll probably want to take back your stuff from Marcus, just in case he decides to split...

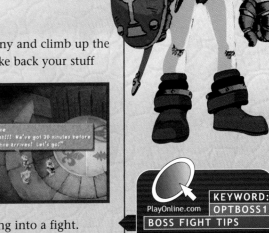

In the chamber above, Steiner and the rest of the crew are reunited. With a party of Steiner, Vivi, Freya and Zidane, you're ready to take on anything. However, you only have 30 minutes until the Queen's ship arrives. Although this may seem like a lot of time, you'll spend a decent amount of time in conversations, so you must keep moving.

Make sure you stay clear of the female Alexandrian guards to avoid getting into a fight. Luckily for you, the Knights of Pluto will not engage you in combat. Instead, they may provide you hints as to where you can find Dagger.

Exit the left tower and run to the courtyard. Each time you enter an area, the guards on duty will give chase. Enter the castle and fight your way upstairs. Quickly scale the circular stairs,

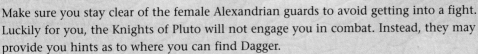

and head through the double doors at the top. Run straight back to the next double doors into the Queen's chamber.

Search the back corner of the area, where the strange candle casts a purple glow. Moving the candle triggers a switch that opens a secret passage. Charge down the steps and wait for the wildly rotating bridge to stop in front of you. Jump when the "!" appears. Hop off on the other side, wait for the bridge to rotate around, and then get on again.

This should deposit you on the platform at the top. Hop back to the right platform and run down the spiraling stairs.

PlayOnline.com

KEYWORD: OPTBOSS1

BOSS FIGHT TIPS

There's an optional Boss you can fight at this point of the game. To learn more about it, go to PlayOnline.

Upon reaching the bottom of the pit, move to the stairs on the right and then head through the double doors at the top of the circular platform. The Princess is unconscious on the altar at the back, and the jester twins will attempt to thwart your rescue.

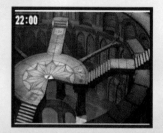

KEYWORD: ZRNTRN1

BOSS FIGHT TIPS

Check out PlayOnline for further Zorn and Thorn Boss strategies.

BOSS FIGHT

ZORN AND THORN

HP	4896 (Zorn), 2984 (Thorn)	AP	0	Weak vs.	Ice
Steal Items	(*Thorn:*) Mythril Armlet, Mythril Armor; (*Zorn:*) Stardust Rod, Partisan			Spoils	None

BATTLE TACTICS:

- Attack the twin with the Meteor ability to nullify to Meteor spell

- Use high-powered cold attacks

 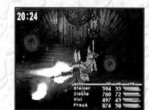

A DARING PLEA

Carrying the comatose Princess, Zidane must now return the way he came to the Queen's chambers. Mosh the moogle stands in the ceremonial chamber now, and may have a letter from Kupo to read. This is also an excellent time to save your game.

When the party gets back upstairs, the Twins lead the indomitable Beatrix right to the heroes! Get ready for another intense showdown with this holy warrior.

GENERAL BEATRIX (FINAL DUEL)

HP 5709	AP 0	Weak vs. Ice
Steal Items Survival Vest, Ice Brand, Phoenix Down		**Spoils** None

BATTLE TACTICS:

- Have Vivi rely on magic, like Slow and Blizzara
- Use Steiner's Blizzara Sword attack
- Make sure Zidane attempts to steal from Beatrix

KEYWORD: BEATRX3
BOSS FIGHT TIPS
For more Boss strategy, refer to PlayOnline.

THE TIDE TURNS

Once Zidane convinces Beatrix to protect the Princess, Freya and the ultra-powerful General join forces to battle a Bandersnatch set upon them by the Jesters. Have Beatrix perform her Climhazzard attack to end the battle swiftly. Let's hope she joins the party permanently...

The action cuts back and forth during this pulse-pounding sequence. With Zidane leading, jump across the spinning bridge and run down the steps before another Bandersnatch attacks the group. In the next portion of the pit, Black Mages emerge to do battle.

Near the bottom, the Bandersnatches finally catch up with the group. Fire magic seems to be what ails them most, so roast these overgrown doggies and continue downward. Steiner will then split off to rejoin Freya and Beatrix, who are taking on additional Bandersnatches.

MOSH THE MOOGLE
Once the party gets back down the stairs, make sure you return to the chapel because Mosh the moogle has a letter for you to deliver at this time.

In the meantime, Zidane, Vivi and Dagger board the gargant and head for Treno. However, the big worm that the Princess chased away earlier seems to have evolved and become much more threatening.

KEYWORD: RALV2

PlayOnline.com

BOSS FIGHT TIPS

More Boss tactics for this fight are at PlayOnline.

RALVUIMAGO

BOSS FIGHT

HP	3352	AP	7	Weak vs.	Ice

Steal Items	Oak Staff, Adaman Vest, Phoenix Down	Spoils	Ether

BATTLE TACTICS (PART 1):

- Cast Shell and Protect on the entire party
- Use Vivi's Ice spells

BATTLE TACTICS (PART 2):

- Avoid physically attacking the Boss when it coils up
- Steal and heal while the Boss is coiled up
- You can cast Vivi's Blizzara even when the Boss is coiled up

After the fight, Ralvuimago still gets back up and chases the gargant down the tunnel. The group crashes at Pinnacle Rocks, where the epic quest resumes.

PINNACLE ROCKS

ENEMIES:	KEY ITEMS:	ITEMS:	CARDS:
SAND SCORPION, ZAGHNOL, SEEKER BAT	NONE	THE OGRE, MYTHRIL VEST, MYTHRIL ARMLET, PERIDOT	NONE

OBJECTIVES

Accept the challenge of Ramuh

Search for the Eidolon's five ghosts

Assemble the hero's tale

Race back to Lindblum

THE SPECTER OF RAMUH

As Dagger, Vivi, and Zidane recover from the crash-landing of the gargant, the Eidolon of Ramuh appears and challenges the group to a trial. If you assemble the story correctly, you'll receive a **Peridot**, which enables Dagger to summon Ramuh in battle.

The group is led by Dagger throughout this event. Following the encounter with Ramuh, Dagger walks into an area where Monty the moogle waits to record your game. Make sure you give him the letter that you received from Mosh. After doing so, return to the first area, where Ramuh will appear again and recite the **'Hero'** part of the story. Now return to where Monty sits and head up the top branch. Ramuh appears in your path and recites the **'Beginning'** part.

Continue across the branch, head to the right across a bridge, and then jump down when the "?" appears. Moving to the left causes Ramuh to appear once more, reciting the **'Silence'** part of the story. Go around the ramping branch, head toward the chest, and Ramuh should appear in the corner. This time he recites **'Cooperation.'**

Head down from that area to the place just below Monty's perch. Now run under the window set into the tree, and Ramuh should appear for the last time just behind it. He now recites **'Human,'** the last piece of the story.

To finish the event, you must find Ramuh at the exit from Pinnacle Rocks near the location where you jumped off the branch. He now expects Dagger to assemble the narrative in a coherent manner.

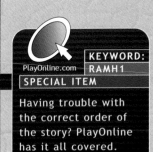

After putting together the pieces of the story, Ramuh reviews the story as you assembled it and asks if you want to correct it. He will point out any errors in assembling the first three parts, and let you try again if need be. When you're satisfied, Ramuh will examine your choice of ending. No matter which ending you choose, Ramuh bestows his abilities upon Dagger in the form of a **Peridot** to be equipped on Dagger as an Add-on.

LINDBLUM IN RUINS

ENEMIES:
NONE

KEY ITEMS:
WORLD MAP

ITEMS:
ETHER, PHOENIX
PINION, ORE,
BANDANA

CARDS:
LINDBLUM CARD

OBJECTIVES

Meet Artania in the Business District

Confer with Regent Cid

Prepare for the Outer Continent

Bid farewell to Regent Cid

THE RAVAGES OF WAR

Lindblum is in shambles. Queen Brahne's attack force has left most of the town in tatters, and the Industrial District is completely wiped out. Move Zidane and Dagger through the Business District. The Alexandrian Soldiers will not attack, and you can speak to them if you want.

The destruction has caused a few items to become scattered in amongst the debris, so explore every aspect of the area before continuing.

Proceeding into the mall area, Minister Artania finds Dagger and Zidane and escorts them to Regent Cid. A plan is formed to find and defeat Kuja on the Outer Continent. You must travel there via a series of underground caverns known as "Fossil Roo."

KEYWORD:
PlayOnline.com | **ITMS5**
SPECIAL ITEM

There are a few items of interest to gain at this point. Visit PlayOnline before going any further!

REMAINS OF THE CITY

Thereafter, a man awaits for you to prepare yourself in the Business District's mall. There are plenty of shops to visit, so check your inventory and determine what you'll need to continue your adventure. A complete inventory appears at the end of this section. When you're ready, return to this man and tell him you're all set to go.

The Lindblum Inn is still standing, and the price is still 100 Gil to rest. Upstairs, Moodon the moogle has an important letter for Zidane from Ruby about recruiting Lowell for her theater in Alexandria. The air cab system will still take you to the Theater District for free, but signs posted indicate that a fare will be implemented by the Queen shortly.

In the Theater District, you can find the actor Lowell just below the Tantalus Theater. If Zidane has read Ruby's letter, then he will convince Lowell to take off for Alexandria.

When you're finished exploring, set off for the Qu's Marsh north of the conquered city, where a rumored excavation site may take you to the Outer Continent.

At the Lindblum Grand Castle's base level, Regent Cid will give your group the **World Map** to help. The Merchant remains stationed at the Dragon's Gate, selling a combination of items and potions. Moonte the moogle will happily save your game before you head off once more.

DRAGOOS' WEAPON SHOP

Item	Gil
Dagger	320
Mage Masher	500
Mythril Dagger	950
Ice Brand	3780
Partisan	1600
Multina Racket	750
Stardust Rod	760
Flame Staff	1100
Ice Staff	980
Lightning Staff	1200
Leather Wrist	200
Glass Armlet	250
Bone Wrist	330
Mythril Armlet	500
Mythril Gloves	980
Thunder Gloves	1200
Headgear	330
Magus Hat	400
Bandana	500
Mage's Hat	600
Mythril Helm	1000
Silk Shirt	400
Leather Plate	530
Bronze Vest	670
Chain Plate	810
Mythril Vest	1180
Chain Mail	1200
Mythril Armor	1830

ALICE'S MEDICINE SHOP

Item	Gil
Potion	50
Phoenix Down	150
Echo Screen	50
Soft	100
Antidote	50
Eye Drops	50
Annoyntment	150
Tent	800

TORRES' SYNTHESIS SHOP

Item	Gil	Required Items
Butterfly Sword	300	Dagger, Mage Masher
The Ogre	700	2 Mage Mashers
Exploda	1000	Mage Masher, Mythril Dagger
Cotton Robe	1000	Wrist, Steepled Hat
Silk Robe	2000	Silk Shirt, Bandana
Desert Boots	300	Leather Hat, Leather Shirt
Yellow Scarf	400	Feather Hat, Steepled Hat
Glass Buckle	500	Glass Armlet, Leather Wrist
Germinas Boots	900	Desert Boots, Fork
Cachusha	1000	Magus Hat, Rubber Helm
Coral Ring	1200	Lightning Staff, Rod
Gold Choker	1300	Linen Cuirass, Soft
Magician Shoes	1500	Germinas Boots, Bone Wrist
Barette	1800	Needle Fork, Barbut
Power Belt	2000	Glass Buckle, Chain Mail

DRAGON'S GATE MERCHANT

Item	Gil
Ice Brand	3780
Partisan	1600
Multina Racket	750
Stardust Rod	760
Mythril Armlet	500
Thunder Gloves	1200
Bandana	500
Mage's Hat	600
Mythril Helm	1000
Chain Plate	810
Mythril Vest	1180
Adaman Vest	1600
Mythril Armor	1830
Potion	50
Phoenix Down	150
Echo Screen	50
Soft	100
Antidote	50
Eye Drops	50
Remedy	300
Annoyntment	150
Tent	800

QU'S MARSH EXCAVATION SITE

ENEMIES:
GIGAN TOAD,
AXOLOTL

KEY ITEMS:
NONE

ITEMS:
NONE

CARDS:
NONE

OBJECTIVES

1
Find Quina safe by
the frog pond

2
Check with Quale
for clues

3
Enter the marshes to
look for Fossil Roo

4
Quina leads you to
the entrance

HOME IS WHERE THE FROGS ARE

KEYWORD:
CHOCO6
PlayOnline.com
SIDE QUESTS
Remember the Chocobos!
Go to PlayOnline for
further details.

Zidane runs into Quina at the frog pond, griping about the
hard trip back from Cleyra. Quina rejoins the party and
brings your group back up to four strong, so you may want
to re-recruit Quina before doing any leveling up or Ability
learning on the surrounding plains. There's also bound to be
a new brood of frogs that need catching at the pond.

ENTRANCE TO THE UNDERWORLD

Return to Quale's hut to see if the elder Qu has any knowledge of an excavation site. Quale does give a few sketchy clues, but doesn't know much more
than you do. From Quale's hut, exit to the right into the brush. Quina will
pick up the scent of more frogs, and takes Zidane straight to the entrance of
the excavation site. Enter the tunnel and descend the steps into Fossil
Roo, the treacherous underground passage to the Outer Continent.

FOSSIL ROO

ENEMIES:
ARMODULLAHAN, LANI
(BOSS), ABOMINATION,
GRIFFIN, SEEKER BAT,
FEATHER CIRCLE

KEY ITEMS:
NONE

ITEMS:
ELIXIR, FAIRY
EARRINGS, ETHER,
LAMIA'S TIARA,
SURVIVAL VEST

CARDS:
NONE

OBJECTIVES

1 Run from Fossil Roo's guardian

2 Square off against the gorgeous bounty hunter

3 Ride the gargants through the passage

4 Use the switches to change course

5 Dig for treasures with the miner

6 Throw the final switch to exit forever

GUARDIANS OF THE ROO

As you're innocently making your way through the first passage, a gate opens behind the party and the enemy Armodullahan begins pursuit in which you must navigate a gauntlet of swinging pendulums. If Zidane gets struck by a pendulum, the creature might catch up to you. This supernatural creature can withstand an infinite number of battles, has little to steal, and can slay your characters instantly by summoning the visage of Death. Therefore, you don't want to get caught.

The treacherous path you must cross is divided into three sections. You'll have better luck clearing this area without incident if you *cross along the upper side of the pendulums in the first area, the lower side in the second, and the upper side again in the last area.* Don't be afraid to stop for a moment to keep from getting hit by the pendulums.

However, before you have time to shake the dust from your shanks, the Queen's bounty hunter steps into your path. Intent on taking Dagger's pendant, the desirable femme fatale doesn't care if the Princess cooperates or not. The pendant can be removed from Dagger's corpse as easily as handed over.

KEYWORD:
ARMD1
BOSS FIGHT TIPS

This enemy isn't too difficult to disable, but if you're still having trouble, visit PlayOnline for more help.

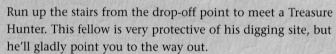

BOSS FIGHT	**HP** 5708	**AP** 0	**Weak vs.** None
	Steal Items Coral Sword, Gladius, Ether		**Spoils** None

LANI

This fight consists of three separate confrontations, resulting in an explosive finish. This fight really isn't that difficult, so to make it through unscathed follow these suggestions.

BATTLE TACTICS

- Using Dagger, cast Ramuh
- Cast second level spells on Lani
- Make sure you steal!
- Use Shell and Protect on Dagger

ANCIENT PASSAGE

At the bottom of the stone steps, head to the left. There are some wild yellow flowers growing in front of a gigantic tunnel. Pick one and move to the right until a "!" appears. Press the X button to make Zidane raise the flower. This summons an untamed gargant, which carries Zidane to the excavation site.

Run up the stairs from the drop-off point to meet a Treasure Hunter. This fellow is very protective of his digging site, but he'll gladly point you to the way out.

Down the steps to the right, you might bump into everyone's favorite striped moogle, Stiltzkin. He'll gladly sell you some more useful medicines, at his usual markup. Stiltzkin's friend Mogki will let you rest up or save, and has just received a letter from Kuppo. Mogki also sells a variety of potions and medicines, listed for convenience at the end of this section.

THE GARGANT EXPRESS

Getting through Fossil Roo to the Outer Continent requires you to ride back and forth on different gargant paths, using a number of switches to alternate each path.

Start off by heading down to the right from the moogles' position. There are some yellow flowers growing on a platform. Pick one and walk toward the edge until you see a "!." Press the X button to call a gargant.

As you travel on the gargant, you will notice that this path has a divergence that is controlled by Switch 2. On this first trip, the gargant will drop you off at a ledge where you can pull **Fairy Earrings** out of a treasure chest. Then return to the drop-off point and call a gargant to ride back to the excavation chamber.

Now go through the tunnel past the Treasure Hunter, and call another gargant to take you on the path controlled by Switch 1. From this drop-off point, head to the right out to a platform, where you'll find Switch 1. Flip the switch so that you can travel the second leg of the path. Return to the drop-off point, pick a flower, and move to the center of the cave to call the gargant.

The gargant drops you off at a cavern with two levels. First, climb the steps and follow the top path to a ledge where you'll find an item. Now return to the drop-off point, and follow the lower path through a series of twists and turns to a platform where you'll find Switch 2. Flip this switch, then return to the drop-off point and ride back to Switch 1. Position Switch 1 so that the gargant will now return you to the cave with the moogles and the Treasure Hunter.

Now move to the bottom-right cave and ride the gargant again. This time, you're dropped off in a new area, only to find that another Treasure Hunter is already here.

Take the stairs up to reach a platform where you'll find Switch 4. Flip the switch and head through the right-hand tunnel to call the gargant. This takes you to a platform where you'll find a treasure chest. Ride the gargant back to Switch 4, flip it back to its original position, and ride the gargant again.

This time, you arrive in a chamber where the back wall is covered with vines and a few water spouts. To climb across any part of the wall without getting knocked down by water, you must crawl *directly under* the spouts. However, you should get knocked down once. You want to reach the cave exit on the upper part of the right-hand wall, so climb the vines on that side of the room to reach it. In summary, just stick to the bottom of the vines.

Inside this cave, another Treasure Hunter has beaten you to the scene once more. He'll let you dig in this area in exchange for a Potion, so take him up on his offer.

When you're done digging, head through the lower-right exit from the dig cavern to find a storage area. You are now ready to leave Fossil Roo. Return to the chamber with the vine wall, and climb up to Switch 3 on the upper-left ledge. Turn the switch to the path marked "Exit." Now climb, or fall, to the bottom of the vine wall and exit the lower cave. Call a gargant and ride out to the final cave of Fossil Roo.

MOGKI'S AND KUPPO'S MOGSHOPS

Item	Gil
Potion	50
Phoenix Down	150
Echo Screen	50
Soft	100
Antidote	50
Eye Drops	50
Annoyntment	150
Tent	800

TREASURE HUNTER'S INVENTORY

Item	Gil
Ice Brand	3780
Partisan	1600
Multina Racket	750
Stardust Rod	760
Mythril Armlet	500
Thunder Gloves	1200
Bandana	500
Mage's Hat	600
Mythril Helm	1000
Chain Plate	810
Mythril Vest	1180
Adaman Vest	1600
Mythril Armor	1830
Potion	50
Phoenix Down	150
Echo Screen	50
Soft	100
Antidote	50
Eye Drops	50
Remedy	300
Annoyntment	150
Tent	800

OUTER CONTINENT

ENEMIES:
GRIFFIN, CACTUAR,
ZAGHNOL, GOBLIN MAGE

KEY ITEMS:
NONE

ITEMS:
NONE

CARDS:
NONE

OBJECTIVES

1

*Circle the area to reach the
suspended building*

THE WASTE LANDS

The Outer Continent is a series of vast desert islands with a few mountains and a couple of scattered forests with small patches of green land scattered about. The first and most notable landmark is a structure suspended on what looks like two gigantic tree roots. Follow the canyon under this structure, and stick to the cliffs as they curve to the east.

KEYWORD:
QUIN1

ABILITIES

Quina can learn a couple of useful abilities in this area. Make sure you visit PlayOnline to find out what s/he can learn.

To reach the strange building, you must follow the cliffs as they gradually slope downward to meet the lower land level near the eastern shore. Then you can move west up the long slope toward the suspended structure.

> **REST UP!**
> The journey through Fossil Roo probably left your party in bad shape, and the trek across the desert is no picnic either. Don't hesitate to use a Tent when needed and save your game. There are strong enemies in the area that might take advantage if your characters are weak.

CONDE PETIE

ENEMIES:
NONE

KEY ITEMS:
NONE

ITEMS:
PHOENIX PINION, DIAMOND

CARDS:
NONE

OBJECTIVES

1

2

3

4

Give a hearty "Rally-ho" at the entrance

Talk to the dwarves blocking the exits

Follow Vivi into the Grocer's

Pursue the Black Mage

HOME OF THE DWARVES

The suspended structure is the dwarf village known as Conde Petie. The party is greeted at the door with the boisterous dwarven greeting, "Rally-ho!" Only those who return the greeting can enter the town, and so Zidane is separated from the others by his resistance to do so.

Zidane asks the dwarves if they know of Kuja, and some of the answers are quite hilarious. From the entrance, head through the left door across the corridor to find the Conde Petie Inn, where 100 Gil is a nice price to rest up and get your crew back in shape.

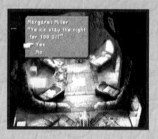

The stairs leading up from the top of the area lead to the central part of the village, where the locals are joined in marriage. There is a dwarf blocking the exit in the upper-right corner, and you can't get through at this time.

You'll then see Vivi talking to two individuals on the bridge at the bottom of the square, after which he runs off. Follow him into a store, where Zidane spots a Black Mage shopping at the counter. Vivi and Zidane chase the Black Mage out of Conde Petie. The folks at the door know the Black Mages well, and they direct the party to find them in the forest to the southeast.

Before leaving, restock your necessities in Conde Petie's Grocery Store or in the Weapon Shop located behind it. Both stores' inventories are listed at the end of this section. The moogle Mogmatt in the Grocery Store has a letter he needs you to take to Suzuna. You'll come across her soon enough, so be a pal, *kupo!*

GROCERY STORE MEDICINES	
Item	**Gil**
Potion	50
Phoenix Down	150
Echo Screen	50
Soft	100
Antidote	50
Eye Drops	50
Annoyntment	150
Tent	800

GOLDPILER'S WEAPONS SHOP	
Item	**Gil**
Poison Knuckles	5000
Multina Racket	750
Stardust Rod	760
Flame Staff	1100
Ice Staff	980
Lightning Staff	1200
Oak Staff	2400
Mythril Fork	4700
Mythril Armlet	500
Lamia's Tiara	800
Ritual Hat	1000
Adaman Vest	1600
Magician Cloak	1850

BLACK MAGE VILLAGE

ENEMIES: ZEMZELETT, MYCONID

KEY ITEMS: VIRGO STELLAZZIO

ITEMS: ELIXIR, GYSAHL GREENS, ETHER, BLACK BELT

CARDS: NONE

OBJECTIVES

1 Follow the signs to the village

2 Find Dagger at the Synthesis Shop

3 Talk to No. 288 at the cemetery

4 Check in with Vivi at the Inn

5 Regroup in the morning

THE OWLS ARE NOT WHAT THEY SEEM...

Leave Conde Petie and run to the southeast. The large bulge in the forest, visible from the high plateau, is your destination. The party must run all the way back down the slope, and then hang a right and travel west through a long, forest-filled canyon. Press the X button to enter the bulging area of the forest.

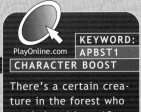

KEYWORD: APBST1
CHARACTER BOOST
PlayOnline.com

There's a certain creature in the forest who can help with an AP boost. Go to PlayOnline to find out more.

Zidane finds a forked path with a sign in the middle. Read the sign, and then head in the direction "where there are no owls." One of the owls in the trees overhead will fly away. Then it seems that Zidane enters the exact same area. Read the sign at the fork once more, and again head in the direction without any owls. Another owl will leave its perch. Starting to get the idea?

Each time you enter the area, read the sign in the center and head in the direction indicated, even if it means going back the way you just came in. Eventually, you will see a Black Mage emerge and then run back.

After all the owls have left the area, Zidane will follow the Black Mage to what looks like a spot of dead trees in the forest. But this is really a magical cloaking that protects the Black Mage Village.

"Pyntie-Hets"

The Black Mages are a bit alarmed to see humans entering their village, and they quickly run for cover. Vivi chases after them in his continuing quest for answers. Naturally, Dagger and Quina abandon Zidane to explore the village on their own and to find something good to eat.

You can explore the village before or after following Vivi. To the left of the village entrance is No. 239's Weapon & Armor Shop.

There's a house on the far right side of the village where a couple of Black Mages have taken up raising a baby chocobo. A moogle named Mogryo is stationed outside to save your game if you want, and he would very much like for you to take a letter to Mocchi.

KEYWORD:
PlayOnline.com   STELLA5
SPECIAL ITEM

There's another Stellazzio available here. Visit PlayOnline for its location.

The building to the right of the Weapon Shop houses No. 163's Medicine Shop, where you can purchase Hi-Potions for the first time ever at a cost of 200 Gil a piece. A complete inventory is at the end of this section.

The building behind the Medicine Shop to the left is the Black Cat Synthesis shop. Zidane will find Dagger here, and he helps to smooth out the ruckus she accidentally caused earlier.

As you continue to the left of the Synthesis shop, Vivi dashes past. Talk to the Black Mages at the cemetery to find out what's going on, and then catch up with Vivi at the Inn.

When Dagger enters and suggests that the party rest, take her up on the suggestion. Vivi leaves in the middle of the night to find out more information. In the morning, Zidane joins Dagger and a Black Mage by the village entrance. She's learned that Kuja has been seen in the Northwest of the Outer Continent. To reach that area, the party will somehow have to get past the dwarves blocking the western exits from Conde Petie.

NO. 163'S MEDICINE SHOP

Item	Gil
Potion	50
Hi-Potion	200
Phoenix Down	150
Echo Screen	50
Soft	100
Antidote	50
Eye Drops	50
Remedy	300
Annoyntment	150
Tent	800

NO. 239'S WEAPON & ARMOR SHOP

Item	Gil	Item	Gil
Mage Masher	500	Feather Hat	200
Mythril Dagger	950	Steepled Hat	260
Gladius	2300	Headgear	330
Stardust Rod	760	Magus Hat	400
Mage Staff	320	Bandana	500
Flame Staff	1100	Mage's Hat	600
Ice Staff	980	Lamia's Tiara	800
Lightning Staff	1200	Ritual Hat	1000
Oak Staff	2400	Silk Shirt	400
Mythril Fork	4700	Leather Plate	530
Leather Wrist	200	Bronze Vest	670
Glass Armlet	250	Chain Plate	810
Bone Wrist	330	Mythril Vest	1180
Mythril Armlet	500	Adaman Vest	1600
Magic Armlet	1000	Magician Cloak	1850
Leather Hat	150	Survival Vest	2900

BLACK CAT SYNTHESIS SHOP

Item	Gil	Required Items	Item	Gil	Required Items
Butterfly Sword	300	Dagger, Mage Masher	Cachusha	1000	Magus Hat, Rubber Helm
The Ogre	700	2 Mage Mashers	Coral Ring	1200	Lightning Staff, Rod
Exploda	1000	Mage Masher, Mythril Dagger	Gold Choker	1300	Linen Cuirass, Soft
Rune Tooth	2000	2 Mythril Daggers	Magician Shoes	1500	Germinas Boots, Bone Wrist
Cotton Robe	1000	Wrist, Steepled Hat	Barette	1800	Needle Fork, Barbut
Silk Robe	2000	Silk Shirt, Bandana	Power Belt	2000	Glass Buckle, Chain Mail
Desert Boots	300	Leather Hat, Leather Shirt	Madain's Ring	3000	Bone Wrist, Stardust Rod
Yellow Scarf	400	Feather Hat, Steepled Hat	Fairy Earrings	3200	Magic Armlet, Soft
Glass Buckle	500	Glass Armlet, Leather Wrist	Extension	3500	Lamia's Tiara, Multina Racket
Germinas Boots	900	Desert Boots, Fork	Reflect Ring	7000	Anklet, Madain's Ring

BLISS IN CONDE PETIE

ENEMIES:	KEY ITEMS:	ITEMS:	CARDS:
NONE	NONE	PHOENIX PINION	NONE

OBJECTIVES

1

Talk to the dwarf at the exit

2

Find Father Heavenguard in the corridor

3

Make the commitment of a lifetime

4

Follow the little thief west into the mountains

PRENUPTIAL ARRANGEMENTS

Return to Conde Petie on the double. Move through town and find Shamis Gatekeeper, the dwarf blocking the exit from the ceremonial area. He's a bit more forthcoming with information this time, and directs Zidane to find the village priest.

You can find Father David Heavenguard wandering the corridor between the entrance and the Inn. Zidane learns from him that only those who are married in the village can go west from here. Dagger walks in and instantly agrees to undergo the ceremony with Zidane.

Following the crazy nuptials and depending on if you chose to watch the first ATE in this section, Vivi and Quina decide to get married too. Is Quina so happy because s/he is married, or because s/he might get to eat Vivi? If you chose the second ATE, they will just sneak past the guards.

MOUNTAIN PATH

ENEMIES:
GNOLL, OCHU, TROLL, HILGIGARS (BOSS)

KEY ITEMS:
BLUE STONE, RED STONE, YELLOW STONE, GREEN STONE

ITEMS:
REMEDY, TENT, ETHER, MOONSTONE

CARDS:
NONE

OBJECTIVES

① Rescue the little thief

② Collect the four colored stones

③ Topple the green giant

④ Head to Eiko's house

THE LAST OF THE SUMMONERS

As the group heads west of Conde Petie through the mountains, a little purple-haired person is chased out of town by the dwarves. The party stumbles across the tiny girl, who had been stealing food from Conde Petie to survive.

Her name is Eiko, and she permanently joins the party. You'll notice right away that she knows absolutely no abilities, but she can summon like Dagger. Eiko can learn Fenrir to start, and then she will pick up the awesome Phoenix summon from a Phoenix Pinion, if you have any in stock. Make sure you equip Eiko with armor and a bracelet right away, so that she's well protected and begins to learn abilities.

Climb up the left slope, and use the vine to reach to the upper ledge. Head to the left until you reach a statue. Take the **Blue Stone** out of the icon and return to the starting point.

Head to the right until you see another vine to climb. On this lower ledge, head to the left. Another statue nearby holds the **Red Stone**.

Return to the lower path and continue to the right. Up a sharp slope you'll meet the moogle Suzuna, whom you may hold a letter for. You may also encounter Stiltzkin, who offers to sell some more items. Move down to the left, climb up the ladder, and cross the giant tree root to the right.

You've certainly been wondering about the origin of the tree roots and their meaning. Now the answer lies before you, as Zidane spots the massive Iifa Tree far off in the distance. However, as you continue across the root to the end, you realize that getting there may be a tough battle.

KEYWORD: HILGG1
PlayOnline.com
BOSS FIGHT TIPS

For more Boss strategy, go to PlayOnline.

BOSS FIGHT

HILGIGARS

HP 8106	**AP** 9	**Weak vs.** Thunder
Steal Items Fairy Flute, Mythril Fork, Phoenix Down		**Spoils** Elixir, Tent

BATTLE TACTICS:

- Have Dagger or Eiko cast Float on the entire party
- Cast Ramuh
- Make Vivi cast Bio

EIKO'S HOME

After the Boss fight, Eiko invites everyone to her house in the nearby town of Madain Sari. First, examine the statue in the fork in the path to get the **Yellow Stone**. Then proceed along the right path. Curve off onto the bottom path and swing down to a statue containing a **Green Stone**. Now go back to the fork and continue to the right until you leave the Mountain Path area.

KEYWORD: CSTONE1
PlayOnline.com
SPECIAL ITEM

Want to know what all of the colored stones are for? PlayOnline has everything covered on this subject.

MADAIN SARI

ENEMIES:
(surrounding area)
BLAZER BEETLE,
GOBLIN MAGE,
TROLL, YETI

KEY ITEMS:
LIBRA STELLAZZIO,
KIRMAN COFFEE

ITEMS:
TENT, ORE,
PHOENIX PINION

CARDS:
NONE

OBJECTIVES

① Relax at Eiko's home

② Go with Morrison to the Eidolon Wall

③ Bring Dagger to the wall

④ Cook a hearty meal

⑤ Clear Eiko's table

⑥ Convince Eiko to go to the Iifa Tree

LOST HOME OF THE SUMMONERS

Follow Eiko into the ancient ruins of the once-powerful village. After the little lady puts Zidane through a detailed screening, explore the area to find a few special items.

Take the path to the left to talk to Vivi, or head to the right to see what Quina's up to.

PlayOnline.com | **KEYWORD: STELLA6**
SPECIAL ITEM

To add to your Stellazzio collection, go to PlayOnline. There's another one in this area.

PlayOnline.com | **KEYWORD: EKCOOK1**
SPECIAL ITEM

You must cook the right amount of food for the *entire* group. When you reach this point, go to PlayOnline for the correct answer.

If you attempt to enter Eiko's house, the moogle Morrison will prevent entry. He asks you to follow him back to the Eidolon Wall. Upon hearing the purpose of the wall, Zidane decides to go find Dagger. When she joins Zidane, head back to speak with Morrison again. During a short scene, the moogle lets them view the mysterious Eidolon Wall.

LONELY HEARTS

Zidane and Dagger should return to Eiko's house after visiting the Eidolon Wall. Everyone begins eating, and the group discusses Madain Sari, Eiko's abilities, and summoning. Following dinner, Eiko asks Zidane to bring the pot into the kitchen.

On the back patio, Zidane and Eiko briefly discuss the Iifa Tree. Quina and a moogle are fishing off the lower part, so go back inside. As you're leaving the hut, Momatose enters and offers to let you rest.

During the night, Vivi and Zidane discuss the importance of having a past, and share a male bonding ritual. In the morning, Eiko decides to join Zidane's group and go to the Iifa Tree. The group then leaves Madain Sari.

Before returning to the Mountain Path, roam the area around Eiko's home, defeating enemies, leveling up and learning abilities. The Iifa Tree provides quite a challenge, so it's good to work out and level up. If you need items, return to the lost village and Morrison will greet you at the gate with a full inventory. If the party becomes worn down from excessive battles, you can rest in Madain Sari for free by speaking with Momatose in Eiko's dining room.

MORRISON'S MOGSHOP

Item	Gil	Item	Gil
Dagger	320	Magician Cloak	1850
Mage Masher	500	Survival Vest	2900
Mythril Dagger	950	Potion	50
Gladius	2300	Phoenix Down	150
Poison Knuckles	5000	Echo Screen	50
Multina Racket	750	Soft	100
Golem's Flute	2700	Antidote	50
Pinwheel	200	Eye Drops	50
Magic Armlet	1000	Magic Tag	100
Lamia's Tiara	800	Annoyntment	150
Ritual Hat	1000	Tent	800
Adaman Vest	1600		

IIFA TREE, PART ONE

ENEMIES:
STROPER,
MYCONID, ZOMBIE,
DRACOZOMBIE,
SOULCAGE (BOSS),
NYMPH

KEY ITEMS:
NONE

ITEMS:
RUBY, PHOENIX DOWN,
HI-POTION, ETHER,
LAMIA'S FLUTE, REMEDY,
ELIXIR, BRIGANDINE

CARDS:
NONE

OBJECTIVES

Penetrate the Eidolon seal

Ride the circular platform down

Brave the endless spiral

Evaporate the Mist maker

Investigate the trouble in Madain Sari

ANCIENT TREE OF LIFE

Arriving at the massive tree, which may be Kuja's hangout, the group finds the entrance barred by an Eidolon's force field. You can have Zidane poke or body-slam (just once!) the barrier as much as you like to get your kicks. Eventually, you'll want to ask Eiko to intervene. The little summoner breaks the seal and receives a **Ruby.**

As you travel along the winding tree root, the party will encounter various plant-based and undead enemies weak against Fire. After slowly descending a steep slope, Zidane stumbles across Mocchi the moogle, whom you might have a letter for. From this point forward, you'll encounter mostly undead enemies.

The group eventually reaches a circular platform with strange markings. Choose for Zidane to stand on it, and he will discover that it is a magical elevator down into the trunk.

PlayOnline.com

KEYWORD: EKSUMM1

SPECIAL ITEM

The Ruby enables Eiko to call upon a new summon, which is covered at PlayOnline.

PlayOnline.com

KEYWORD: UNDED2

FIGHTING TIPS

There's an easy way to defeat undead monsters. Go to PlayOnline for the answer.

ROOTS OF EVIL

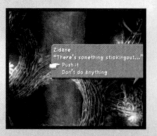

As Zidane and the heroes fight their way down the winding roots inside the trunk, you'll eventually come to a pair of off-shoots on the right. Go to the bottom one first, and trigger a switch that drops a treasure chest from above. Make sure you explore the area to pick up all the items, some of which are off the main path.

Continue downward but make sure you explore every path as you descend to the bottom of the Iifa Tree. The crew hops on, and the long descent begins. During the ride, you can expect

several encounters, but you also have at least one chance to revive characters, equip new items and abilities, or use Potions outside of battle.

KEYWORD:
PlayOnline.com **ARMZID1**

ARMOR UPGRADE

There's some new armor for Zidane in this area. To find its location, go to PlayOnline.

When the leaf-like platform stops at the bottom of the long and spiraling column, you have the option to go back up to the top if you want. The party separates momentarily, so search for items as Zidane.

When you examine the far-left edge of the area, something terrible rises from below, and then falls to annihilate the Iifa Tree's intruders.

KEYWORD:
PlayOnline.com **SCAGE1**

BOSS FIGHT TIPS

This is a tough Boss fight. If you're still having trouble with it, go to PlayOnline for further details.

BOSS FIGHT

SOULCAGE

HP 9765	AP 9	Weak vs. None
Steal Items Brigandine, Magician Cloak, Oak Staff		**Spoils** Elixir, Phoenix Pinion

BOSS PREPARATIONS:

↓ Equip the Auto-Potion ability

↓ Learn Eiko's Auto-Regen ability

BATTLE TACTICS:

↓ Using Eiko, summon Fenrir or cast Reflect on the other party members

↓ Summon Phoenix to revive KO'd characters; it also causes big damage to the Boss

↓ Have Vivi cast Bio

TROUBLE IN MADAIN SARI

ENEMIES:
SCARLET
HAIR (BOSS)

KEY ITEMS:
MEMORY
EARRING

ITEMS:
SURVIVAL VEST,
PHOENIX DOWN,
PHOENIX PINION,
EXPLODA, ELIXIR

CARDS:
NONE

OBJECTIVES

Return to Eiko's house

Strategize with the moogles

Duel against Scarlet Hair

Agree to let Eiko go with Zidane

Form a shaky alliance

CODE OF THE HUNTER

Following the destruction of the Mist monster, Eiko is called back to Madain Sari by her moogle friends. Apparently, someone has stolen her village's precious stone. The whole party agrees to come along.

In her village, follow Eiko back to her house. Move through the back door, and descend the steps to the lower patio. Pass through the gathered moogles, and enter the tiny room under the porch to find Eiko lamenting her lost heirloom. As she runs out, an intruder captures her. Before leaving the house and heading for the Eidolon Wall, search the small room for a couple of items.

Morrison meets the group outside the wall. He will completely restore HP and MP to everyone and remove any lingering status effects. Then peek inside to see that Lani, the irrepressible bounty hunter, holds little Eiko hostage. Back outside the wall, try talking to Mog, and then agree to save Eiko.

The situation takes a sudden U-turn when the Red-haired bandit suddenly thwarts Lani and steals the gem. However, this scabrous wretch isn't here to save the day; he just doesn't agree with Lani's methods. Zidane must now fight the odd stranger in a one-on-one duel.

AMARANT

BOSS FIGHT

HP	8985	AP	9	Weak vs.	None

Steal Items	Poison Knuckles, Ether	Spoils	Tent

BOSS PREPARATIONS:

↓ Equip Zidane with Auto-Potion and High Tide

BATTLE TACTICS:

↓ Only attack Amarant when he returns to the center position and says "Here I go!"

↓ When Zidane goes into Trance, use his highest-power Dyne ability

RETURN OF THE DREAM

When Amarant retreats, Vivi and Eiko return to her house. Follow with Zidane and Dagger, and talk to Momatose in the dining room to rest up. You can find Eiko in the room under the back porch, where she decides to leave Madain Sari and take the **Memory Earring** with her. Dagger disappears at some point during the scene.

Just outside the house, find a spot where the "?" appears over Zidane's head. He will hear Dagger's song, and follows it to a boat dock. After some intense memory recall, the party gathers at the entrance of town to leave. The Flaming Amarant, not satisfied with the outcome of the duel, agrees to join Zidane in his quest. You must decide who fights in the party and who doesn't. Putting Eiko and Amarant in the party is recommended, along with Vivi.

You'll want to do some leveling up and ability learning in the area surrounding Madain Sari and in the Mountain Path. This is suggested especially for Amarant and Eiko's benefit, because they are the two newest characters and possess almost no abilities. When you're ready, return to the Iifa Tree to see if your archenemy has shown up.

BATTLE AT IIFA TREE

ENEMIES:	KEY ITEMS:	ITEMS:	CARDS:
STROPER, MYCONID, MISTODON	NONE	AUQAMARINE	NONE

OBJECTIVES

1. Chase Kuja high into the tree

2. Outrun the scoundrel's beasts

3. Call upon Leviathan for aid

4. Witness the battle between evils

ANGEL OF DEATH

At the entrance to the tree of life, the nemesis Kuja flies overhead on his silver dragon. You'll have the option of arranging your party as you wish before continuing. Use Amarant, Vivi, and one of the ladies to have a balanced crew.

A few enemies will cross your path as you're winding across the tree roots. You won't have to go far, however, as Zidane decides to scale a high area. Once the group reaches Kuja, you can again choose your party. Stick with the previous recommendation.

Although the heroes confront Kuja, the villain has his hands full with bigger problems. He summons the powerful Mistodon enemies to keep you entertained.

A sequence follows in which you must run down a long tree root pursued by Mistodons. Mocchi is partially hidden at the very top of the root, so save your game with him before heading down to the left.

As you descend the root, run at top speed. Mistodons will overtake the party at amazing speeds, so a few battles are unavoidable. However, keep running at all times to avoid fighting any unnecessary battles.

At the bottom of the root, Dagger receives the **Aquamarine** to teach her the Leviathan summons. However, not even this is enough to stop the demonic Kuja from exacting a terrible revenge.

RETURN TO ALEXANDRIA

ENEMIES:
NONE

KEY ITEMS:
LEO STELLAZZIO,
ATHLETE QUEEN

ITEMS:
OPAL, TOPAZ,
AMETHYST,
PHOENIX
PINION (x2),
LAPIS LAZULI

CARDS:
(if not taken previously)
IRONITE, FANG,
GOBLIN, SHIVA,
RAMUH

OBJECTIVES

1 Follow the heroes back to Alexandria

2 Entertain yourself with mini-games around town

3 Speak with Marcus and Blank at the mini-theater

4 Collect new items that have appeared

5 Stop the fight at the boat dock

6 Hold audience with the soon-to-be queen

7 Check out the card tournament in Treno

HANGIN' OUT IN THE BIG TOWN

While a bewildered Dagger is prepared by the castle staff to become queen, Zidane drowns his sorrows at the pub. Eventually, his buddies give up cheering him up and run into Vivi on the street. Now that you're controlling Vivi, there are a number of other things you can do in Alexandria.

Blank and Marcus are waiting for Vivi in the alley where Puck stole the ladder from Dante. You can walk past the two bandits, or you can speak to them. If you want to finish all of the mini-games, make sure you refuse their request to see Ruby's play. If you accept their request, it triggers a long sequence of events that take you out of Alexandria.

KEYWORD:
HIPP01

PlayOnline.com

MINI-GAMES

Help Hippaul get some exercise, plus win some stuff. For all the details, go to PlayOnline.

SHOPPING IN ALEXANDRIA

Since there's no performance at this time, the shops are open for business. Make sure you stop by Doug's Item Shop, the Alchemist's Synthesis Shop, and the Alexandria Weapon Supply.

How Are the Moogles?

Stiltzkin may be hanging out with Kupo at the bell tower. In spite of the seemingly peaceful times, it's a good idea to continue purchasing items from him. You might have an overdue letter from Kuppo to deliver to Kupo.

Moving Along...

Head to the left out of the square. Blank and Marcus are hanging out at the entrance to the mini-theater where Ruby now works. They ask Vivi to run interference while they sneak in, but there's no getting past a smart actress! In the meantime, Dagger is trying to get her act together before the coronation. Dr. Tot helps out by giving her an **Opal**, a **Topaz**, and an **Amethyst**. I'm sure the princess can use these items...

Eventually, Baku and the rest of Tantalus get tired of Zidane moping around. When Vivi joins Zidane, you must guide the two toward the castle. Make sure you explore the area thoroughly for items and Gil.

Head upward from the square to the place where a venetian-style boat takes travelers across the moat to the castle. After Freya and Amarant have a muscle-flexing contest, pick up any spare items in the area. Upon boarding the boat, you head to the castle.

After scouring the outside area, return to the castle's entrance, where Eiko is being forcibly ejected. The group then enters the castle and a long series of scenes commences. Eventually, the party decides to attend the card tournament currently underway in Treno.

Doug's Item Shop	
Item	**Gil**
Potion	50
Hi-Potion	200
Phoenix Down	150
Echo Screen	50
Soft	100
Antidote	50
Eye Drops	50
Remedy	300
Annoyntment	150
Tent	800

ALCHEMIST'S SYNTHESIS SHOP

Item	Gil	Required Items
The Ogre	700	2 Mage Mashers
Exploda	1000	Mage Masher, Mythril Dagger
Rune Tooth	2000	2 Mythril Daggers
Angel Bless	9000	Mythril Dagger, Gladius
Cotton Robe	1000	Wrist, Steepled Hat
Silk Robe	2000	Silk Shirt, Bandana
Magician Robe	3000	Mage Staff, Magician Cloak
Glass Buckle	500	Glass Armlet, Leather Wrist
Germinas Boots	900	Desert Boots, Fork
Cachusha	1000	Magus Hat, Rubber Helm
Coral Ring	1200	Lightning Staff, Rod
Gold Choker	1300	Linen Cuirass, Soft
Magician Shoes	1500	Germinas Boots, Bone Wrist
Barette	1800	Needle Fork, Barbut
Fairy Earrings	3200	Magic Armlet, Soft
Extension	3500	Lamia's Tiara, Multina Racket
Reflect Ring	7000	Anklet, Madain's Ring
Anklet	4000	Gold Choker, Peridot
Feather Boots	4000	Magician Shoes, Phoenix Pinion
Black Belt	4000	Twist Headband, Survival Vest
Pearl Rouge	5000	Moonstone, Elixir

ALEXANDRIA WEAPON SUPPLY

Item	Gil	Item	Gil
Mythril Dagger	950	Bone Wrist	330
Gladius	2300	Mythril Armlet	500
Ice Brand	3780	Magic Armlet	1000
Partisan	1600	Mythril Gloves	980
Ice Lance	2430	Thunder Gloves	1200
Cat's Claws	4000	Lamia's Tiara	800
Poison Knuckles	5000	Ritual Hat	1000
Stardust Rod	760	Twist Headband	1200
Healing Rod	1770	Barbut	600
Lamia's Flute	3800	Mythril Helm	1000
Flame Staff	1100	Gold Helm	1800
Ice Staff	980	Magician Cloak	1850
Lightning Staff	1200	Survival Vest	2900
Oak Staff	2400	Brigandine	4300
Pinwheel	200	Mythril Armor	1830
Glass Armlet	250	Plate Mail	2320

CARD TOURNAMENT IN TRENO

ENEMIES:
NONE

KEY ITEMS:
(*Auction Items*) DOGA'S ARTIFACT, UNE'S MIRROR, RAT TAIL, GRIFFIN'S HEART, MINI-CID, FEATHER BOOTS, ANKLET, MADAIN'S RING, DARK MATTER, BURMAN COFFEE

ITEMS:
CHIMERA ARMLET, REBIRTH RING

CARDS:
(CARD TOURNAMENT WINS)

OBJECTIVES

Navigate smartly through the ATEs

Become a finalist in the Treno card tournament

HIGH ROLLERS IN THE BIG TOWN

Upon speaking to Dr. Tot in Treno, he offers to loan you some cards if you need them. There's a three-part card challenge to win at this point of the game. You must win the first and second challenges, and you only get *one shot* to win the third match, which is against the champion. For the game to proceed, you must take part in the card tournament.

If you haven't been paying much attention to the card game up to this point, it's not a real problem. If you've picked up every card and if you've gained cards by defeating enemies, then you shouldn't have much trouble blowing away the competition. However, if your collector status is low and you haven't had much luck with cards, then you'll need to take some cards from Doctor Tot.

KEYWORD: VATE1
PlayOnline.com
VIEW ATES

The ATEs in Treno play an important role. To find out how to view them, go to PlayOnline.

Arriving in Dr. Tot's tower, everyone runs off as usual to explore the area for themselves. *It is very important to watch the ATEs that occur in Treno.* Not only can you gain some insight into the pasts of Zidane and Vivi, but there's one scene in particular ("How He Ended Up Here") where you can send Vivi to Quan's Dwelling.

KEYWORD: ATENAM7
PlayOnline.com
HIDDEN ATE

During the card tournament, a hidden ATE will trigger a special event later. See PlayOnline for details.

LOW ON CARDS?
If you're running low on cards, you can always purchase some from the vendor in front of the card stadium. The vendor sells four types of cards for 100 Gil apiece.

VISIT THE QUEEN!
Don't forget to trade in the Stellazzios you've found since your last stop in Treno. Queen Stella rewards you with a lot of Gil and some great items.

AUCTION AT THE KING'S MANSION

The last time you were in Treno, this is where Steiner finally caught up to Dagger. From there, you were probably taken straight into the Supersoft quest. Now you finally have the chance to bid on some rare and expensive items at the Treno Auction house.

KEYWORD: FRE01
PlayOnline.com
SPECIAL

You can get an old party member back at this point. If you're curious, go to PlayOnline for details.

Each time you enter the mansion, the auctioneer lists the items to be sold. Of particular interest is the **Dark Matter**, which enables a character to summon Odin. Also of interest are rare items such as the **Mini-Cid**, **Rat Tail**, **Doga's Artifact**, **Une's Mirror**, and the **Griffin's Heart**.

KEYWORD: CHARM1
PlayOnline.com
SIDE QUESTS

Remember the Four-armed Man? He drops an item if you do just the right things. PlayOnline covers it all

A good strategy for bidding is to wait patiently as the nobles bid back and forth on the item. When it seems that the item is about to be sold, outbid the highest offer and you will instantly purchase the piece. However, you want to be sure that you don't overbid!

After purchasing all of the items you want, the auction offers a lot of Add-on items that prove useful in battle. However, you should set a limit on how much you'll bid for these items. To do this, find the price of what it would cost to synthesize the item and add the cost of each material needed. Don't bid any higher than what it would cost you to buy the necessary items and synthesize the Add-on yourself. It may be a fancy auction, but you can still get ripped off.

OFFERS FOR YOUR GOODS

If you purchase items in the Treno Auction and then speak to the citizens near the Café Carta, they will offer to purchase the items that they want. If you sell the item to them, it will reappear at the auction later in the game. Usually, their offers are just a little better than what is listed as the best bid for each item in the table shown earlier. Once the nobles buy each rare item from you once, they don't offer to buy them again. Always decline their first offer, and they'll then raise their offer.

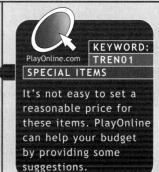

PlayOnline.com
KEYWORD: TRENO1
SPECIAL ITEMS
It's not easy to set a reasonable price for these items. PlayOnline can help your budget by providing some suggestions.

SHOPPING IN TRENO

Treno is a much better place to shop than it was previously. The Synthesist is now the best in the game, producing items not even made in Alexandria. If you're not completely depleted after the Treno Auction, then lay down some Gil on some good new weapons and Add-ons. Buy a few presents for Steiner and Dagger, too. You may be seeing them again sooner than you think.

MONSTERS IN THE CAGE
You can still fight the monsters in the cage under the Knight's Residence Weapon Shop; however, the battles are fairly tough.

PlayOnline.com
KEYWORD: KNCAG1
SPECIAL ITEMS
You can receive some cool items for defeating the monsters. Find out what and how to do it at PlayOnline.

DOWN TO BUSINESS

When you're ready, head to the card stadium and show the card-playing "pros" your skills. Speak to the Card Seller on the left side of the entrance to register in the competition.

Getting through the card tournament requires that you play at least three card games. You must win against the first two challengers to go up against the champion. You only get one shot at the title, so if you don't win, you don't get a second chance. Frankly, it's not that difficult to win the entire tournament with just a mediocre collection of cards.

The first opponent is Attic Man Wake. This guy uses a lot of magic cards, but they're only 1M. Pick five cards that have 2M, 3M, 3P, or 4P attack ratings and fairly decent defense ratings. That way, you're covered if your cards get into a battle. The best strategy is to play by the arrows before depending on the card's stats. For example, if he puts down a card that doesn't have an arrow in the lower-left corner, and you have a card that has an arrow in the upper-right corner, then you can turn his card blue without a fight. He will, of course, pursue the same strategy, so if you happen to have a lot of cards that are 2M, it might be better to ignore the previous strategy and instead place your cards arrow to arrow with his so that you win the fight.

WHAT IF I LOSE?
Losing the first or second round forces you to play a rematch. If you lose a lot and start to run out of cards, you can purchase more from the Card Seller outside the stadium. If you get down to less than five, Dr. Tot will give you better cards than the Card Seller.

The second round pits you against Cardona Bishop, who's a bit better than the first contestant. It becomes important to pick cards that not only have strong stats, but a lot of arrows, too. Cardona plays the arrows of the cards quite well, so having a lot of arrows on each of your cards proves to be a good defensive measure. You're better off placing your cards arrow to arrow with his, starting a card battle to resolve things.

After winning two rounds, the Usher reminds you that you have but one chance to defeat the opponent. Before proceeding to the final match, return to the moogle at the Knight's Residence and save. That way, you can try again if you happen to lose.

Sailor Erin is your next opponent and she uses all Oglop cards. These are rare cards, so it will be good to try to win one. Her cards are all 1P or 2P and have a physical defense of 1, and *no magical defense!*

The key to winning is to employ cards of 1M, 2M, 3P or 4P. Try to win with the arrows first, and battle it out only if you must. Winning this round lets you pick an Oglop card, and you get the **Rebirth Ring**, which teaches all characters the valuable Auto-Life skill. If the round comes to a draw, you immediately play again. Lose and you get nothing. That's why it's important to break away and save before the third round! Afterward, Eiko rushes in with some terrible news.

TRENO SLUMS MEDICINE SHOP

Item	Gil	Item	Gil
Potion	50	Antidote	50
Hi-Potion	200	Eye Drops	50
Phoenix Down	150	Remedy	300
Echo Screen	50	Annoyntment	150
Soft	100	Tent	800

ALCHEMIST'S SYNTHESIS SHOP

Item	Gil	Required Items
The Ogre	700	2 Mage Mashers
Exploda	1000	Mage Masher, Mythril Dagger
Rune Tooth	2000	2 Mythril Daggers
Angel Bless	9000	Mythril Dagger, Gladius
Cotton Robe	1000	Wrist, Steepled Hat
Silk Robe	2000	Silk Shirt, Bandana
Magician Robe	3000	Mage Staff, Magician Cloak
Desert Boots	300	Leather Hat, Leather Shirt
Yellow Scarf	400	Feather Hat, Steepled Hat
Glass Buckle	500	Glass Armlet, Leather Wrist
Germinas Boots	900	Desert Boots, Fork
Cachusha	1000	Magus Hat, Rubber Helm
Coral Ring	1200	Lightning Staff, Rod
Gold Choker	1300	Linen Cuirass, Soft
Magician Shoes	1500	Germinas Boots, Bone Wrist
Barette	1800	Needle Fork, Barbut
Power Belt	2000	Glass Buckle, Chain Mail
Madain's Ring	3000	Bone Wrist, Stardust Rod
Fairy Earrings	3200	Magic Armlet, Soft
Extension	3500	Lamia's Tiara, Multina Racket
Reflect Ring	7000	Anklet, Madain's Ring
Anklet	4000	Gold Choker, Peridot
Feather Boots	4000	Magician Shoes, Phoenix Pinion
Black Belt	4000	Twist Headband, Survival Vest
Pearl Rouge	5000	Moonstone, Elixir

KNIGHT'S RESIDENCE ARMORY SHOP

Item	Gil
Dagger	320
Mage Masher	500
Mythril Dagger	950
Gladius	2300
Ice Brand	3780
Coral Sword	4000
Partisan	1600
Ice Lance	2430
Cat's Claws	5000
Poison Knuckles	5000
Multina Racket	750
Stardust Rod	760
Healing Rod	1770
Lamia's Flute	3800
Oak Staff	2400
Magic Armlet	1000
Mythril Gloves	980
Thunder Gloves	1200
Lamia's Tiara	800
Ritual Hat	1000
Twist Headband	1200
Mythril Helm	1000
Gold Helm	1800
Magician Cloak	1850
Survival Vest	2900
Brigandine	4300
Linen Cuirass	800
Mythril Armor	1830
Plate Mail	2320

THE BATTLE OF ALEXANDRIA

ENEMIES:	KEY ITEMS:	ITEMS:	CARDS:
MISTODON, TANTARIAN (OPTIONAL BOSS)	NONE	NONE	NONE

OBJECTIVES

1 Order the Knights of Pluto into action

2 Plow the monsters off main street

3 Follow the music to the top of the castle

4 Evacuate the castle dwellers

5 Challenge a mysterious monster

6 Save Dagger and Eiko from destruction

DISC THREE

THE BATTLE OF ALEXANDRIA

MUSTERING THE TROOPS

The beautiful city of Alexandria is besieged by the black horrors unleashed by Kuja. Dagger must quickly and precisely give out orders to the Knights of Pluto. You can tell that you're giving orders properly when the knights respond enthusiastically. If you give the knights the wrong tasks, they will be unsure of their orders.

PlayOnline.com
KEYWORD:
KOP03
SPECIAL ITEM
Save the townspeople and be rewarded. Head to PlayOnline for the scoop.

The answer harks back to the very beginning of the game, when Captain Steiner had to give orders to all of the Knights of Pluto. If you spoke to Breireicht twice on the stairs, he rattled off a list of the knights and their personalities. Judging by their interests and abilities, you should know which order to give to which two knights.

SAVE THE QUEEN

Beatrix and Steiner run down Alexandria's main street, protecting the townsfolk from the evil Mist monsters invading the city. You will have a battle in each area, and your party will consist only of Beatrix and Steiner. Considering Beatrix's abilities, that's not necessarily a bad thing.

Equip Steiner with an Ice Brand and the Add Status ability. This may allow you to freeze a Mistodon, so that Beatrix can crush it on the next turn. Otherwise, Beatrix and Steiner should be able to attack a Mistodon once each and survive to the next battle.

When fighting two Mistodons at once, have Beatrix perform Climhazzard to bring them both down. You may only need one more blow to finish them off. Between each battle, use Hi-Potions and Ethers to keep both warriors energized.

Before this series of battles ends, you may want to consider exchanging some of your weaker equipment for the more beneficial fare Beatrix is wearing. You can use the Cross Helm, Thunder Gloves, Plate Mail, and Yellow Scarf that she's wearing to the benefit of Steiner or Freya later. However, Beatrix's Save the Queen sword is the only weapon she can equip, plus only she can use it.

KEYWORD: SVQN01
PlayOnline.com
SPECIAL ITEM

Want to know how to get Beatrix's Save the Queen sword at the end of the game? If so, go to PlayOnline and check out the **Side Quests** section.

In the last battle, an enraged Steiner automatically Trances. This takes place even if he Trances in the previous fight. He should be able to take out one Mistodon on his own, and Beatrix can perform Shock to take out the other.

CALL OF THE EIDOLON

Dagger feels a strange energy emanating from the entire castle and senses a calling from upstairs. Any route she attempts to take that isn't correct becomes blocked by a wall of invisible force, so it's really easy to determine where to go.

Lead Dagger up the circular steps to the third floor, and go through the double doors toward the Queen's chambers. Veer to the left, and go up a series of circling staircases. Each one becomes sealed off by the swords of two knight statues, preventing Dagger from turning back.

At the top, the castle transforms into a new shape. Lead Dagger up the stairs until the game takes over.

EVACUATE ALEXANDRIA

Zidane and the party arrive just in time to rescue Dagger and Eiko. Your fellow warriors are Vivi, Freya, and Amarant. Before following Dagger's path to the top of the castle, you may want to play the hero and clear everyone out. There's even an optional Boss to fight, if you think you're prepared!

KEYWORD: OPTBOSS
PlayOnline.com
BOSS FIGHT STRATEGY

If you're willing, you can fight an optional Boss in Alexandria. To find out its location, go to PlayOnline.

BOSS FIGHT

TANTARIAN (OPTIONAL BOSS)

HP 21,997	AP 30	Weak vs. None
Steal Items Demon's Mail, Silver Fork, Elixir, Ether		**Spoils** Running Shoes

BOSS PREPARATIONS:

- Equip everyone with Antibody and Auto-Regen or Auto-Potion

- Equip Amarant with the Poison Knuckles

- Equip the Bandit ability on Zidane

BATTLE TACTICS:

- Need to cause between 150 and 200 HP of damage to the book; this causes the book to show its true form

- Try Amarant's Spare Change ability

- Once the book opens and shows its true form, don't physically strike the book; instead, use only magic and skills

- Beware of the Boss's Paper Storm or Edge attacks

PlayOnline.com
KEYWORD: TANTB01
BOSS FIGHT TIPS
For additional help against this Boss, check out PlayOnline.

PREPARATIONS IN LINDBLUM

ENEMIES:
NONE

KEY ITEMS:
STRANGE POTION, UNUSUAL POTION, BEAUTIFUL POTION, SAGITTARIUS STELLAZZIO

ITEMS:
EGOIST'S ARMLET, ELIXIR (x2), LAPIS LAZULI, REMEDY, CHIMERA ARMLET

CARDS:
NONE

OBJECTIVES

1 Find out Dagger's location from Blank

2 Go to Dagger at the telescope

3 Join Regent Cid's conference

4 Check on Dagger's condition

5 Ride the air cab to the Theater District

6 Search the art studio for the Strange Potion

7 Talk to Cinna to get the Unusual Potion

8 Get the Beautiful Potion from Alice in the Business District

9 Return to the throne room with the three potions

10 Ride to the Serpent's Gate

11 Board the Blue Narciss

The Silence of Sorrow

After the rescue, Zidane awakes in the Guest Room at Lindblum. The chests are all full of items, so make sure you pillage them and speak to Mogki. He has a letter for you to deliver to Moodon over at the Business District Inn.

As you head toward the stairs, Blank enters. If you ask him about Dagger, he'll tell you she's by the telescope on the roof. If you select the other option, he remembers to tell you to head to the Regent's throne room. Either way, you can speak to Dagger first or proceed directly to the throne room. You can also find your friends waiting in the conference room before going to see Cid.

Leave the conference room and return to the mid level of the castle. Return to the guest room, where everyone shows their concern for the princess. When the meeting recommences in the throne room, everyone discusses plans to return Regent Cid to human form. It's up to Zidane to search Lindblum for three items: Unusual Potion, Strange Potion, and Beautiful Potion.

A Flask Full of Hope

Cinna has the Unusual Potion, and the ATE that follows the throne room scene shows that he is helping repair the Tantalus hideout. Board the air cab and ride from the castle to the Theater District.

Before going to Tantalus, visit Michael's studio to the right. Ask the artist about it, and he will tell you to search his studio. Search the corner by the stairs to find the **Strange Potion**.

Now visit the Tantalus hideout. During the short scene, Cinna gladly gives Zidane the **Unusual Potion**. But after Zidane leaves the area, you may want to double-back and search inside the hideout for some more Gil.

Now there's just one more potion to find, and it's somwhere in the Business District. Ride the air cab there, but don't forget to give the letter to Moodon at the Inn.

Continue into the market square, where Alice's shop is under reconstruction. Ask Alice about the potion and she'll hand it over! Now with the **Beautiful Potion** in hand, you're ready to return to the castle.

GO SHOPPING!
Before you return to the castle, visit the Synthesist and other local shops. It's always a good idea to stock up on your inventory.

With the three potions in hand, return to Regent Cid's throne room in the castle. Unfortunately, the mixture has a different effect on Cid than what was hoped for. However, the Regent is undaunted and continues the meeting from where it left off.

Cid and the party determine that the group should return to the Black Mage Village on the Outer Continent to determine the connection between the mages and Kuja. Leave the throne room and take the elevator to the base level. Ride the trolley on the right side to the Serpent's Gate. The Blue Narciss is docked at the end of the pier.

THE BLUE NARCISS

Once onboard the Blue Narciss, Quina rejoins the party and Cid tells you to select your party members.

SWITCHING PARTY MEMBERS
If you want to switch out the fighting team, press the Triangle button while on the World Map on the ship and speak with Cid to select new party members.

You can now visit any beach on the World Map. The only new outside town you can visit is Esto Gaza, which is on the Lost Continent, covered with ice (it lies to the north). Or, you can visit Alexandria by landing at the harbor on the eastern side of the Mist Continent. These sections are covered later.

BLUE NARCISS CONTROLS

Button	Controls
X	Forward
Triangle	Return to the deck
Square	Reverse
Circle	Disembark
SELECT	Switch navigation map
L1, R1	Camera control
L2	Align camera
R2	Switch perspective
Left stick	Move left and right
Right stick	Move forward and backward

WAYNE'S SYNTHESIS SHOP

Item	Gil	Materials
The Ogre	700	2 Mage Mashers
Exploda	1000	Mage Masher, Mythril Dagger
Rune Tooth	2000	2 Mythril Daggers
Angel Bless	9000	Mythril Dagger, Gladius
Cotton Robe	1000	Wrist, Steepled Hat
Silk Robe	2000	Silk Shirt, Bandana
Magician Robe	3000	Mage Staff, Magician Cloak
Desert Boots	300	Leather Hat, Leather Shirt
Yellow Scarf	400	Feather Hat, Steepled Hat
Glass Buckle	500	Glass Armlet, Leather Wrist
Germinas Boots	900	Desert Boots, Fork
Cachusha	1000	Magus Hat, Rubber Helm
Coral Ring	1200	Lightning Staff, Rod
Gold Choker	1300	Linen Cuirass, Soft
Magician Shoes	1500	Germinas Boots, Bone Wrist
Barette	1800	Needle Fork, Barbut
Power Belt	2000	Glass Buckle, Chain Mail
Madain's Ring	3000	Bone Wrist, Stardust Rod
Fairy Earrings	3200	Magic Armlet, Soft
Extension	3500	Lamia's Tiara, Multina Racket
Reflect Ring	7000	Anklet, Madain's Ring
Anklet	4000	Gold Choker, Peridot
Feather Boots	4000	Magician Shoes, Phoenix Pinion
Black Belt	4000	Twist Headband, Survival Vest
Pearl Rouge	5000	Moonstone, Elixir

DRAGOOS' WEAPON/ MEDICINE SHOP

Item	Gil
Coral Sword	4000
Partisan	1600
Ice Lance	2430
Poison Knuckles	5000
Magic Racket	1350
Healing Rod	1770
Lamia's Flute	3800
Cypress Pile	3200
Mythril Fork	4700
Pinwheel	200
Chimera Armlet	1200
Thunder Gloves	1200
Twist Headband	1200
Mantra Band	1500
Dark Hat	1800
Gold Helm	1800
Magician Cloak	1850
Survival Vest	2900
Brigandine	4300
Mythril Armor	1830
Plate Mail	2320
Potion	50
Hi-Potion	200
Phoenix Down	150
Echo Screen	50
Soft	100
Antidote	50
Eye Drops	50
Magic Tag	100
Remedy	300
Annoyntment	150
Tent	800

THE BLACK MAGE VILLAGE, DESERTED

ENEMIES:
NONE

KEY ITEMS:
NONE

ITEMS:
BLACK BELT

CARDS:
NONE

OBJECTIVES

 **1**

 **2**

 **3**

 **4**

Return to the deserted Black Mage Village

Follow Vivi to the cemetery

Witness a chocobo hatching

Figure out the next move at the entrance

NO ONE IN SIGHT

Pilot the Blue Narciss to Gegalrich Shores, just southeast of the Black Mage Village. You must still cross through the forest on foot, unless you head to the chocobo tracks far to the northeast of Qu's Marsh and call for a ride.

The Black Mage Village is mostly deserted. Vivi immediately takes off for the cemetery, but you don't have to follow him just yet.

Number 288 is still at the cemetery, and he explains why the Black Mages are assisting Kuja. Afterwards, follow Vivi to the hut, where the other two mages are nurturing the chocobo egg.

The scene then returns to the entrance of town, where the group determines to follow No. 288's tip and go to the desert on the eastern end of the Outer Continent.

> **KEYWORD:**
> **BBITEM1**
> **SPECIAL ITEM**
> There's a special item in the Village, if you didn't get it previously. To find out where it is and how to get it, go to PlayOnline.

QUICKSAND IN THE DESERT

ENEMIES:
ANTLION, GOBLIN MAGE,
GRIFFIN, TROLL, OGRE,
GRIMLOCK

KEY ITEMS:
NONE

ITEMS:
NONE

CARDS:
NONE

OBJECTIVES

1
Land on the east side
of the Outer Continent

2
Move to the northern
sinkhole

3
Make a deal with
the devil

4
Board the airship

5
Land on the Forgotten
Continent

SWIRLING SINKHOLES IN THE DESERT

Pilot the Blue Narciss to the far eastern end of the Outer Continent to a strip of beaches on the southeast end. Just north of this location is another beach, which is the best place to land. This should put you very close to four whirling sinkholes in the desert.

Move around the outside of the quicksand area, heading to the furthest area to the north. If you go to the wrong sinkhole, you'll get attacked repeatedly by Antlions. Look for the sinkhole without the "puffs" or "whisps" of sand coming out of it. When you reach the northernmost sinkhole, a "?" appears. Press the X button to enter.

AN OFFER YOU CAN'T REFUSE

After a short sequence between Zidane and Kuja, the Black Mages teleport Zidane to Kuja's room in the Desert Palace. The demonic overlord threatens to annihilate the heroes unless Zidane retrieves an item called the **Gulug Stone** from Oeilvert, an ancient fortress on the Forgotten Continent in the far west. Zidane must pick a party that doesn't rely on magic, because Kuja mentions that magic cannot be used in Oeilvert.

Choosing a party for this mission is a big decision. Whomever you leave behind forms a second party. Since magic doesn't work in Oeilvert, leave all of your magic users behind. This means that the best party to take to the Forgotten Continent would consist of Zidane, Steiner, Freya, and Amarant. However, Steiner is more useful when in the same party as Vivi. The decision is yours! You may want to place Quina in your party, because s/he can "eat" enemies and learn new Blue Magic.

MORE ABILITIES FOR QUINA
Quina can learn some fantastic abilities by eating the new enemies on the Forgotten Continent.

THE HILDA GARDE 1

The party heading to Oeilvert is teleported to the mountain airship dock. The massive Hilda Garde 1 is docked there, which is Cid's long-lost craft.

DEFEATING THE GRIMLOCKS
The Grimlocks with blue heads are weak against physical attacks and strong against magic. If they rearrange themselves so that they have pink heads, they can only be damaged effectively by magic.

148   Disc Three

Head over to the large craft and board. The vessel immediately departs for the Forgotten Continent. When the ship sets down in the grassy area north of Seaways Canyon, Zidane automatically disembarks, after which you won't be able to board again.

From the landing point, press the SELECT button until the mini-map appears in the lower-right corner of the screen. Proceed directly south and follow the Seaways Canyon, which spirals west and then inward.

KEYWORD: **QUMAR4**

HIDDEN AREA

Tired of always going to the same Qu's Marsh? PlayOnline can tell you where to find another one!

FORGOTTEN CONTINENT

ENEMIES:

JABBERWOCK, CATOBLEPAS, ADAMANTOISE, ARMSTRONG, CACTUAR

KEY ITEMS:

NONE

ITEMS:

NONE

CARDS:

NONE

OBJECTIVES

Fight your way south

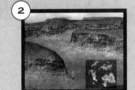

Enter the canyons and curve to the west

At the sea, turn east and follow the spiraling canyon

THE UNFORGIVING DESERT

Upon disembarking from the Hilda Garde 1, you should stock up on medicine by purchasing it from the jester twins on the ship. You should equip each character with the Clear Headed ability, as well as Loudmouth and Bright Eyes.

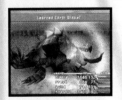

QUINA SO HUNGRY!

If you made the choice to bring Quina along, work hard to satisfy that appetite. You can learn Limit Glove by eating Catoblepases or Jabberwocks, and the intimidating Adamantoise will yield the Earth Shake ability. If you haven't done so yet, learn the 1,000 Needles ability by eating a Cactuar.

SEAWAYS CANYON

The day becomes dusky and night threatens to fall when you reach the Seaways Canyon area. To reach Oeilvert, head into the canyons and veer off to the west. This canyon leads your party out to the western seashore. There, another canyon forms that spirals inward to the mysterious fortress, which is surrounded by high canyon walls.

THORN AND ZORN'S MEDICINE SHOP

Item	Gil
Potion	50
Hi-Potion	200
Phoenix Down	150
Echo Screen	50
Soft	100
Antidote	50
Eye Drops	50
Magic Tag	100
Vaccine	100
Remedy	300
Annoyntment	150
Tent	800

OEILVERT

ENEMIES:	KEY ITEMS:	ITEMS:	CARDS:
OGRE, EPITAPH, GARUDA, ARK (BOSS)	GULUG STONE	REMEDY, RISING SUN, ELIXIR, DIAMOND SWORD, SHIELD ARMOR, POWER VEST, FEATHER BOOTS, GAIA GEAR	NONE

OBJECTIVES

1 Meet the moogle outside

2 Enter the mysterious fortress

3 Activate the globe on the upper level

4 View the gigantic hologram

5 Turn on the projectors in order

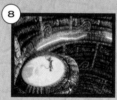

6 Catch the slide show

7 Stand before the witnesses

8 Find the spiraling platform

9 Bring down the floating Ark

10 Take the Gulug Stone from the altar

FRIENDLY GREETING AT THE GATE

Eiko's friend Mimoza is outside of Oeilvert, patiently waiting for your arrival. The moogle has a letter she'd like you to deliver to Mooel. Mimoza also runs a Mogshop, and the items are listed at the end of this section.

THE COSMIC PUZZLE

At the front gate, the doors magically open by themselves. Make sure you search the area inside to find a couple of items. Plus, you may find something useful for Amarant to throw in your next Boss fight.

Follow the top platform through a doorway to the left, and then examine the magic globe. This causes it to mysteriously change from blue to red.

Return to the lobby, go back downstairs, and proceed through the lower doorway to the left. As you continue to the right, a holograph appears in the center of the room. Circle around behind the image and search for treasure chests. There are a few doorways to the far left; ignore them for now, and proceed through the exit at the bottom of the screen.

There are two projectors set into the floor on this platform. Examining them causes nothing to happen at the moment, though. Head up the steps to find two more floor projectors. As Zidane suspects, there is a certain order to activating the projectors. Start with the top-left one, and work your way clockwise down to the one nearest the entrance. This reveals a bit of the history of airships, but not the ones used in Gaia. Following this, head out the top exit to explore further.

Zidane must cross a series of arching bridges. In the center of the two spans, search the global object and a short slide show begins. Then continue across the bridge to the left. This exits back into the area with the large hologram, just outside the previously locked blue door. Inside this chamber, a host of spooky faces enlighten the party about the plight of another world.

With these clues firmly in hand, return to the lobby and continue through the door on the far right. Another moogle stands at the back of this chamber, so save your game. As you proceed around the chamber to the right, another hologram appears in the center of the room.

Stepping through the final doorway, it seems you've reached a dead end. However, upon examining the platform, you activate an ancient mechanism that causes you to spiral down into a gigantic pit. At the bottom, Zidane finds the **Gulug Stone**. But something large and hostile shows up, attempting to prevent you from taking Kuja's prize.

ARK

BOSS FIGHT

HP	20,002	AP	11	Weak vs.	Shadow

Steal Items	Holy Lance, Power Vest, Elixir	**Spoils**	Pumice Piece

BOSS PREPARATIONS:

- Equip the Clear Headed ability on your entire party

BATTLE TACTICS:

- Have Freya act as Medic, casting Reis's Wind
- Have Amarant throw weapons
- If Steiner is in your party, his Power Break and Armor Break abilities make things a bit easier

After the fight, take the **Gulug Stone** from the altar; this causes the scene to shift back to your comrades in captivity at the Desert Palace.

MIMOZA'S MOGSHOP

Item	Gil	Item	Gil	Item	Gil
Diamond Sword	4700	Egoist's Armlet	2000	Gold Armor	2950
Trident	3580	Thunder Gloves	1200	Hi-Potion	200
Mythril Claws	6500	Diamond Gloves	2000	Phoenix Down	150
Magic Racket	1350	Mantra Band	1500	Soft	100
Healing Rod	1770	Dark Hat	1800	Antidote	50
Fairy Flute	4500	Green Beret	2180	Eye Drops	50
Cypress Pile	3200	Gold Helm	1800	Magic Tag	100
Silver Fork	7400	Cross Helm	2200	Remedy	300
Pinwheel	200	Brigandine	4300	Annoyntment	150
Chimera Armlet	1200	Judo Uniform	5000	Tent	800
		Plate Mail	2320		

DESERT PALACE

ENEMIES:
OGRE, GRIMLOCK, DRAKAN, TORAMA, VALIA PIRA (BOSS)

KEY ITEMS:
HOURGLASS KEY

ITEMS:
PROMIST RING, ANKLET, SHIELD ARMOR, N-KAI ARMLET, BLACK HOOD, VENETIA SHIELD

CARDS:
NAMINGWAY CARD

OBJECTIVES

1
Cid must sneak over to the key

2
Move through the Palace, activating bloodstones

3
Use the braziers to make windows and objects disappear

4
Light candelabras to open the path

5
Destroy the security guard

6
Chase Kuja to the airship dock

7
Use the rope ladder to exit the Palace

TREACHERY OF THE WICKED

While Zidane is away treasure hunting for Kuja, the maniacal double-crosser proves that his word is not worth a penny. The lives of the heroes left in the Desert Palace are limited by an hourglass.

Since Regent Cid is the only one who is free to save the others, he must hop over to the hourglass and flip it over before the four remaining party members meet their fate. Move Cid to the center of the prison area, where he overhears a conversation between two Black Mages. An important clue is discussed. The Black Mages exit to the left, meaning Cid must go to the right.

FROG IN PERIL

A small mini-game ensues, with the heroes' lives in the balance. Using the Circle button, move Cid carefully and quietly across the floor toward the **Hourglass Key**, which is hanging on the back of a Hedgehog Pie's cage. You have only six minutes to get the key and determine how to unbalance the scales so that Cid can hop up to the hourglass. If the Hedgehog Pie sees you moving, you must start over again with whatever time is remaining.

If the six minutes expire and you haven't reached the key yet, the mini-game simply starts over again with Cid back at the beginning.

After successfully snatching the key, Cid makes his way to the scales in the back. Choose to examine the weights, so that Cid can determine what they're made of.

PlayOnline.com

KEYWORD: SCAL01

MINI-GAMES

Need help aligning the proper weights on the scale? If so, check out PlayOnline for more coverage.

EIKO IN CHARGE

With the Hourglass Key in your possession, the remaining four party members meet in the center of the prison area. Eiko is automatically in the lead, and hopefully you have Vivi in the party as well.

First, head to the right again, into the room with the hourglass. From a taller perspective, you can see that there is a moogle named Mojito in here. Save your game and agree to deliver mail to Mogsam. Mojito also runs a Mogshop, and his inventory appears at the end of this section. Head back through the prison area, and proceed up the stairs to the far left.

"TURN THEM ALL ON..."

Light the candelabra under the angel on the left-hand side. This activates a bloodstone under the right-hand angel. Examine the bloodstone, which describes the properties of the object that powers the device. Remove the **Promist Ring**, which contains the Mag Elem Null ability.

Up the stairs, Eiko encounters the statue of an angel between two demon statues. Run to the far right, and then run to the left as if you're going to exit. This causes a magical staircase to appear. This hidden path leads to a balcony. Light the candelabra here, and then return to the previous room and continue off to the left.

A lavish staircase winds up to a patio area. The left side is cut off from the center and the right by a row of statues. Light all three braziers in the left area, which should cause the stained glass in the back on the left and on the right to disappear. Now, Eiko can move across the balcony to the right side.

Once there, only light the brazier in the bottom-left corner next to the statues. This causes the left three statues to disappear. Go back across the balcony to the center area, and read the inscription on the central mosaic: "The path will open when all lamps are lit."

Light the two braziers at the top of the central staircase, which causes the right set of statues to disappear. Light the two remaining braziers on the right, and then descend the central steps and light the large brazier on the small circular platform. This causes the stained glass on the far right to disappear, and the bloodstone under the mosaic activates. Extract the **Anklet** from the bloodstone, and then exit through the right doorway.

Halfway around this circular corridor, search for a candelabra to light. Then extract the **Shield Armor** from the blood-stone and continue to the back of the semi-circle. From there, move Eiko a little forward to go up the stairs.

Lighting the candelabra at the top of the steps causes a huge stained glass window overhead to light up. Circle around to the forefront of the screen, and then enter the library.

Move across the library and light the candles on the far left. This makes a staircase magically appear on the right. Ascend the stairs to the top level, and light the fixture on the left. This causes a section of bookcase to rise, revealing a hidden doorway. Extract the **N-Kai Armlet** from the bloodstone.

WATER SPELL
The N-Kai Armlet reduces Magic Eva to zero, so it would be better to equip just prior to the upcoming Boss fight.

Return to the library and descend the stairs on the right. Now move up the smaller staircase on the left, which leads to the mid level. A message on the left portion of the bookcase section gives an important clue about lighting all of the stained glass. Igniting the candelabra on the right raises the mid level section of bookcase to reveal yet another doorway.

Follow this balcony as it runs a circular course around the large central chamber. Stop off to light the candelabra, which illuminates the stained glass panel on the wall. Continue up the ramp to the top. Light another candelabra, which causes a new section of stained glass to appear. Now return to the library.

Move to the bottom level of the giant bookcase and light the candles on the right. This raises the bottom section, revealing a final balcony with another candelabra to light. This opens the left-hand wall in the library, and the moogle Mogsam is glad for it. Deliver the letter from Mojito, and save your game. Continue to the left past the moogle to the next candle-lighting challenge.

Examine the gargoyle on the back wall to find out that it's the "Apostle from the Underworld." Lighting the two candles causes the bloodstone on the balcony to activate. Extract the **Black Hood** from it, and then head through the door across the balcony to the other side of the high chamber. Light all three candles on the left side of the chamber to activate yet another bloodstone. This one contains the **Venetia Shield**.

Now for the tricky part. Extinguish the left candle under the angel statue, and then cross back to the right side of the room and extinguish the left candle under the demon. This makes a staircase appear in the middle of the room. Ascend the staircase to the final area. Climb up the steps to the candelabra at the top. Examining the final candelabra triggers the security system, and the monolithic Valia Pira descends to counteract the intruders.

BOSS FIGHT

VALIA PIRA

HP	12,119	AP	11	Weak vs.	Water
Steal Items	None			Spoils	Ether, Elixir

BOSS PREPARATIONS:

- Make sure Dagger can summon Leviathan
- Equip Vivi with the N-Kai Armlet
- Make sure Eiko can cast Reflect or summon Carbuncle

BATTLE TACTICS:

- Have Vivi cast Water and make Steiner perform Water Sword
- Make Dagger summon Leviathan every round
- Have Eiko serve as the party's medic

After the struggle, light the final candelabra, step into the glowing circle, and press the X button to teleport out.

DESPERATE REUNION

The scene shifts back to the airship dock, where Zidane and the other party have just returned from Oeilvert. Return to use the teleporter.

This time, the magical device deposits Zidane and the crew outside Kuja's room. Only Zidane is allowed to enter, so that Kuja can collect his prize. When the other party members teleport in from the opposite direction, the heroes attempt to storm Kuja's chamber with disastrous results!

Now you must form a combat party and chase the diabolical villain back to the airship dock. We highly recommend a party of Zidane, Steiner, Vivi, and Amarant.

Run back out to the teleporter on the left, and beam back down to the airship dock. The gigantic Hilda Garde 1 is already gone! Fight your way to the end of the path, and keep running until you reach a cliff.

After the party resolves to chase Kuja by sea, kick the switch to lower the rope ladder and descend to the sandy surface. Move quickly, albeit carefully, toward the exit at the top of the screen.

MOJITO'S MOGSHOP

Item	Gil	Item	Gil	Item	Gil
Diamond Sword	4700	Chimera Armlet	1200	Potion	50
Trident	3580	Egoist's Armlet	2000	Hi-Potion	200
Mythril Claws	6500	Diamond Gloves	2000	Phoenix Down	150
Magic Racket	1350	Mantra Band	1500	Echo Screen	50
Healing Rod	1770	Dark Hat	1800	Soft	100
Fairy Flute	4500	Green Beret	2180	Antidote	50
Cypress Pile	3200	Cross Helm	2200	Magic Tag	100
Silver Fork	7400	Brigandine	4300	Remedy	300
Pinwheel	200	Judo Uniform	5000	Annoyntment	150
Rising Sun	500	Gold Armor	2950	Tent	800

THE LOST CONTINENT

ENEMIES:
WHALE ZOMBIE, GREEN VEPAL,
BLAZER BEETLE, FEATHER
CIRCLE, GIGAN OCTOPUS

KEY ITEMS:
NONE

ITEMS:
NONE

CARDS:
NONE

OBJECTIVES

Cross the continent toward the mysterious structure near the mountains

HILLS OF SNOW AND ICE

The Blue Narciss chases Kuja in the Hilda Garde 1 across the ocean to the Lost Continent. There are few people in this region due to the frigid conditions on the plains. However, there is a small citadel on the continent called Esto Gaza, where the inhabitants have formed a religion based on the magic emanating from the Shimmering Island to the south.

When the ship lands at the south shore of the continent, run to the west to reach Esto Gaza. The toughest monsters of the continent seem to appear more frequently in the south end.

If you want to reach Esto Gaza with less hassle, there are some chocobo tracks in the snow just north of the landing spot.

PlayOnline.com
KEYWORD:
QINA4
NEW ABILITIES
Quina can learn a few new abilities outside Esto Gaza. To find out which ones, refer to PlayOnline.

ESTO GAZA

ENEMIES:	KEY ITEMS:	ITEMS:	CARDS:
GARUDA	NONE	WING EDGE	NONE

OBJECTIVES

1

Exchange pleasantries with the Bishop

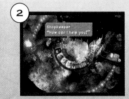

2

Check out Esto Gaza's shop

3

Cross the back patio area

4

Enter the volcano

THE CULT OF THE SHIMMERING ISLE

COME PREPARED
The outer portion of Esto Gaza is currently swarming with flying enemies called Garuda. Prepare your party by equipping the Locomotion ability on everyone, so that they won't succumb to the Stop spell cast by these enemies.

As quickly as possible, enter the main building. Inside, the party encounters the Bishop, the leader of the town. He begrudgingly admits that Kuja and the Black Mages went straight through town to Mount Gulug, an extinct volcano. You can follow them by heading out to the back patio through the left exit.

However, you should head to the right first, where you'll find most of the citizens of Esto Gaza holed up. There's an Equipment Shop with an inventory of new items for each of your characters. Also, explore the area thoroughly just in case there are some hard-to-find treasure chests.

Upon returning to the main hall, the area is teeming with people. The Bishop stands on the left side and will let you rest for 100 Gil. Catching a few Z's is not a bad idea before following Kuja to Mount Gulug.

On the series of platforms behind the town, Mogrika stands by to let you save your game. She has a disturbing letter about Mognet, and desperately needs you to deliver a letter to Moolan. Step to the highest platform to catch a breathtaking view of the place the worshippers call the "Shimmering Island," or the "Path of Souls." Head down the steps to the right to proceed.

You will quickly find the entrance to Mount Gulug. Sealed for many thousands of years, the doors now stand open. What perils await inside?

Esto Gaza Equipment Shop

Item	Gil	Item	Gil	Item	Gil
Gladius	2300	Octagon Rod	4500	Judo Uniform	5000
Zorlin Shape	6000	Silver Fork	7400	Power Vest	7200
Diamond Sword	4700	Rising Sun	500	Gold Armor	2950
Flame Saber	5190	Egoist's Armlet	2000	Shield Armor	4300
Heavy Lance	4700	N-Kai Armlet	3000	Hi-Potion	200
Scissor Fangs	8000	Jade Armlet	3400	Phoenix Down	150
Magic Racket	1350	Diamond Gloves	2000	Magic Tag	100
Asura's Rod	3180	Venetia Shield	2800	Vaccine	100
Hamelin	5700	Black Hood	2550	Remedy	300
Cypress Pile	3200	Red Cap	3000	Annointment	150
		Cross Helm	2200	Tent	800

MOUNT GULUG

ENEMIES:
GRENADE, RED VEPAL, WRAITH, WORM HYDRA, RED DRAGON, MELTIGEMINI (BOSS)

KEY ITEMS:
NONE

ITEMS:
ETHER, RED HAT, GOLDEN HAIRPIN, WING EDGE, GAIA GEAR, DEMON'S MAIL, ELIXIR, RIBBON

CARDS:
NONE

OBJECTIVES

① Search the abandoned mine for treasures

② Be wary of Red Dragon attacks

③ Pull the lever to descend into the well

④ Eiko faces the jesters

⑤ Face the horror of Meltigemini

ECHOES IN THE DARKNESS

Kuja has dragged Eiko into a truly dark and foreboding underworld. The enemies here strike with a lot of fire-based magic. Make sure Vivi is in your party along with Steiner. This duo enables you to retaliate with Ice and Water magic, simplifying your battles. Dagger is still not the best person to bring along. Her magic and attacks continue to fail half the time. Also, prepare everyone with the Body Temp and Antibody abilities.

KEYWORD:
PlayOnline.com   **QINA5**
NEW ABILITIES

Quina can always learn new abilities. To find out which ones s/he can learn here, go to PlayOnline.

From the entry point, head into the house on the left. Search amongst the rubble for some goodies and note the message on the bulletin board. Return to the entrance and continue to the right.

Proceed through the next dilapidated hut, and then find a rope to slide down. Before descending, you may want to examine the rest of the cavern just in case there are some more items available.

In the top corner is another bulletin board that explains how to operate a lever somewhere. Now slide down the rope into the chasm. This deposits you near a well; the lever that controls it is on the left-hand side. There are some items to get on this level before you pull the lever and continue to descend.

Head to the right first. This is where Moolan the moogle stands vigilant. Give him the letter from Mogrika, which contains more clues about Mognet. He then asks you to deliver a letter to Mogtaka in return. In the bottom-right corner, search the area for another cool item. Save your game, and then continue to the right.

Another dilapidated house has a staircase to climb on the far right. There's another message at the top in the corner with a clue about the lever. Continue up the steps and head out the top-left exit. Follow this platform to the end to find some new armor. As you return to the well area, a couple of Red Dragons burst through the roof and attack.

  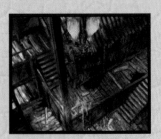

It's time to explore the area to the left of the well. Go past the cave opening into the crumbling house. Search to the right inside the condemned building, and then check the wall to the left to find another message. This one indicates that the true solution to the well is to pull the lever three times.

Exit the left house and go through the opening in the wall. Up the stairs is Mogtaka, for whom you have a letter. Mogtaka also runs a Mogshop. Stock up on Hi-Potions and then continue up the stairs. On the top level, another Red Dragon bursts through the wall and attacks.

GREED OF THE DARK SPAWN

Finally, return to the well and pull down the lever three times to lower the rope. Climb down into the well bottom, where another set of Red Dragons break through the wall, creating an exit. Defeat the dragons and step through the dust. The party can see that the jester twins, Zorn and Thorn, are attempting to extract the Eidolons from Eiko.

The scene shifts down to the floor for a quick Boss fight between Eiko and the jesters. However, the battle immediately ends when Eiko summons Madeen.

EIKO'S NEW SUMMON
The Ribbon enables Eiko to summon Madeen. Keep this in mind for future Boss fights.

BOSS FIGHT

MELTIGEMINI

HP	24,348	AP	11	Weak vs.	Mini
Steal Items	Demon's Vest, Golden Hairpin, Vaccine			**Spoils**	Vaccine (x2)

BOSS PREPARATIONS:

- Equip your party with Antibody

BATTLE TACTICS:

- When afflicted with the virus, quickly administer Vaccines
- Cast Mini againt Meltigemini

PlayOnline.com
KEYWORD: MELT1
BOSS FIGHT TIPS

For additional Boss fight strategy, check out PlayOnline.

After finding Lady Hilda in a nearby room, the scene shifts back to Lindblum.

THE MISSING PRINCESS AND THE HILDA GARDE 3

ENEMIES:
NONE

KEY ITEMS:
NONE

ITEMS:
GARNET, TENT, ELIXIR

CARDS:
ELIXIR CARD

OBJECTIVES

1

Meet everyone in the conference room

2

Search for Dagger in Alexandria

3

Board the amazing Hilda Garde 3

KUJA'S MASTER SCHEME

The following morning, Zidane is awakened by a Lindblum palace guard. On the upper level, Mogki has a letter he'd like you to deliver to Kumool, if you're willing.

Lady Hilda holds a meeting in the conference room. Your new objectives are to search Ipsen's Castle on the Forgotten Continent for clues as to how to open the gateway to the villain's home world, Terra.

The only problem is, Dagger can't be found anywhere in Lindblum. Just when Zidane is ready to give up, Baku takes him to find Beatrix, who hands over the **Garnet** for Dagger.

Not long afterward, Zidane finds Dagger by her mother's grave. The princess has regained her ability to speak, so her magic abilities will no longer be hampered. Meanwhile, Regent Cid has finished his masterpiece airship, making travel across the world quite a breeze.

THE HILDA GARDE 3

After a brief reunion on board the airship, command of the Hilda Garde 3 is turned over to you. Your next destination is Ipsen's Castle on the Forgotten Continent, which is now marked on the World Map. To get there, press the SELECT button until the World Map appears. Move the cursor to Ipsen's Castle and press the X button to fly there immediately.

THINGS TO DO WITH YOUR NEW TOY

At the first chance, return to the bridge of the ship and exit through the left doorway. Continue down to the deck, and move forward until you see a ladder. Explore the area to find any items.

There are two cities to consider visiting at this point in the game. One is Alexandria, since you may not have had the chance to return there and hunt for items amongst the debris. The other city is Daguerreo, and it's only accessible by airship or with a Gold Chocobo. Read

further to find out what there is to gain from visiting these two cities. You can skip to the description of Ipsen's Castle when you are ready to continue the adventure.

ENEMIES:	KEY ITEMS:	ITEMS:	CARDS:
NONE	NONE	ETHER, TENT, OPAL, PERIDOT, SAPPHIRE, REMEDY	ALEXANDRIA CARD

OBJECTIVES

1

2

Console the citizens of the crushed city

Find items and Gil scattered amongst the Debris

THE ACROPOLIS IN ASHES

Players can visit the ruins of the once grand city any time after the party has fully recuperated in Lindblum. You can pilot the Hilde Garde 3 to Alexandria Harbor on the eastern side of the Mist Continent, or you can touch down on the plains just outside of town.

The Memorial Square is no more. When you enter town, the first area is now the main street leading into the square. Doug's Medicine shop is completely gone, and there no longer seems to be a way to purchase Potions and such in Alexandria anymore. What a tragedy…

PlayOnline.com **KEYWORD: CARDG2**

RARE CARD

Are you a card game guru? If so, there's a rare card to find in this part of town. Visit PlayOnline for the details.

However, the Shopkeeper who used to run the Armory now stands just outside of the Inn, on the left side of the square. His inventory remains the same until the end of the game.

PlayOnline.com **KEYWORD: KUPCH2**

MINI-GAME

Kupo's alone for now. However, if you return on Disc 4, you'll notice a difference. To find out what it is, visit PlayOnline.

Things seem sort of grim even in the mini-theater, where the destruction Alexandria has suffered seems not apparent at all. Lowell has traveled from Lindblum to work with Ruby and her friend, and he's giving them all the attitude one might expect from a prima donna. In the alley leading back to the bell tower, you can stop and talk to the old man strolling by. He is the Synthesist, and despite the destruction of his shop, he can still forge items for you. Inside the bell tower, Kupo survived the battle and he's still hanging out inside.

Head upward from the square to the boat dock and search the area for some items. Ride the boat across the channel to where the grand castle once stood.

The left tower is all that stands of the castle, and even that has taken quite a beating. Move past the two Knights of Pluto sifting through the rubble, and enter the double doors on the left. The chamber containing the Neptune statue is still intact, and you can still ride it down to the Harbor. This enables a landing by sea, if you're still confined to ocean travel.

SHOPKEEPER OUTSIDE THE INN

Item	Gil
Mythril Dagger	950
Gladius	2300
Ice Brand	3780
Partisan	1600
Ice Lance	2430
Cat's Claws	4000
Poison Knuckles	5000
Stardust Rod	760
Healing Rod	1770
Lamia's Flute	3800
Flame Staff	1100
Ice Staff	980
Lightning Staff	1200
Oak Staff	2400
Pinwheel	200
Glass Armlet	250
Bone Wrist	330
Mythril Armlet	500
Magic Armlet	1000
Mythril Gloves	980
Thunder Gloves	1200
Lamia's Tiara	800
Ritual Hat	1000
Twist Headband	1200
Barbut	600
Mythril Helm	1000
Gold Helm	1800
Magician Cloak	1850
Survival Vest	2900
Brigandine	4300
Mythril Armor	1830
Plate Mail	2320

SYNTHESIST WANDERING THE ALLEY

Item	Gil	Materials
The Ogre	700	2 Mage Mashers
Exploda	1000	Mage Masher, Mythril Dagger
Rune Tooth	2000	2 Mythril Daggers
Angel Bless	9000	Mythril Dagger, Gladius
Cotton Robe	1000	Wrist, Steepled Hat
Silk Robe	2000	Silk Shirt, Bandana
Magician Robe	3000	Mage Staff, Magician Cloak
Desert Boots	300	Leather Hat, Leather Shirt
Yellow Scarf	400	Feather Hat, Steepled Hat
Glass Buckle	500	Glass Armlet, Leather Wrist
Germinas Boots	900	Desert Boots, Fork
Cachusha	1000	Magus Hat, Rubber Helm
Coral Ring	1200	Lightning Staff, Rod
Gold Choker	1300	Linen Cuirass, Soft
Magician Shoes	1500	Germinas Boots, Bone Wrist
Barette	1800	Needle Fork, Barbut
Power Belt	2000	Glass Buckle, Chain Mail
Madain's Ring	3000	Bone Wrist, Stardust Rod
Fairy Earrings	3200	Magic Armlet, Soft
Extension	3500	Lamia's Tiara, Multina Racket
Reflect Ring	7000	Anklet, Madain's Ring
Anklet	4000	Gold Choker, Peridot
Feather Boots	4000	Magician Shoes, Phoenix Pinion
Black Belt	4000	Twist Headband, Survival Vest
Pearl Rouge	5000	Moonstone, Elixir

DAGUERREO

ENEMIES:	KEY ITEMS:	ITEMS:	CARDS:
NONE	CAPRICORN STELLAZZIO, RANK S AWARD	ELIXIR (X2)	FLARE CARD, METEOR CARD

OBJECTIVES

Meet the citizens of Daguerreo

Engage in the debate near the medicine shop

Find the secret passage to the mid level

Fix the lift in front of the weapon shop

CITADEL OF THE WATER GOD

Daguerreo is located at the top of a mountain on an island in the Salvage Archipelago south of the Forgotten Continent. Pilot the Hilda Garde 3 to the largest landmass below the western frontier to find the entrance of the city. Land the airship on the plains, and move across the bridge to the large cave.

Consider visiting this mountain dwelling before proceeding with the adventure. Daguerreo has a full stock of new and powerful weapons and armor, some of which you can only find here. You can also find some useful items and a few tasks to perform.

LEVELING UP
The monsters around Daguerreo are tough, but after a dozen or so battles, you won't notice anymore. Since you can fully regain your strength just inside at the Library, Daguerreo is a very attractive area for leveling up your characters to a powerful status.

KEYWORD: STELLAX
PlayOnline.com
SPECIAL ITEM
There's yet another Stellazzio to add to your collection here. Visit PlayOnline for the answers.

Inside Daguerreo, head off the center platform down to the right. Search the sunken path for some goodies, and then continue into the passageway. A clever, hydraulic-powered lift elevates you to the upper ledge. A moogle named Noggy always hangs out up here.

Directly across from the lift is the Synthesis Expert, who makes a whole slew of new weapons and items. You should browse through his inventory, which is listed at the end of this section.

THE MASTER TREASURE HUNTER

Near the Synthesis Expert, you'll encounter the mysterious Four-armed Man once more. This arrogant fellow assesses your Treasure Hunter Rank, which is a summary of all the treasures you've collected in the game up to this point, including those found in the Chocobo Hot and Cold side quest.

PlayOnline.com | KEYWORD: **TRSHUNT1**

SPECIAL ITEM

You can get a cool reward from the Four-armed Man. To find out what it is, refer to PlayOnline.

DAGUERREO'S LIBRARY

The bookshelves at Daguerreo are legendary, containing a copy of every volume ever written on every subject imaginable. Near the right entrance is Engineer Zebolt from Lindblum, who is studying hydraulics. To his left are two people arguing; one is the Sales Clerk who runs the Medicine store (her inventory is listed at the end of this section).

PlayOnline.com | KEYWORD: **RARCRD2**

RARE CARDS

If you join in the argument near the Medicine store, you could earn a rare card. To find out what to do, go to PlayOnline.

SUPPLY PROBLEMS IN DAGUERREO

The left exit from the library takes you to the Weaponsmith's Shop. However, he can't sell you anything because he's having trouble with his supplies. You must fix his problem before he can sell you anything. And believe me, you *want* to help this guy because he's got the good stuff!

To get his supplies flowing again, head back across the second floor library after speaking to the Weaponsmith. Go down to the first floor, and head straight across the entrance chamber to access the area beneath the Weaponsmith.

Examine the three lifts on the left wall. The levers on the top wall operate the lift, however, there's a malfunction that prevents the top lift from going all the way up to the second level. This is the heart of the Weaponsmith's problem.

Examine the levers. The Right lever raises and lowers the top lift, while the Left lever raises and lowers the bottom lift. Lower the Left lever until the bottom lift is at bottom floor level. Examine the bottom lift, and Zidane will spot a hole in the wall just above the platform. Now examine the staff leaning against bookshelves. Zidane will take it across the room and insert it into the hole. This keeps the bottom lift from raising.

Return to the levers and lower the Right lever until the top lift is at floor level. Move Zidane to it, and press the X button. He will get on and ride up to the second floor. Speak to the Weaponsmith and he will express his relief. He will immediately sell you equipment, and his inventory of amazing items appears at the end of this section.

PlayOnline.com | KEYWORD: **NAMCRD3**

HIDDEN AREA

You can rename a character if you have the correct item in your inventory. PlayOnline can show you how it's done!

BLESSING OF THE DRAGON GOD

After spending some time in Daguerreo, return to the entrance and examine the mosaic depicting the Water Dragon God. This causes something new to occur.

SYNTHESIS EXPERT'S SHOP

Item	Gil	Materials
Angel Bless	9000	Mythril Dagger, Gladius
Sargatanas	12000	Gladius, Zorlin Shape
Cotton Robe	1000	Wrist, Steepled Hat
Silk Robe	2000	Silk Shirt, Bandana
Magician Robe	3000	Mage Staff, Magician Cloak
Glutton's Robe	6000	Mythril Fork, Cotton Robe
White Robe	8000	Gaia Gear, Jade Armlet
Black Robe	8000	Gaia Gear, N-Kai Armlet
Cachusha	1000	Magus Hat, Rubber Helm
Coral Ring	1200	Lightning Staff, Rod
Magician Shoes	1500	Germinas Boots, Bone Wrist
Barette	1800	Needle Fork, Barbut
Power Belt	2000	Glass Buckle, Chain Mail
Mandain's Ring	3000	Bone Wrist, Stardust Rod
Fairy Earrings	3200	Magic Armlet, Soft
Extension	3500	Lamia's Tiara, Multina Racket
Reflect Ring	7000	Anklet, Madain's Ring
Anklet	4000	Gold Choker, Peridot
Feather Boots	4000	Magician Shoes, Phoenix Pinion
Black Belt	4000	Twist Headband, Survival Vest
Pearl Rouge	5000	Moonstone, Elixir
Promist Ring	6000	Chimera Armlet, Ruby
Battle Boots	6500	Feather Boots, Wing Edge
Rebirth Ring	7000	Diamond, Anklet
Angel Earrings	8000	Fairy Earrings, Barette
Garnet	350	Ore, Remedy
Amethyst	200	Ore, Annoyntment
Peridot	100	Ore, Soft
Sapphire	200	Ore, Antidote
Opal	100	Ore, Potion
Topaz	100	Ore, Eye Drops
Thief Gloves	50000	Mythril Armlet, Sargatanas

ARGUING SALES CLERK'S MEDICINE SHOP

Item	Gil
Potion	50
Hi-Potion	200
Phoenix Down	150
Echo Screen	50
Soft	100
Antidote	50
Eye Drops	50
Magic Tag	100
Remedy	300
Annoyntment	150
Tent	800

WEAPONSMITH'S SHOP

Item	Gil
Mage Masher	500
Mythril Dagger	950
Gladius	2300
Zorlin Shape	6000
Rune Blade	8900
Obelisk	6000
Tiger Fangs	13500
Mythril Racket	2250
Asura's Rod	3180
Hamelin	5700
Octagon Rod	4500
Rising Sun	500
Bone Wrist	330
Mythril Armlet	500
Magic Armlet	1000
Chimera Armlet	1200
Egoist's Armlet	2000
N-Kai Armlet	3000
Jade Armlet	3400
Venetia Shield	2800
Defense Gloves	6000
Lamia's Tiara	800
Twist Headband	1200
Golden Hairpin	3700
Coronet	4400
Diamond Helm	3000
Gaia Gear	8700
Demon's Vest	10250
Demon's Mail	5900
Diamond Armor	8800

IPSEN'S CASTLE

ENEMIES:
AGARES,
GARGOYLE,
CERBERUS,
VETERAN,
TONBERRY,
TAHARKA (BOSS)

KEY ITEMS:
AQUARIUS
STELLAZZIO,
EARTH MIRROR,
FIRE MIRROR,
WIND MIRROR,
WATER MIRROR

ITEMS:
DAGGER, CAT'S
CLAWS, JAVELIN,
BROADSWORD, ROD,
BARETTE, MAIDEN
PRAYER, AIR RACKET,
GOLEM'S FLUTE,
ANCIENT AROMA,
FORK, MAGE STAFF

CARDS:
NONE

OBJECTIVES

1 Choose and equip your party, and ascend the steps

2 Slide down the pole

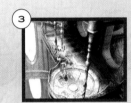

3 Navigate the upside down castle

4 Find the weakest items possible

5 Open the fresco secret door

6 Take the mirrors from the map room

7 Overcome the guardian of the mirrors

8 Engage trap doors to find the secret of Odin

9 Return inside to rescue Amarant

THE PARADOX PALACE

The bewildering Ipsen's Castle looks like two castles smashed together, causing one to look upside down while the other part looks right side up. This indicates something about the nature of the place.

Until you reach a certain height in the castle, everything *is* upside down! Plus, your strongest weapons will cause a pitiful amount of damage to enemies. To remain strong, you must equip each character in the battle party with the WEAKEST WEAPON POSSIBLE!

Outside the entrance, Amarant rebels and decides to go at it on his own. You must now choose three other characters to accompany you inside. The best mixture of magic and physical force seems to be achieved by a party consisting of Zidane, Dagger, Steiner, and Vivi. They seem to be capable of the best teamwork, as well. However, if Quina has learned the LV4 Holy spell, then take him/her along. If Eiko has Madeen, that will also come in handy.

KEYWORD: WEAP3
NEW WEAPONS

You need weak weapons to progress in this area. PlayOnline can show you where to find them.

KEYWORD: AGGAR4
FIGHTING STRATEGIES

Need some help against the Agares and Gargoyle combo? If so, PlayOnline has some excellent tips.

LIKE WALKING BACKWARDS

Take a deep breath and proceed up the long steps into Ipsen's Castle. Inside the foyer, explore the area for some items. Head up the steps in the back to venture into a courtyard of sorts.

The moogle Kumool stands in the bottom-left corner of the area. You might have a letter for Kumool from Mogki. Kumool also runs a very convenient Mogshop. Kumool sells Vaccines, so stock up while you have the opportunity!

There's a doorway across the courtyard from Kumool that overlooks an expansive area. As you can see, everything below this level is a mirror image of all that is above. Slide down the pole on the far-right side of the courtyard.

Move along the arches to the ladder, and climb up to the balcony. Follow the balcony out to a small overlook, and go through the next doorway and hop onto the ladder. Climb the ladder up and press the X button when the icon appears. Select to jump off to the left, and run around the gallery looking for items. Return to the ladder, but this time jump off to the right.

When you get back to the ladder this time, climb to the bottom and hop off. Cross the lower balcony and climb the steps on the right. Hop on the next ladder and climb up. Jump off this ladder and circle the other side of the balcony. Then climb the ladder to the top, and enter the archway on the top balcony.

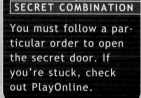
Move to the bottom of the red-carpeted room and examine the fresco on the right. Sure enough, it's a secret door, but it's tough to open. Each time you try something, a new option becomes available.

Leaning on the fresco causes it to open right up, but it's a matter of making the correct options appear. Take the elevator near the back staircase up to the top floor.

A cocky Amarant has beaten Zidane here, and he considers this victory enough to be able to abandon the party. After the rascal stalks away, search the wall in the back and take the **Fire Mirror**, **Water Mirror**, **Wind Mirror**, and the **Earth Mirror**. Each Key Item is inscribed on the back with a clue as to the location of a shrine.

Using each of these items at each of their respective shrines opens the gateway to Terra. However, the guardian of the mirrors isn't willing to let you take away its treasures. Taharka materializes from its two-dimensional world, and a tough battle ensues.

BOSS FIGHT

TAHARKA

HP	29,186	AP	11	Weak vs.	Flare
Steal Items	Orichalcon, Mythril Claws, Elixir	Spoils	None		

BOSS PREPARATIONS:

- Equip your party with Auto-Potion or Auto-Regen

BATTLE TACTICS:

- Have Vivi cast Flare
- Summon Bahamut with Dagger
- Use Steiner's Flare Sword
- When the Boss reduces in size, have Zidane use skills like Thievery

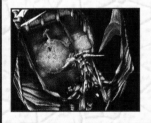

PlayOnline.com

KEYWORD: TAHR1

BOSS FIGHT TIPS

For additional Boss fight strategy and tactics, refer to PlayOnline.

MORE DISCOVERIES WHILE EXITING

Go back out the same way you came in, and climb the pole back up to the courtyard. There is a trap door that is barely visible just below the chest at the top of the courtyard.

Drop through this trap, and Zidane will land on the upside-down chandelier in the dark room below. Hop down and climb the pole back up to the courtyard.

Another trap door is under the balcony on the top-left side. This one drops you onto the upper level of the lower room. You might want to avoid this trap door as there is no reward for triggering it.

Return to the entrance and take note of the staircase that appeared on the left side going up to the top balcony as well. A new entrance is in-between the staircase and the first arch you entered on the right. This leads to the courtyard in the balcony area, and during your trip, look for some chests on the chandelier high above. Continue across the balcony to the upper archway, and descend the steps inside into a whole new area.

 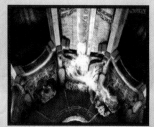

Ride the elevator in the center of the room down to find yourself in a room with Odin's electrified sword chained to the back wall. There are also two flower vases and three shelves on which to arrange them. Rearrange the vases, moving them from shelf to shelf in a counter clockwise direction. The electrical energies will fill the vase, and then you'll receive the **Ancient Aroma**.

You can now return to the courtyard and climb the pole up to the chandelier.

KUMOOL'S MOGSHOP	
Item	**Gil**
Mage Masher	500
Iron Sword	660
Mythril Spear	1100
Poison Knuckles	5000
Multina Racket	750
Mythril Rod	560
Lamia's Flute	3800
Oak Staff	2400
Needle Fork	3100
Rising Sun	500
N-Kai Armlet	3000
Jade Armlet	3400
Venetia Shield	2800
Red Hat	3000
Golden Hairpin	3700
Cross Helm	2200
Diamond Helm	3000
Power Vest	7200
Gaia Gear	8700
Shield Armor	4300
Demon's Mail	5900
Potion	50
Hi-Potion	200
Phoenix Down	150
Echo Screen	50
Soft	100
Antidote	50
Eye Drops	50
Magic Tag	100
Vaccine	100
Annoyntment	150
Tent	800

THE LOST ALLY

Exit Ipsen's Castle and rejoin your friends at the bottom. Zidane receives the alarming news that Amarant has not yet emerged. As Zidane, return to the courtyard and slide down the pole. Amarant can be heard groaning at the very bottom of the room and rejoins the party. Now, Zidane and Amarant must fight their way back out of the castle. Make sure you equip Amarant with the Cat's Claws beforehand.

Outside the castle, a plan is formed to utilize the four mirrors found inside. The player has the option of exploring more of the World Map, fulfilling a few side quests, or moving straight on to the Four Shrines challenge. Just make sure you take the first opportunity to re-equip your characters with the best weapons available!

THE FOUR SHRINES

ENEMIES: EARTH GUARDIAN (BOSS)   **KEY ITEMS:** NONE   **ITEMS:** NONE   **CARDS:** NONE

OBJECTIVES

1 Drop off Dagger and Eiko at the Water Shrine

2 Leave Amarant and Freya at the Fire Shrine

3 Steiner and Vivi will head to the Wind Shrine

4 Zidane is stuck with Quina at the Earth Shrine

5 Avoid the traps in the ancient temple

6 Face the four Guardians of Terra simultaneously

ONE IS ALL, ALL IS ONE

Upon boarding the Hilda Garde 3, Zidane and the party review the clues uncovered in the Taharka's chamber. The party must conquer all four locations at the exact same time. This means splitting the party off into pairs and depositing them at the four shrines, located in four different locations around the world. The only challenge to this is finding the four shrines and defeating one of the four shrine guardians.

- The shrine closest to Ipsen's Castle is the Water Shrine, located in the waters in the center of the "hook" on the Forgotten Continent. Let the airship hover over the area and press the Circle button to drop off Dagger and Eiko.

- The Fire Shrine is located north of Esto Gaza, on the Lost Continent. Fly into the volcano and press the Circle button to release Amarant and Freya.

- As Zidane indicates, the next location is the Wind Shrine, located on the southeastern part of the Forgotten Continent. Press the Circle button to assign Vivi and Steiner to attack this shrine.

The Earth Shrine is located in the grassy area on the eastern part of the Outer Continent. Hover above the quaking area and press the Circle button to enter the shrine.

The game follows Zidane's and Quina's adventure, with brief cut-scenes to highlight the plights of the others.

FOCUS ON THE EARTH SHRINE

After the duo converse at the entrance, take one last chance to ensure that both are equipped with their strongest weapons. Ipsen's Castle has a way of leaving you with a weak armament, and you don't want that here.

A LITTLE HELP

Equip the following abilities on both characters, if possible: Auto-Float, Auto-Regen or Auto-Potion, High Tide, and Counter. They are listed in order of priority, in case you can't equip them all. Also, equip Quina with any items that absorb Earth damage.

When you're ready, proceed down the steps. As the mismatched pair makes their way down the corridor, a trap springs causing the walls to close from different directions. Press the X button when a "!" appears over Zidane's head to outmaneuver the sliding stones.

In the main chamber, follow Quina and examine the altar. At the same instant in all four shrines, the characters come face-to-face with the Guardians of Terra, the protectors of the four shrines. The only one you'll actually fight is the Earth Guardian.

KEYWORD: ERTHG1
BOSS FIGHT TIPS

PlayOnline has additional Boss strategy if you're still having trouble defeating the Earth Guardian.

BOSS FIGHT

EARTH GUARDIAN

HP	20,756	AP	11	Weak vs.	Wind
Steal Items	Rubber Suit, Avenger			Spoils	Phoenix Pinion

BATTLE TACTICS:

- Have Quina cast Mighty Guard and then cast Bad Breath
- When Zidane Trances, use Grand Lethal once or twice

TERRA

ENEMIES:
HECTEYES,
MOVER,
RING LEADER,
MALBORO

KEY ITEMS:
NONE

ITEMS:
CORONET, DRAGON
WRIST, ELIXIR, REMEDY,
MYTHRIL RACKET,
DEMON'S VEST,
MINERVA'S PLATE

CARDS:
NONE

OBJECTIVES

① *Pilot the airship to the Shimmering Island*

② *Transport to Terra*

③ *Follow the mysterious girl to Bran Bal*

CROSSING OVER

Following the simultaneous defeat of the four Guardians of Terra, it's time to cross dimensions and explore that other world for more answers. Pilot your airship to the Shimmering Island, which is the glowing iceberg just south of the Lost Continent. When you press the Circle button, the party gets drawn off the ship and into the new world.

STRANGERS IN A STRANGE LAND

The ominous Garland greets the party at their landing site on Terra. Select your party and head downward along the path. Random battles with powerful enemies begin almost immediately.

KEYWORD: ABLTY5
FIGHTING STRATEGY
You must come to this area properly equipped. For some tips, refer to PlayOnline.

A strange blonde girl runs away from Zidane in the next area. The object is to pursue her, but there are valuable items off the path she follows. Don't worry, she'll wait up ahead.

KEYWORD: KEYIT4
SPECIAL ITEMS
To find the locations of the items mentioned here, refer to PlayOnline.

Follow the mysterious girl over an alien bridge, and then climb down the webbing at the end. There is another web directly below the first one that leads down to a platform. Climb

back up and follow the ledge around to the gap at the left. Jump across the gap and search for the hidden trunk around the corner, which contains a **Mythril Racket**. From this side of the gap, you have the option to climb down the webbing.

On the lower level around the corner, Zidane attempts to confront the blonde-haired girl once more. She leads Zidane onto another bridge and encourages him to go ahead. At the

end of the bridge is a stairway leading up to a platform. A nondescript tunnel on the left side of this platform spirals downward. Continue up the stairs to the right to reach Bran Bal.

BRAN BAL

ENEMIES:	KEY ITEMS:	ITEMS:	CARDS:
NONE	NONE	WING EDGE, ELIXIR, FLASH HAT, ANGEL EARRINGS, MINERVA'S PLATE	NONE

OBJECTIVES

1

Find the Inn for Dagger so Dagger can recuperate

2

Meet the blonde-haired girl in the basement lab

3

As Eiko, find the party members and follow Zidane

CULTURE SHOCK

At the entrance to the town of Bran Bal, Dagger has a serious flashback as the Invincible rises into the sky. Zidane must explore Bran Bal and find a place for Dagger to rest.

Pick a party of four, one without Steiner or Dagger. There is a green force field covering the portal in front of Zidane, so there's obviously no getting through this location for the time being.

Head down the stairs to the left, where Zidane will make a startling observation. From the left side of the pond, take a path under the stairs, and cross under the stairs where you will run into a "!" sign. Talk to the two people located to the left of the pond. The one who seems to be staring at the pond tells Zidane that the Inn is directly behind him. When you examine the Inn, Zidane goes back to get Dagger while Eiko bothers everyone for some medicine. Dagger wakes up and explains why she fainted, and then Zidane wanders off to explore the community.

Move Zidane across town to the doorway on the far right. In this small storage room, look for the moogle trapped in a basket. Moorock wants you to deliver mail to Mozme, if you're willing. The appreciative moogle also opens a rather complete Mogshop for you to purchase new equipment (the inventory follows this section).

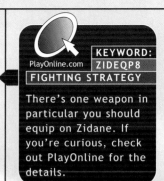

KEYWORD:
ZIDEQP8
PlayOnline.com

FIGHTING STRATEGY

There's one weapon in particular you should equip on Zidane. If you're curious, check out PlayOnline for the details.

In a house to the right of the Inn, a group of individuals stands around a triangular stone and stares. Speaking to everyone here gives you some idea as to the kind of society that exists on Terra. A staircase on the right side of the room goes down to a lab, where the young blonde-haired woman waits for Zidane.

Conversing with the girl opens a floodgate of secrets and truths. The girl eventually leads Zidane out of Bran Bal to find out more of the truth.

In the meantime, Dagger asks an impatient Eiko to go find Zidane. You can leave Bran Bal and take part in some more random battles if you're interested. But to keep the story moving, meet Amarant near the entrance and follow Zidane through the green portal on the platform. Eiko then learns that Zidane has already left for Pandemonium.

MOOROCK'S MOGSHOP

Item	Gil	Item	Gil
Dagger	320	Adaman Hat	6100
Mage Masher	500	Platinum Helm	4600
Mythril Dagger	950	Demon's Vest	10250
Gladius	2300	Minerva's Plate	12200
Zorlin Shape	6000	Platina Armor	10500
Orichalcon	17000	Hi-Potion	200
Defender	9340	Phoenix Down	150
Holy Lance	11000	Echo Screen	50
Avenger	16000	Soft	100
Mythril Racket	2250	Antidote	50
Bistro Fork	10300	Eye Drops	50
Rising Sun	500	Vaccine	100
Dragon Wrist	4800	Remedy	300
Defense Gloves	6000	Annoyntment	150
Coronet	4400	Tent	800
Flash Hat	5200		

PANDEMONIUM

ENEMIES:
AMDUSIAS, MALBORO,
SHELL DRAGON, MOVER,
ABADON, SILVER DRAGON
(BOSS), GARLAND (BOSS),
KUJA (BOSS)

KEY ITEMS:
NONE

ITEMS:
HOLY MITER,
CARABINI
MAIL, ELIXIR,
BATTLE BOOTS

CARDS:
NONE

OBJECTIVES

Follow Garland across the pod platforms

Fight through the corridor

Help Zidane seek an attitude adjustment

Activate the pulsating lights

Cross the bridge before time runs out

Use the control to adjust the elevator

Determine how to move from floor to floor

Use the teleporters to reach the items

Prepare for three powerful enemies

EVIL DESIGNS

Garland meets Zidane at the entrance of Pandemonium and leads him on a kind of twisted tour of the place. You must hop from platform to platform, following Garland as the evil wizard talks about social issues on Terra and the meaning of life, among other things.

KEYWORD: WEAPON1
PlayOnline.com
FIGHTING STRATEGY

One particular weapon proves beneficial in this area. To find out which enemies it's effective against, refer to PlayOnline.

Zidane passes out and is awakened by Eiko and Vivi, who finally managed to find him. Unfortunately, the weight of the truth is too much for our furry-tailed hero, and he tries to set off on his own. Outside the first chamber, Zidane encounters an Amdusias.

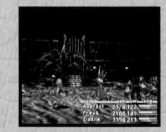

Afterward, Zidane rejects their friendship as well and staggers on. In the next area, Steiner and Quina are having difficulties in a fight against a monster. Zidane then joins in.

After stomping on their feelings, Zidane goes in the next room and picks a fight with a Shell Dragon. His bad mood causes him to sag in the saddle quite suddenly, and Dagger steps in to help. Finally, Dagger, Steiner, and Quina convince Zidane to keep fighting for what he believes in, going against the current of fate.

As you run back into the previous area, the rest of the group rejoins Zidane. Witnessing this glad occasion is the faithful Moorock, who offers to sell the same items as in Bran Bal. In addition, Moorock also switches out your party members. Return to the throne, where Zidane's self loathing culminated to find a **Holy Miter**.

Continue along the path Zidane was taking alone, heading to the left. This takes you to an area covered with dormant blue lights. The control panel is next to the entry point. Activating this causes the blue lights on the floor to turn off and on in alternating patterns.

HURRY UP!
You have 30 seconds to get across the floor and the holographic bridge beyond. If you don't make it in time, the bridge disappears, meaning you must start over. Also, if you touch one of the lights while it's lit, you're forced to fight a monster, and your 30 seconds will definitely run out.

To cross this area without incident, activate the control panel and spend the entire 30 seconds watching the pattern of the lights on the floor. It repeats the same pattern every time! Now activate the panel again, and cross the area avoiding all the lights as they come on.

Across the holographic bridge, you'll find another alien control device of some type. There's not much purpose to it right now, but you'll find out what it does when you proceed into the next room.

This large chamber houses several levels of interconnected platforms and a single elevator which connects to them all. The trick is that the control panel is in the previous room. Therefore, you must run back there and change the setting so that the elevator platform turns to face the dock you want to leave from or get to.

Since the explanation of which platform rides up to which one would be too wordy and difficult to understand, please refer to the screenshots and travel from dock to dock accordingly.

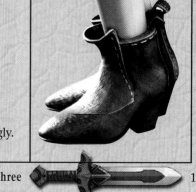

When you return to the control room and adjust the angle of the elevator enough times, half the group offers to stay in the control room and adjust the platform for you. This is great, because then you can just press the SELECT button and change the controls with the sub party rather than having to run back out there. Once you've mastered the system, ride out the top of the room.

 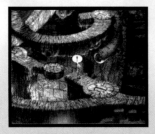  

From the landing platform, head to the teleporter on the right and go up one floor. This moves you to the center of a series of teleporters. From your arrival point, go to the left and teleport down to the lower platform. Search the area for treasure chests, and then teleport back up to the home platform, cross to the far right, and teleport down to another

platform. When you return to the home platform this time, move to the top teleporter, jump up to the red platform, and teleport back to the landing platform.

From there, move down from the elevator and curve over to the left teleporter. Go up one floor to enter the same teleporter-filled room again, only on a different series of platforms. Move down and to the right from the landing pad, and teleport upward twice.

Teleport back down to the lowest path, move to the upper-right platform and teleport up twice. Standing here is Mozme, for whom you should have a message. This is your last opportunity to save, so prepare accordingly and get the proper characters in your party.

KEYWORD: SLVDRG5
PlayOnline.com
BOSS FIGHT TIPS

PlayOnline has more strategy on the Boss fight with Silver Dragon.

SILVER DRAGON

BOSS FIGHT

HP 24,055	AP 13	Weak vs. None

| Steal Items | Kaiser Knuckles, Dragon Mail, Elixir, Ether | Spoils | Wing Edge |

BOSS PREPARATIONS:

- Equip everyone with the Insomniac ability, if Quina can cast the Night spell
- Equip abilities that prevent status ailments

BATTLE TACTICS:

- Summon Madeen using Eiko
- Summon Bahamut using Dagger
- Save some MP for upcoming Boss fights

BOSS FIGHT — GARLAND

HP	40,728	AP	0	Weak vs.	None

Steal Items	Dark Gear, Ninja Gear, Battle Boots	Spoils	None

BOSS PREPARATIONS:

- Equip Locomotion on your party

BATTLE TACTICS:

- Using Eiko, summon Carbuncle to cast Reflect on the party
- Use Skills and Spells
- Make Zidane steal from the Boss

KEYWORD: GARLD8
BOSS FIGHT TIPS

Still having a bit of trouble against this Boss? If so, visit PlayOnline for additional strategy.

BOSS FIGHT — KUJA

HP	42,382	AP	0	Weak vs.	None

Steal Items	Light Robe, Carabini Mail, Ether	Spoils	None

BATTLE TACTICS:

- Using Carbuncle, cast Ruby Light on the entire party
- Use boosted versions of Madeen and Bahamut
- Have Quina use Mighty Guard and White Wind

KEYWORD: KUJAB6
BOSS FIGHT TIPS

For more strategy and tips, go to PlayOnline.

ESCAPE FROM TERRA

As Kuja ravages the area with his terrifying new powers, there's only one thing to do: get the heck outta here! Zidane resolves to save the people of Bran Bal, so you must take a new path across a holobridge to a large teleporter with blinking eyes. Then run Zidane back to Bran Bal and search in the basement lab for the blonde-haired girl.

Once this is accomplished, the party hops onto the Invincible and returns to Gaia. You now have the most awesome airship in existence at your disposal!

ENEMIES:	KEY ITEMS:	ITEMS:	CARDS:
NONE	NONE	NONE	NONE

OBJECTIVES

The Black Mage Village welcomes the Terra refugees

KEYWORD: BMVDAG7
POWERFUL WEAPONS

Don't leave too soon, because there are other things to do. To find out what, visit PlayOnline.

KEYWORD: CHOCQU7
SIDE QUESTS

The mist has made it more difficult to locate Chocographs. For assistance in completing this Side Quest, refer to PlayOnline.

WINDS OF CHANGE

While the world is now completely dark under the thick veil of the Mist, things are shaping up quite nicely in the Black Mage Village. The former soldiers of Kuja now welcome the survivors of decimated Terra. After a series of brief scenes, the party immediately heads out in the Invincible, the ultimate airship!

WORLD OF SHADOWS

Significant changes have occurred in the world since your trip to Terra. The entire planet is now shrouded in Mist, making everything darker and more difficult to see.

Roots of the Iifa Tree have surfaced in new areas all over the world. Several locations that you might have been able to revisit previously are now sealed off permanently. Closed areas include: Conde Petie, Desert Palace, Oeilvert, Observatory Mountain, Esto Gaza, Ice Cavern, and Pinnacle Rocks.

However, the biggest difference is the giant ball of destruction hovering over the Iifa Tree, blackening the sky and blotting out the sun. This swirling ball of evil is your final destination. To "begin the end," equip your characters properly and pilot the Invincible into the burning globe.

No.239's EQUIPMENT SHOP	
Item	**Gil**
Wizard Rod	3990
Siren's Flute	7000
High Mage Staff	6000
Thief Hat	7100
Holy Miter	8300
Dark Gear	16300

No. 163's MEDICINE SHOP	
Item	**Gil**
Potion	50
Hi-Potion	200
Phoenix Down	150
Echo Screen	50
Soft	100
Antidote	50
Eye Drops	50
Magic Tag	100
Vaccine	100
Remedy	300
Annointment	150
Tent	800

BLACK CAT SYNTHESIS SHOP

Item	Gil	Materials	Item	Gil	Materials
Butterfly Sword	300	Dagger, Mage Masher	Light Robe	20000	Magician Robe, Glass Armlet
The Ogre	700	2 Mage Mashers	Grand Armor	45000	Mythril Sword, Mythril Armor
Exploda	1000	Mage Masher, Mythril Dagger	Desert Boots	300	Leather Hat, Leather Shirt
Rune Tooth	2000	2 Mythril Daggers	Yellow Scarf	400	Feather Hat, Steepled Hat
Angel Bless	9000	Mythril Dagger, Gladius	Glass Buckle	500	Glass Armlet, Leather Wrist
Sargatanas	12000	Gladius, Zorlin Shape	Germinas Boots	900	Desert Boots, Fork
Masamune	16000	Zorlin Shape, Orichalcon	Gold Choker	1300	Linen Cuirass, Soft
Duel Claws	16000	Dragon's Claws, Tiger Fangs	Running Shoes	12000	Battle Boots, Emerald
Priest's Racket	11000	Air Racket, Cachusha	Rosetta Ring	24000	Madain's Ring, Holy Lance
Bracer	24000	Battle Boots, Venetia Shield	Garnet	350	Ore, Remedy
Gauntlets	8000	Mythril Gloves, Dragon Wrist	Amethyst	200	Ore, Annoyntment
Golden Skullcap	15000	Gold Helm, Golden Hairpin	Peridot	100	Ore, Soft
Circlet	20000	Coronet, Rosetta Ring	Sapphire	200	Ore, Antidote
Grand Helm	20000	Cross Helm, Power Belt	Opal	100	Ore, Potion
Rubber Suit	20000	Minerva's Plate, Egoist's Armlet	Topaz	100	Ore, Eye Drops
Brave Suit	26000	Mythril Vest, Mythril Rod	Lapis Lazuli	400	Ore, Dead Pepper

MEMORIA

ENEMIES:

NOVA DRAGON (BOSS), ASH, CHIMERA, IRON MAN, VETERAN, STILVA, BEHEMOTH, MALIRIS (BOSS), TIAMAT (BOSS), KRAKEN (BOSS), LICH (BOSS), DEATHGUISE (BOSS), TRANCE KUJA (BOSS), NECRON (BOSS)

KEY ITEMS:

NONE

ITEMS:

KAIN'S LANCE, THE TOWER, ANGEL FLUTE, RUNE CLAWS, MACE OF ZEUS

CARDS:

NONE

OBJECTIVES

1 Overcome the guardian at the gate

2 Search for hidden weapons

3 Upset the four Chaos Guardians

4 Learn the secrets of the universe

5 Defeat the enemies of the world

WAR IN HEAVEN

PlayOnline.com
KEYWORD: CRDMST7
CARD MASTERS

Having trouble finding all five Card Masters? PlayOnline will lead you to all of them!

A LITTLE HELP

In Memoria, exclamation marks will appear over Zidane's head in various corners and niches. If you press the action button to examine these areas, Zidane will shake his head in confusion. These areas are where you may battle a Card Master's ghost. Press the Square button to initiate a card battle with a ghost. Certain rare cards can only be obtained in this manner.

At first, you'll think you've made a terrible mistake. No matter how ready you think you are, you cannot be prepared for the spectacle that greets the Invincible at the gates of Memoria. Only with the aid of all the airships in the world can the Invincible land.

Memoria is populated with monsters so powerful, each battle is like a Boss fight. It's important to use Dagger's Scan spell on each new enemy you face. Pinpointing the enemy's weaknesses and exploiting them is tantamount to survival in this surrealistic lair.

PlayOnline.com
KEYWORD: NOVDR3
BOSS FIGHT TIPS

If you're still having trouble with the Nova Dragon, log on to PlayOnline for more strategy.

NOVA DRAGON

BOSS FIGHT

HP	59,940		AP	13		Weak vs.	None

Steal Items	Grand Armor, Dragon Wrist, Remedy	Spoils	Wing Edge

BOSS PREPARATIONS:

- Use a party of Zidane, Dagger, Steiner, and Vivi
- Equip Vivi with the Black Robe and Reflectx2 ability

BATTLE TACTICS:

- Use a Tent on the Nova Dragon; this may cause it to go blind
- Have Dagger summon Bahamut

CASTLE OF DREAMS

Zidane and the party now find themselves at the entrance of a place created entirely from their deepest fears and their long-forgotten pasts. Garland acts as a tour guide throughout the area when necessary.

Move up the brick path to the next screen. You'll notice that an icon appears near the entrance. If you want to leave, return to this spot and you can go straight back to the Invincible. Just ahead is a magic globe. These globes serve as save points throughout Memoria. There are also several hidden save points along the way.

Continuing past the magic globe, you'll learn your first big lesson about exploring Memoria. As you search along the right wall, you'll slip into a hidden niche, where you'll find a new weapon for Freya.

Continue along the path until you reach a gothic area full of spires and arched window panes. There's a small platform you can explore at the top of this area. Thoroughly explore the area to find another powerful weapon.

As you start to ascend a long and curving bridge, Maliris attacks without warning. This is the first of several Bosses who closely resemble the Guardians of Terra.

BOSS FIGHT

MALIRIS

HP 59,497	AP 10	Weak vs. Ice, Water
Steal Items Masamune, Ultima Sword, Genji Armor		Spoils Phoenix Pinion

BOSS PREPARATIONS:

- Equip the party with the Body Temp ability

BATTLE TACTICS:

- Have Dagger and Vivi team up to use his Reflectx2 ability, using Blizzaga spells

- Use Steiner's Shock ability or Blizzaga Sword

KEYWORD:
PlayOnline.com **MALRS3**
BOSS FIGHT TIPS

For more strategy and tips on the Maliris Boss fight, check out PlayOnline.

SONGS OF YESTERDAY

The next chamber presents the party with a reenactment of Alexandria's destruction. Place Eiko in the party for the upcoming Boss fight, and continue onward to the right when prepared.

Memories and regrets continue to haunt those who experienced them. When you reach the area with the eye floating at the top of the steps, be advised that the Boss fight will occur once you ascend.

KEYWORD:
PlayOnline.com **RNCLW3**
POWERFUL WEAPON

Before leaving, make sure you explore the area thoroughly. There's a cool item you can pick up.

TIAMAT

KEYWORD: TIAMT5

BOSS FIGHT TIPS

For more Boss fight tips against Tiamat, refer to PlayOnline.

BOSS FIGHT

HP 59,494	AP 10	Weak vs. Earth

Steal Items	Grand Helm, Feather Boots, Blood Sword	Spoils	Wing Edge

BOSS PREPARATIONS:

- Equip party members with equipment that protects or absorbs Wind damage
- Equip the Clear Headed ability

BATTLE TACTICS:

- Have Vivi cast Meteor
- Let Eiko summon the boosted version of Fenrir
- Have Steiner perform Shock
- Let Dagger act as a medic for the party

CLOUD CITY

Continue up and around a series of endless staircases, and then cross the platform to the stairway that goes up into the sky. The next chamber contains a twisting path that is difficult to navigate.

KEYWORD: OPTBOS7

BOSS FIGHT TIPS

You can fight an optional Boss at this point of the game. To find out what to do, log on to PlayOnline.

A magic globe rests on a bridge beyond the twisting path, and you should rest up and save before continuing. Walk under the waterfall into a room where Quina tries to swim.

 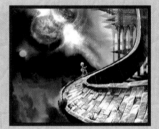

As you continue up the stairs, you'll be surprised by another Boss, the Kraken.

KRAKEN

KEYWORD: KRAKN0

BOSS FIGHT TIPS

If you're still having difficulties against this Boss, check out PlayOnline for more help.

BOSS FIGHT

HP 59,496	AP 10	Weak vs. Fire

Steal Items	Glutton's Robe, Wizard Rod, Genji Helmet	Spoils	Ether, Phoenix Pinion

BOSS PREPARATIONS:

- Equip armor that protects against Water or absorbs it
- Equip the Body Temp ability

BATTLE TACTICS:

- Take out the two tentacles first
- Use Fire magic (summons)

PERSISTENCE OF TIME

Proceeding past the Kraken's remains, Zidane enters an area where a strange clock displays an unreadable hour. There is a small niche to the right before going up the steps, where you can find a hidden save point. After an event, explore the area thoroughly; you may just uncover another powerful weapon!

Continue to the room at the top. As you step forward, the room dissolves away to reveal its true form. Lich then salutes your party and commences attack.

BOSS FIGHT

LICH

HP 60,000	**AP** 10	**Weak vs.** Thunder, Wind

Steal Items Black Robe, Siren's Flute, Genji Gloves	**Spoils** Phoenix Down, Phoenix Pinion

BOSS PREPARATIONS:

↓ Equip the Locomotion ability

BATTLE TACTICS:

↓ Have Dagger or Eiko cast Reflect on a party member and have Vivi bounce Flare off them

↓ Make Eiko summon Madeen

↓ Have Steiner perform Shock

↓ If you've learned it, use Quina's Twister spell

PlayOnline.com **KEYWORD: LICHB9**

BOSS FIGHT TIPS

For more detailed Boss fight strategy, refer to PlayOnline.

SPACE COWBOYS

After defeating Lich, check the left side of the room to find a hidden save point. Then step off the ledge into what looks like deep space. As Zidane floats, press up on the directional button to direct him toward the top of the screen.

When you reach the light at the top, Zidane enters the Crystal World. The random monsters encountered here are all lesser versions of the four Chaos Guardians you just defeated, all made of crystal. They yield a high amount of AP, but no EXP.

Follow the crystalline path until it swoops upward in a semi-loop. Finally! You've reached the last platform of Memoria. A magic globe here enables you to rest, save, or select your party.

> **TELEPORTATION**
> *An added feature enables you to teleport back to the entrance of Memoria. However, you cannot teleport back to this location from the entrance. If you leave, you must follow the same path all over again to return to this point.*

When you cross through the barrier, you'll experience the Deathguise Boss fight. After that, you have an opportunity to leave and return before facing Trance Kuja and Necron, but there is no break between those two. Good luck!

DEATHGUISE

BOSS FIGHT

HP 55,535	**AP** 0	**Weak vs.** None
Steal Items Duel Claws, Black Belt, Elixir		**Spoils** Wing Edge

BATTLE TACTICS:

¡ Equip your party with the Insomniac ability

¡ Command everyone to attack, and then have Quina end each round by casting Night

¡ Use Steiner's Shock attack or Vivi's Reflectx2 tactic

BOSS FIGHT

TRANCE KUJA

HP	42,382		AP	0		Weak vs.	None
Steal Items	Rebirth Ring, White Robe, Ether					**Spoils**	None

BOSS PREPARATIONS:

- Equip Freya with Kain's Lance and the High Jump ability
- Use Steiner if he has the Ragnarok
- Equip Auto-Life, Auto-Reflect, Counter, and High Tide

BATTLE TACTICS:

- Use Eiko to cast Carbuncle to protect your party
- Use Quina's White Wind ability to heal your party
- Use your party's strongest attacks

PlayOnline.com

KEYWORD:
TRNCKUJ1

BOSS FIGHT TIPS

For more Boss fight tips and strategy, log on to PlayOnline.

NECRON

The final Boss awaits. Equipping Jelly, Antibody, Clear-Headed, and Loudmouth will help prevent the myriad of status effects that Necron is capable of inducing all at once. You must figure out ways to quickly cure the Mini status as well.

We hope that this guide has helped you get the most out of the *FINAL FANTASY IX* experience, and that you enjoyed the game more thoroughly with our help. And now, enjoy the dramatic and well-deserved ending!

PlayOnline.com

KEYWORD:
GAIA

SECRET

Check out a special, exclusive preview of FINAL FANTASY: The Spirits Within, just for our readers

SIDE QUESTS, MINI-GAMES, AND SECRETS

This section details some of the side quests, mini-games, and secrets contained within this epic adventure called FINAL FANTASY IX.

JUMP ROPE

KEYWORD:
JUMPR3
PlayOnline.com
SPECIAL ITEMS

A complete list of the items you receive for jumping rope appears at PlayOnline.

The first mini-game encountered during FINAL FANTASY IX is the jump rope mini-game in Alexandria. To participate, have Vivi approach the little girls jumping rope to the left of the ticket booth. Once he has done so, the girls offer to let him join. This is a good opportunity to earn some Gil, get extremely rare cards, and obtain a Key Item very early in the game.

CHOCOBO HOT AND COLD GAME

Upon setting out from Lindblum's Dragon's Gate, you can venture due east over land to the Chocobo's Forest. This is where you get to meet Mene and his pal Choco.

KEYWORD:
CHOC01
PlayOnline.com
SIDE QUESTS

For more information on the Chocobo Hot and Cold game, log on to PlayOnline.

Many of the side quests described in this section depend entirely upon your progress in FFIX and in the Chocobo Hot and Cold game. Your party will not be able to reach certain areas or find some powerful items until you have commandeered certain vehicles and Choco has acquired the necessary skills to swim, climb mountains, or fly.

Each time you pay Mene 60 Gil, you get 60 seconds to search the Chocobo Forest for valuable items and Gil.

CHOCOGRAPHS

KEYWORD:
CHOC2
PlayOnline.com
SIDE QUESTS

For more information on Chocographs and Chocobo abilities, go to PlayOnline.

There are certain items buried deep beneath the ground in the forest called **Chocographs**. Chocographs are items that provide clues as to the whereabouts of buried treasure that Choco can dig up on the World Map. During your first visit to the Chocobo Forest, you may find the first Chocograph within 3 or 4 games.

CHOCOGRAPH LOCATIONS AND TREASURES

There are a total of 24 Chocographs in the game. Do your best to uncover them all!

PlayOnline.com
KEYWORD: CHOC3
SIDE QUEST

If you want to find all the Chocographs, go to PlayOnline for all the details.

OTHER THINGS CHOCOBO

There are additional aspects to the Chocobo Hot and Cold side quest. For example, Chocobo's Lagoon, Chocobo's Air Garden, and Chocobo's Paradise among many others.

For the most compete coverage of all things chocobo, please refer to PlayOnline.

MOGNET CENTRAL

The "Chocobo Hot and Cold" game, along with all the treasure hunting it entails, is by far the most complex side quest in FINAL FANTASY IX. Yet completing the side quest and getting the gold Choco is essential to unlocking so many other side quests. One such quest that depends on the gold Choco is the revival of Mognet.

On your way through Esto Gaza to Mount Gulug, delivering a letter to Mogrika the moogle causes her to indicate that Mognet is shutting down because of an accident. From this point on, most of the moogles will not have any letters to deliver and won't ask you to deliver any due to problems at the home office, Mognet Central.

The crack crumbled and opened up a hole!

Artemicion
"I only did it because it makes my coat so soft and shiny..."

To fix Mognet Central, you must travel to and from quite a few different locations delivering letters from moogle to moogle. For completing this huge task, you receive a nice item.

PlayOnline.com
KEYWORD: MOOGL8
SIDE QUEST

This task is somewhat time consuming. To find out the specifics of completing it, log on to PlayOnline.

FEED THE MOOGLE FAMILY

Each time you receive a Kupo Nut for delivering mail between the moogles, return to Gizamaluke's Grotto and feed it to the father of the moogle family. You'll receive a random item in return. During the Chocograph treasure hunt, one of the stashes contains a full set of Hawaiian gear, but only **7 Aloha T-shirts**. That leaves one of your characters out of the luau!

Moguta
"Thanks, Kupo! Take this!"

PlayOnline.com
KEYWORD: MOOGL9
SIDE QUEST

To feed the entire moogle family and earn a nice reward, visit PlayOnline.

STELLAZZIO

There are 12 Stellazzio coins, plus a thirteenth hidden coin, to find in different areas at any point during the game, even on Disc 4. Take these coins to Treno and offer them to Queen Stella. You receive a reward for each coin you hand over to her. The prizes get better with each coin you hand over, regardless of the order in which you do so.

Queen Stella
"Then why do I feel that I am missing one...?"
"Because there is one more it's just your imagination"

Zidane
"Hmm?
There's something under where the Scorpio used to be..."

PlayOnline.com
KEYWORD: STELLCN4
SIDE QUEST

PlayOnline has the entire scoop on the Stellazzio side quest.

TRENO AUCTION

After the group's initial visit to Treno, return to the King's Mansion and the auction. Some Key Items and some extremely useful equipment are auctioned off here, and this sale is the key to receiving a very powerful weapon!

Rare and Key Items that you can bid on at the auction include the following: **Mini-Cid**, **Griffin's Heart**, **Doga's Artifact**, **Une's Mirror**, the **Magical Fingertip**, and the **Rat Tail**. (Some FINAL FANTASY veterans may remember some of these items from previous FINAL FANTASY titles.) These items have some strange uses, plus you can resell them.

KEYWORD:
PlayOnline.com TRNO5
SPECIAL ITEMS

Curious as to the resale value of some of the items in the auction? Go to PlayOnline for complete coverage.

TRENO WEAPON SHOP MONSTERS

Depending on when you visit the Weapons Shop in Treno, you can have one character duel with a monster that the owner has caught and caged under the floor. You can fight one monster during Disc 2, two monsters during Disc 3, and only one monster on Disc 4.

The Weapon Shop monsters don't reward you with any EXP or AP, but the store clerk will give you a prize for each monster you defeat.

KEYWORD:
PlayOnline.com TRNO6
SIDE QUEST

You receive nice prizes for defeating the monsters. Go to PlayOnline for the details.

QUAN'S DWELLING REUNION

After Alexandria Castle experiences a horrific event, return to Quan's Dwelling with Quina and Vivi in the party. After Quina dreams about food, a conversation takes place on the patio. You can find an item in this area if you search thoroughly.

KEYWORD:
PlayOnline.com QUAND6
SPECIAL ITEM

Want to know what item you'll find in Quan's Dwelling? PlayOnline can tell you!

FROG CATCHING

When you enter the frog pond area of any Qu's Marsh, Quina asks to spend some time catching frogs. Quina must be in your party for this to occur. If you agree to let him/her catch frogs, you can control Quina as s/he runs around the pond attempting to catch the frogs that leap onto the ground out of the water. There's no real strategy to this; you just need to be swift.

As Quina catches more and more frogs, Quale appears occasionally and congratulates Quina on his/her progress. The master Qu then bestows items upon Quina as rewards for catching frogs. If you can catch 99 frogs, Quale challenges your party to a battle.

KEYWORD:
PlayOnline.com QUINFR7
SIDE QUEST

Frog catching is very beneficial. To see what you can get, go to PlayOnline.

MR. MORRID'S COFFEE

Before going to Dali after leaving the Ice Cavern, first head to Observatory Mountain near the village. There's an elderly fellow inside the hut named Morrid, who's just dying for a good cup of java. Find the three coffees at different locations in the world and return to Observatory Mountain with them, before the end of Disc 3, and Mr. Morrid will reward you.

FINAL FANTASY ITEMS AND MUSIC

We've mentioned earlier that several items for sale at the Treno Auction House are from previous *FINAL FANTASY* titles. There is some purpose to this, but it takes a bit of work to uncover it.

CRIME AND PUNISHMENT

There is a rarely seen ATE that you can view under the proper circumstances. This ATE only becomes available during your first visit to Treno, after returning to Dr. Tot's tower to get the Supersoft.

RACING HIPPAUL

You can only take part in this mini-game with Vivi at the beginning of Disc 3. Hippaul stands with his mother on the main street in Alexandria. When you speak to Hippaul's mother, Vivi and Hippaul will run a race.

You are rewarded quite well for defeating Hippaul, but it will take some time and effort.

NERO BROTHERS' GAMBLING

You can take part in a gambling mini-game with the Nero Brothers. It resembles the shell game, and you only receive Gil as a reward for playing.

RENAMING CHARACTERS

You can win the rare **Namingway Card** from Mario during the card tournament in Treno. You can also find the card inside Kuja's room during the sequence in the Desert Palace.

You can then use the card to rename a character in your party as long as you complete a specific task.

RANKING IN DAGUERREO

The true identity of the four-armed bandit is revealed after you've collected enough treasures to gain a Treasure Hunting Rank of "S." You can view your rank at any time by speaking to the Four-armed Man or to the woman at the Treno Inn. You must then track down the Four-armed Man to receive a Key Item.

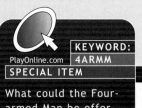

KEYWORD: 4ARMM
SPECIAL ITEM

What could the Four-armed Man be offering? To find out, visit PlayOnline.

SECRET OF THE EIDOLON WALL

One of the big secrets of the game is that Princess Garnet's true name is engraved somewhere in Madain Sari. There is a very complicated way to reveal the truth at the beginning of Disc 4.

The process is quite complicated, and takes some time to complete.

KEYWORD: GRNT4
SECRET

To find out Dagger's true name, go to PlayOnline.

EXCALIBUR

You can get a very powerful sword for Steiner by completing a short side quest. However, take note that this occurs late in the game and will cost you quite a bit of Gil.

KEYWORD: STNREX7
POWERFUL WEAPON

To find out how to get a powerful weapon for Steiner, go to PlayOnline.

EXCALIBUR II

You can even get the Excalibur II, but this secret will take every ounce of your gaming skills. You will need to finish the game within a certain time limit, so good luck!

KEYWORD: EXCAL9
POWERFUL WEAPON

How fast must you complete the game to get this weapon? Only PlayOnline has the answer!

HADES

Extremely late in the game, you can encounter Hades, an optional Boss. In Memoria, the player enters a room where Quina thinks that there is water and tries to swim. After the scene, search the hidden area amongst the coral on the right side of the screen. When an ominous voice begins to ward you off, persist in the conversation to fight Hades.

BOSS FIGHT

HADES (OPTIONAL)

HP	????	AP	30	Weak vs.	None

Steal Items	Robe of Lords, Battle Boots, Running Shoes, Reflect Ring	Spoils	Elixir, Wing Edge

BOSS PREPARATIONS:

- Equip Auto-Regen, Antibody, Clear Headed, Bright Eyes, and Body Temp
- Make sure Vivi and Dagger have the Half-MP ability

BATTLE TACTICS:

- Have Steiner use Shock
- Make Zidane steal and attack
- Have Dagger cast Reflect on herself, and then have Vivi cast Flare on Dagger

KEYWORD: OPTBOSS9

BOSS FIGHT TIPS

This Boss is deadly! If you're still having trouble, go to PlayOnline for additional strategy.

FRIENDLY MONSTERS

At various locations on the World Map, a random battle occurs but the music sounds sweet and melodic. The creatures that appear won't attack either; instead, they beg you to give them a specific jewel. If you give them the jewel, your party receives a ton of AP and sometimes a useful item.

KEYWORD: FRND4

SIDE QUEST

Want to know more about the friendly creatures? If so, log on to PlayOnline.

THE RAGTIME MOUSE

While wandering the forests of the world, you may encounter a strange creature that asks your party true or false questions. To answer a question, attack the large "circle" symbol for "True" or "X" for "False."

For each correct answer, you receive a percentage grade based on the number of questions you've answered right or wrong. For each correct answer, you receive 1000 Gil.

KEYWORD: RAGTIM5

SIDE QUEST

I can't find the Ragtime Mouse! For help finding this strange creature, visit PlayOnline.

Ozma

The most terrifying enemy in the game is not the final Boss, but the creature hidden at the Eidolon grave in Chocobo's Air Garden.

PlayOnline.com

KEYWORD: OZMABSS2

BOSS FIGHT TIPS

PlayOnline has all the details to help find this optional Boss.

To fight Ozma, you must complete most other side quests first. You'll get a few chances to back out, so make sure you only fight it when you're ready.

BOSS FIGHT

OZMA (OPTIONAL)

HP	55,535	AP	0	Weak vs.	Wind, Holy

Steal Items	Elixir, Robe of Lords, Dark Matter, Pumice Piece	Spoils	Pumice Piece, Dark Matter

Battle Tactics:

- Equip Antibody and Clear-Headed
- Equip armor that protects against Shadow damage
- If Zidane Trances, use the Grand Lethal Dyne attack

Tetra Master

PlayOnline.com

KEYWORD: TETRMST9

SIDE QUEST

For more information on the card game Tetra Master, visit PlayOnline.

There is more complete strategy for the card game in the Tetra Master section. Please refer to that section for additional details.

Blackjack

PlayOnline.com

KEYWORD: BLJK1

MINI-GAME

Want to know how to play the game? Go to PlayOnline for all the details.

After finishing the game, let the credits roll until the phrase "The End" appears. There's a cool little mini-game that you can play.

BESTIARY

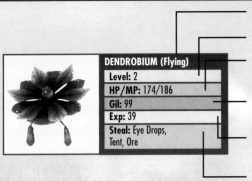

DENDROBIUM (Flying)

Level: 2	
HP/MP: 174/186	
Gil: 99	
Exp: 39	
Steal: Eye Drops, Tent, Ore	

- The enemy's type
- The enemy's level
- The enemy's Hit Points and Magic Points
- Money received for defeating the enemy
- Experience received for defeating the enemy
- Items you can steal from the enemy

REMEMBER...

Some items are easier to steal than others. When referring to an enemy's "Steal" entry, the most common items are listed first, followed by the least common, and finally the rare items. Also, take note that all Bosses appear in red.

PlayOnline.com — **MORE STATS**

KEYWORD: BESTRY3

Find an enemy's weaknesses, strengths, and more at PlayOnline!

Flan (N/A)

Level: 2	
HP/MP: 75/183	
Gil: 110	
Exp: 41	
Steal: Potion, Ore	
Spoils: Potion, Phoenix Down	
Card: Flan	
Fire: Weak	
Ice: Half	
Lightning: N/A	
Earth: N/A	
Water: N/A	
Wind: N/A	
Holy: N/A	
Shadow: N/A	
Status Effect: Vanish	

ABADON (Bug/Flying)

Level: 58	
HP/MP: 12,658/2479	
Gil: 2604	
Exp: 32,073	
Steal: Garnet, Vaccine, Phoenix Pinion	

ABOMINATION (N/A)

Level: 15	
HP/MP: 879/482	
Gil: 388	
Exp: 913	
Steal: Ore, Hi-Potion, Ether	

ADAMANTOISE (N/A)

Level: 31	
HP/MP: 3587/1043	
Gil: 4433	
Exp: 5096	
Steal: Tent, Hi-Potion, Phoenix Down	

AGARES (Demon)

Level: 43	
HP/MP: 6775/1596	
Gil: 1945	
Exp: 14,279	
Steal: Tent, Soft, Ore	

AMDUSIAS (Demon/Flying)

Level: 42/52 (Pand. Event)	
HP/MP: 6578/1568;10,926/9282	
Gil: 0/2316	
Exp: 0/26,376	
Steal: Hi-Potion, Antidote, Phoenix Pinion, Ether/Tent, Ether	

ANEMONE (N/A)

Level: 31	
HP/MP: 3586/1045	
Gil: 1137	
Exp: 5080	
Steal: Ore, Tent	

ANTLION (N/A)

Level: 16	
HP/MP: 3938/3950	
Gil: 1616	
Exp: 0	
Steal: Annoyntment, Mythril Vest, Gold Helm	

ARMODULLAHAN (N/A)

Level: 13	
HP/MP: 818/4598	
Gil: 474	
Exp: 809	
Steal: Ore, Hi-Potion, Ether	

ARMSTRONG (N/A)

Level: 33	
HP/MP: 4204/1165	
Gil: 1456	
Exp: 7150	
Steal: Ore, Hi-Potion, Ether	

ARK (Flying)

Level: 38	
HP/MP: 20,002/1374	
Gil: 5964	
Exp: 0	
Steal: Elixir, Power Vest, Holy Lance	

ASH (Demon/Flying)
Level: 66	
HP/MP: 25,591/3014	
Gil: 2748	
Exp: 40,329	
Steal: Tent	

AXE BEAK (Beast)
Level: 6	
HP/MP: 241/267	
Gil: 224	
Exp: 123	
Steal: Ore, Hi-Potion, Ether	

AXOLOTL (N/A)
Level: 6	
HP/MP: 211/266	
Gil: 236	
Exp: 106	
Steal: Potion, Hi-Potion, Phoenix Pinion	

BAKU (Human)
Level: 2	
HP/MP: 202/1285	
Gil: 0	
Exp: 0	
Steal: Hi-Potion, Iron Sword	

BANDERSNATCH (Beast)
Level: 14	
HP/MP: 899/464	
Gil: 347	
Exp: 787	
Steal: Potion, Tent	

BASILISK (Bug)
Level: 6	
HP/MP: 346/247	
Gil: 233	
Exp: 167	
Steal: Soft, Hi-Potion	

BEATRIX (1st Battle) (Human)
Level: 14	
HP/MP: 3630/3467	
Gil: 0	
Exp: 0	
Steal: Phoenix Down, Chain Plate, Mythril Sword	

BEATRIX (2nd Battle) (Human)
Level: 17	
HP/MP: 4736/3964	
Gil: 0	
Exp: 0	
Steal: Phoenix Down, Thunder Gloves, Ice Brand	

BEATRIX (3rd Battle) (Human)
Level: 19	
HP/MP: 5709/4203	
Gil: 0	
Exp: 0	
Steal: Phoenix Down, Ice Brand, Survival Vest	

BEHEMOTH (Beast) (Memoria)
Level: 71	
HP/MP: 24,123/3338	
Gil: 2764	
Exp: 53,168	
Steal: Phoenix Pinion	

BENERO (Human)
Level: 1	
HP/MP: 28/149	
Gil: 0	
Exp: 0	
Steal: N/A	

BLACK WALTZ NO.1 (Human)
Level: 2	
HP/MP: 229/9999	
Gil: 134	
Exp: 0	
Steal: Remedy, Silk Shirt	

BLACK WALTZ NO.2 (Human/Flying)
Level: 6	
HP/MP: 1030/3017	
Gil: 441	
Exp: 0	
Steal: Steepled Hat, Leather Plate	

BLACK WALTZ NO.3 (Human/Flying)
Level: 7 (Cargo Ship)	
HP/MP: 1128/2080	
Gil: 0	
Exp: 0	
Steal: Steepled Hat, Linen Cuirass, Silver Gloves	

BLACK WALTZ NO.3 (Human)
Level: 9 (South Gate)	
HP/MP: 1272/344	
Gil: 864	
Exp: 0	
Steal: Steepled Hat, Lightning Staff, Flame Staff	

BLAZER BEETLE (Bug)
Level: 19	
HP/MP: 1468/603	
Gil: 740	
Exp: 1548	
Steal: Hi-Potion, Phoenix Pinion, Ether	

BOMB (Flying)
Level: 10	
HP/MP: 526/359	
Gil: 235	
Exp: 178	
Steal: Ore, Hi-Potion, Ether	

CACTUAR (N/A)
Level: 30	
HP/MP: 1939/1018	
Gil: 1021	
Exp: 4208	
Steal: Phoenix Down, Tent, Ether	

CARRION WORM (Bug)
Level: 9	
HP/MP: 259/345	
Gil: 319	
Exp: 329	
Steal: Annoyntment, Tent	

CARVE SPIDER (Bug)
Level: 3	
HP/MP: 123/199	
Gil: 124	
Exp: 48	
Steal: Potion, Tent, Ore	

CATOBLEPAS (Beast)
Level: 32	
HP/MP: 3727/1069	
Gil: 1421	
Exp: 6609	
Steal: Soft, Hi-Potion, Phoenix Pinion, Ether	

CAVE IMP (N/A)
Level: 2	
HP/MP: 74/186	
Gil: 118	
Exp: 35	
Steal: Potion, Phoenix Down	

CERBERUS (Beast)
Level: 44	
HP/MP: 6977/1625	
Gil: 1984	
Exp: 15,181	
Steal: Ore, Tent, Ether	

CHIMERA (Demon)
Level: 67	
HP/MP: 21,901/3,053	
Gil: 2732	
Exp: 42,785	
Steal: Vaccine, Garnet, Remedy	

CLIPPER (N/A)
Level: 7	
HP/MP: 294/278	
Gil: 190	
Exp: 80	
Steal: Ore, Hi-Potion	

CRAWLER (Bug)
Level: 10	
HP/MP: 625/358	
Gil: 323	
Exp: 480	
Steal: Antidote, Phoenix Down, Hi-Potion, Phoenix Pinion	

DEATHGUISE (Demon/Bug/Flying)
Level: 74	
HP/MP: 55,535/9999	
Gil: 8916	
Exp: 0	
Steal: Elixir, Black Belt, Duel Claws	

DENDROBIUM (Flying)		**DRACOZOMBIE**		**DRAKAN (Demon/Flying)**	
		(Dragon/Undead)		Level: 30	
Level: 2		Level: 24		HP/MP: 3292/1018	
HP/MP: 174/186		HP/MP: 2179/760		Gil: 1118	
Gil: 99		Gil: 941		Exp: 5675	
Exp: 39		Exp: 3229		Steal: Antidote	
Steal: Eye Drops, Tent, Ore		Steal: Magic Tag, Hi-Potion, Ether			

DRAGONFLY (Bug/Flying)		**EARTH GUARDIAN (Demon)**		**EPITAPH (Stone)**	
Level: 8		Level: 54		Level: 32	
HP/MP: 348/295		HP/MP: 20,756/2234		HP/MP: 3732/300	
Gil: 307		Gil: 4512		Gil: 0	
Exp: 249		Exp: 0		Exp: 0	
Steal: Eye Drops, Tent		Steal: Avenger, Rubber Suit		Steal: Phoenix Down, Soft	

FALSE (Flying)		**FANG (Beast) (Evil Forest/Hunt)**		**FEATHER CIRCLE (Flying)**	
Level: 11		Level: 1/5		Level: 13	
HP/MP: 594/376		HP/MP: 68/170;216/253		HP/MP: 619/448	
Gil: 0		Gil: 90/0		Gil: 378	
Exp: 23,852		Exp: 23/0		Exp: 629	
Steal: N/A		Steal: Potion, Phoenix Down, Hi-Potion, Phoenix Pinion/N/A		Steal: Ore, Annoyntment, Hi-Potion,Ether	

FEATHER CIRCLE		**FLAN (N/A)**		**GARGOYLE (Stone/Flying)**	
(Flying/Friendly)		Level: 2		Level: 44	
Level: 29		HP/MP: 75/183		HP/MP: 6977/1628	
HP/MP: 3298/994		Gil: 110		Gil: 1958	
Gil: 0		Exp: 41		Exp: 15,181	
Exp: 0		Steal: Potion, Ore		Steal: Hi-Potion, Tent, Phoenix Pinion, Ether	
Steal: N/A					

GARLAND (Human)		**GARUDA (Flying)**		**GARUDA (Flying/Friendly)**	
Level: 62		Level: 35		Level: 42	
HP/MP: 40,728/9999		HP/MP: 3521/1216		HP/MP: 6583/1570	
Gil: 0		Gil: 1279		Gil: 0	
Exp: 0		Exp: 6933		Exp: 0	
Steal: Battle Boots, Ninja Gear, Dark Gear		Steal: Ore, Hi-Potion, Ether, Phoenix Pinion		Steal: N/A	

GHOST (Undead/Flying)		**GHOST (Flying/Friendly)**		**GIGAN OCTOPUS (Flying)**	
Level: 4		Level: 8		Level: 31	
HP/MP: 118/9999		HP/MP: 347/293		HP/MP: 3584/1044	
Gil: 126		Gil: 0		Gil: 1840	
Exp: 48		Exp: 0		Exp: 6096	
Steal: Potion, Ore, Hi-Potion, Phoenix Pinion		Steal: N/A		Steal: Eye Drops, Phoenix Down, Ether	

GIGAN TOAD (N/A)		**GIMME CAT (N/A)**		**GIZAMALUKE (Flying)**	
Level: 7		Level: 36		Level: 16	
HP/MP: 297/280		HP/MP: 4683/1240		HP/MP: 3175/502	
Gil: 288		Gil: 5000		Gil: 800	
Exp: 178		Exp: 4		Exp: 0	
Steal: Ore		Steal: Echo Screen, Tent, Ether		Steal: Elixir, Magus Hat, Ice Staff	

GNOLL (N/A)		**GOBLIN (N/A)**		**GOBLIN MAGE (N/A)**	
Level: 18		Level: 5		Level: 15	
HP/MP: 1375/586		HP/MP: 33/172		HP/MP: 983/485	
Gil: 691		Gil: 88		Gil: 568	
Exp: 1368		Exp: 23		Exp: 913	
Steal: Hi-Potion, Phoenix Pinion, Ether		Steal: Potion		Steal: Potion, Ore	

GRAND DRAGON (Dragon)		**GRENADE (Flying)**		**GRIFFIN (Flying)**	
Level: 60		Level: 36		Level: 16	
HP/MP: 13,206/2550		HP/MP: 4685/1240		HP/MP: 1470/602	
Gil: 2604		Gil: 1336		Gil: 602	
Exp: 35,208		Exp: 7459		Exp: 1858	
Steal: Tent, Ether, Rising Sun		Steal: Ore, Tent, Ether		Steal: Ore	

GRIMLOCK (N/A) (Pink Head)
Level: 30
HP/MP: 3292/1018
Gil: 1363
Exp: 6610
Steal: Ore, Tent, Ether

GRIMLOCK (N/A) (Blue Head)
Level: 30
HP/MP: 3292/1018
Gil: 1363
Exp: 6610
Steal: Hi-Potion, Ether

HADES (Demon/Flying)
Level: 92
HP/MP: 55,535/9999
Gil: 9638
Exp: 65,535
Steal: Reflect Ring, Running Shoes, Battle Boots, Robe of Lords

HAAGEN (Human)
Level: 1
HP/MP: 33/673
Gil: 72
Exp: 0
Steal: N/A

HECTEYES (Demon/Undead)
Level: 51
HP/MP: 9567/2033
Gil: 2049
Exp: 17,096
Steal: Hi-Potion, Vaccine, Phoenix Pinion

HEDGEHOG PIE (N/A)
Level: 7
HP/MP: 295/281
Gil: 187
Exp: 119
Steal: Ore, Hi-Potion, Phoenix Pinion

HILGIGARS (Human)
Level: 28
HP/MP: 8106/908
Gil: 2136
Exp: 0
Steal: Phoenix Down, Mythril Fork, Fairy Flute

HORNET (Bug/Flying)
Level: 7
HP/MP: 293/281
Gil: 194
Exp: 89
Steal: Potion

IRONITE (Dragon/Flying)
Level: 11
HP/MP: 889/374
Gil: 269
Exp: 577
Steal: Hi-Potion, Soft

IRON MAN (Human/Demon)
Level: 68
HP/MP: 21,217/3091
Gil: 2796
Exp: 42,996
Steal: Phoenix Down

JABBERWOCK (N/A)
Level: 30
HP/MP: 3442/1019
Gil: 1156
Exp: 4675
Steal: Ore, Hi-Potion

JABBERWOCK (Friendly)
Level: 31
HP/MP: 3582/1042
Gil: 0
Exp: 0
Steal: N/A

KING LEO (Human)
Level: 1
HP/MP: 186/373
Gil: 0
Exp: 0
Steal: N/A

KRAKEN (Demon) (Memoria)
Level: 72/72 (Crystal World)
HP/MP: 59,496/3380;23,354/3381
Gil: 8628/4338
Exp: 0/0
Steal: Genji Helmet, Wizard Rod, Glutton's Robe/Annoyntment, Eye Drops

KRAKEN (Right Tentacle) (Demon)
Level: 71
HP/MP: 18,168/3338
Gil: 4362
Exp: 0
Steal: Wing Edge

KRAKEN (Left Tentacle) (Demon)
Level: 71
HP/MP: 18,169/3339
Gil: 4386
Exp: 0
Steal: Elixir

KUJA (Human)
Level: 64
HP/MP: 42,382/9999
Gil: 0
Exp: 0
Steal: Ether, Carabini Mail, Light Robe

LADYBUG (Bug/Flying)
Level: 6
HP/MP: 244/266
Gil: 193
Exp: 89
Steal: Eye Drops, Tent, Hi-Potion, Phoenix Pinion

LADYBUG (Bug/Flying/Friendly)
Level: 6
HP/MP: 244/267
Gil: 0
Exp: 0
Steal: N/A

LAMIA (N/A)
Level: 10
HP/MP: 994/358
Gil: 494
Exp: 204
Steal: Ore, Phoenix Down

LAND WORM (Bug)
Level: 29
HP/MP: 5296/997
Gil: 1316
Exp: 5151
Steal: Ore, Hi-Potion

LANI (Human)
Level: 19
HP/MP: 5708/4802
Gil: 0
Exp: 0
Steal: Ether, Gladius, Coral Sword

LICH (Demon) (Memoria)
Level: 71/68 (Crystal World)
HP/MP: 58,554/9999;22,218/3091
Gil: 8436/2828
Exp: 0/0
Steal: Genji Gloves, Siren's Flute, Black Robe/Ore

LIZARD MAN (N/A)
Level: 10
HP/MP: 589/359
Gil: 218
Exp: 173
Steal: Ore, Tent

MAGIC VICE (N/A)
Level: 7
HP/MP: 297/278
Gil: 239
Exp: 213
Steal: Echo Screen, Ether

MALBORO (N/A)
Level: 57
HP/MP: 11,687/2334
Gil: 2572
Exp: 30,579
Steal: Ore, Vaccine

MALIRIS (Demon) (Memoria)
Level: 72/69 (Crystal World)
HP/MP: 59,497/3381;22,535/3127
Gil: 8532/2860
Exp: 0/0
Steal: Genji Armor, Ultima Sword, Masamune/Phoenix Down

MANDRAGORA (N/A)
Level: 9
HP/MP: 662/344
Gil: 595
Exp: 307
Steal: Echo Screen, Tent, Hi-Potion, Phoenix Pinion

MASKED MAN (Human)
Level: 1
HP/MP: 188/223
Gil: 805
Exp: 0
Steal: Potion, Wrist, Mage Masher

MELTIGEMINI (Demon)
Level: 42
HP/MP: 24,348/1570
Gil: 6428
Exp: 0
Steal: Vaccine, Golden Hairpin, Demon's Vest

MIMIC (N/A)
Level: 8
HP/MP: 346/295
Gil: 777
Exp: 320
Steal: Hi-Potion, Antidote

MISTODON (Undead)
Level: 19
HP/MP: 1473/602
Gil: 747
Exp: 2548
Steal: Ore, Hi-Potion

MOVER (Flying)
Level: 52
HP/MP: 7352/2064
Gil: 2300
Exp: 23,801
Steal: Opal, Vaccine, Tent

MU (N/A) (Evil Forest/Hunt)
Level: 2/5
HP/MP: 77/183; 201/253
Gil: 104/0
Exp: 34/0
Steal: Potion/N/A

MU (Friendly)
Level: 2
HP/MP: 78/186
Gil: 0
Exp: 0
Steal: N/A

MYCONID (Flying)
Level: 20
HP/MP: 1372/584
Gil: 726
Exp: 1368
Steal: Eye Drops, Tent

NECRON (Flying)
Level: 69
HP/MP: 54,100/9999
Gil: 0
Exp: 0
Steal: Elixir

NOVA DRAGON (Dragon/Flying)
Level: 67
HP/MP: 54,940/9999
Gil: 9506
Exp: 0
Steal: Remedy, Dragon Wrist, Grand Armor

NYMPH (N/A)
Level: 9
HP/MP: 458/345
Gil: 303
Exp: 329
Steal: Echo Screen, Ore, Hi-Potion, Phoenix Pinion

NYMPH (Friendly)
Level: 9
HP/MP: 463/344
Gil: 0
Exp: 0
Steal: N/A

OCHU (N/A)
Level: 16
HP/MP: 3568/622
Gil: 845
Exp: 2093
Steal: Hi-Potion, Phoenix Pinion, Ether

OGRE (N/A)
Level: 32
HP/MP: 3727/1067
Gil: 1204
Exp: 5507
Steal: Annoyntment, Phoenix Pinion, Ether

OZMA (Flying)
Level: 99
HP/MP: 55,535/9999
Gil: 18,312
Exp: 65,535
Steal: Elixir, Robe of Lords, Dark Matter, Pumice Piece

PLANT BRAIN (N/A)
Level: 7
HP/MP: 916/1431
Gil: 468
Exp: 0
Steal: Eye Drops, Iron Helm

PLANT SPIDER (Bug)
Level: 1
HP/MP: 33/173
Gil: 91
Exp: 22
Steal: Potion, Ore, Hi-Potion

PRISON CAGE (N/A)
Level: 2
HP/MP: 533/1186
Gil: 0
Exp: 0
Steal: Broad Sword, Leather Wrist

PYTHON (N/A)
Level: 2
HP/MP: 75/184
Gil: 106
Exp: 40
Steal: Potion, Ore, Hi-Potion, Phoenix Pinion

QUALE (Human)
Level: 76
HP/MP: 65,535/3680
Gil: 10,800
Exp: 65,535
Steal: Elixir, Ninja Gear, Glutton's Robe, Robe of Lords

RAGTIME MOUSE (N/A)
Level: 31
HP/MP: 3584/1045
Gil: 59,630
Exp: 22,852
Steal: N/A

RALVUIMAGO (N/A)
Level: 18
HP/MP: 3352/584
Gil: 1404
Exp: 0
Steal: Phoenix Down, Adaman Vest, Oak Staff

RALVURAHVA (Dragon)
Level: 13
HP/MP: 2296/3649
Gil: 0
Exp: 0
Steal: Bone Wrist, Mythril Fork

RED DRAGON (Dragon/Flying)
Level: 36
HP/MP: 8000/1242
Gil: 5156
Exp: 22,377
Steal: Tent, Ether, Elixir

RING LEADER (Demon/Flying)
Level: 51
HP/MP: 9569/2030
Gil: 1868
Exp: 18,816
Steal: Echo Screen, Vaccine

SAHAGIN (N/A)
Level: 18
HP/MP: 1375/585
Gil: 684
Exp: 1368
Steal: Hi-Potion, Ether

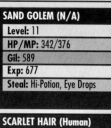

SAND GOLEM (N/A)
Level: 11
HP/MP: 342/376
Gil: 589
Exp: 677
Steal: Hi-Potion, Eye Drops

SAND GOLEM (Core) (N/A)
Level: 11
HP/MP: 1091/377
Gil: 0
Exp: 0
Steal: Ore, Hi-Potion

SAND SCORPION (N/A)
Level: 10
HP/MP: 526/360
Gil: 315
Exp: 400
Steal: Ore, Antidote, Ether

SCARLET HAIR (Human)
Level: 22
HP/MP: 8985/5865
Gil: 4790
Exp: 0
Steal: Ether, Poison Knuckles

SEALION (Flying)
Level: 3
HP/MP: 472/9999
Gil: 205
Exp: 0
Steal: Ether, Mythril Dagger

SEEKER BAT (Flying)
Level: 12
HP/MP: 594/377
Gil: 366
Exp: 449
Steal: Eye Drops, Tent

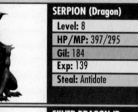

SERPION (Dragon)
Level: 8
HP/MP: 397/295
Gil: 184
Exp: 139
Steal: Antidote

SHELL DRAGON (Dragon)
Level: 58
HP/MP: 12,661/2482
Gil: 2588
Exp: 32,073
Steal: Hi-Potion, Vaccine, Tent, Phoenix Pinion

SHELL DRAGON (Dragon) (Pand.)
Level: 54
HP/MP: 10,921/9335
Gil: 2332
Exp: 26,376
Steal: Phoenix Down, Elixir

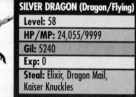

SILVER DRAGON (Dragon/Flying)
Level: 58
HP/MP: 24,055/9999
Gil: 5240
Exp: 0
Steal: Elixir, Dragon Mail, Kaiser Knuckles

SKELETON (Undead)
Level: 8
HP/MP: 400/293
Gil: 209
Exp: 104
Steal: Ore, Hi-Potion, Ether

SOLDIER (Human) (Cleyra)
Level: 10
HP/MP: 523/358
Gil: 311
Exp: 400
Steal: Potion, Phoenix Down, Echo Screen, Phoenix Pinion

SOLDIER (Human) (Alex. Castle)
Level: 9
HP/MP: 459/342
Gil: 292
Exp: 357
Steal: Potion, Phoenix Down, Hi-Potion, Phoenix Pinion

SOULCAGE (Undead)
Level: 26
HP/MP: 9765/862
Gil: 3800
Exp: 0
Steal: Oak Staff, Magician Cloak, Brigandine

STEINER (1st Battle) (Human)
Level: 1
HP/MP: 169/523
Gil: 0
Exp: 0
Steal: Leather Hat, Silk Shirt

STEINER (2nd Battle) (Human)
Level: 1
HP/MP: 167/620
Gil: 355
Exp: 0
Steal: N/A

STEINER (3rd Battle) (Human)
Level: 1
HP/MP: 162/770
Gil: 0
Exp: 0
Steal: N/A

STILVA (Demon)
Level: 67
HP/MP: 21,906/3053
Gil: 2780
Exp: 42,785
Steal: Ether

STROPER (Stone)
Level: 21
HP/MP: 1840/697
Gil: 915
Exp: 2346
Steal: Soft, Peridot, Phoenix Down, Phoenix Pinion

TAHARKA (Flying)
Level: 46
HP/MP: 29,186/1776
Gil: 8092
Exp: 0
Steal: Elixir, Mythril Claws, Orichalcon

TANTARIAN (Demon)
Level: 41
HP/MP: 21,997/1456
Gil: 4472
Exp: 12,585
Steal: Ether, Elixir, Silver Fork, Demon's Mail

THORN (Human)
Level: 16
HP/MP: 2984/9999
Gil: 0
Exp: 0
Steal: Mythril Armor, Mythril Armlet

TIAMAT (Dragon)
Level: 72
HP/MP: 59,494/3381
Gil: 8820
Exp: 0
Steal: Blood Sword, Feather Boots, Grand Helm

TIAMAT (Dragon) (Memoria)
Level: 71 (Crystal World)
HP/MP: 24,127/3338
Gil: 2956
Exp: 0
Steal: Ether, Wing Edge

TONBERRY (N/A)
Level: 46
HP/MP: 7886/1779
Gil: 1513
Exp: 13,297
Steal: Hi-Potion, Phoenix Down, Phoenix Pinion, Ether

TORAMA (Beast/Demon)
Level: 30
HP/MP: 3292/1018
Gil: 1118
Exp: 5675
Steal: Antidote, Phoenix Pinion

TRANCE KUJA (Human/Flying)
Level: 76
HP/MP: 55,535/9999
Gil: 0
Exp: 0
Steal: Ether, White Robe, Rebirth Ring

TRICK SPARROW (Flying)

Level:	5
HP/MP:	191/250
Gil:	198
Exp:	65
Steal:	Ore

TROLL (N/A)

Level:	20
HP/MP:	1469/623
Gil:	854
Exp:	2093
Steal:	Ore, Tent

TRUE (Flying)

Level:	11
HP/MP:	589/377
Gil:	0
Exp:	0
Steal:	N/A

TYPE A (Human)

Level:	8
HP/MP:	398/293
Gil:	199
Exp:	115
Steal:	Phoenix Down, Tent

TYPE B (Human)

Level:	10
HP/MP:	526/361
Gil:	321
Exp:	373
Steal:	Ore, Hi-Potion, Ether

TYPE C (Human)

Level:	13
HP/MP:	623/447
Gil:	336
Exp:	629
Steal:	Potion, Tent

VALIA PIRA (Flying)

Level:	36
HP/MP:	12,119/9999
Gil:	4089
Exp:	0
Steal:	N/A

VEPAL (Flying) (Green)

Level:	34
HP/MP:	4363/1188
Gil:	1270
Exp:	6434
Steal:	Hi-Potion, Phoenix Pinion, Ether

VEPAL (Flying) (Red)

Level:	35
HP/MP:	4022/1214
Gil:	1326
Exp:	6933
Steal:	Hi-Potion, Phoenix Pinion, Ether

VETERAN (Demon/Flying)

Level:	44
HP/MP:	6972/1627
Gil:	1971
Exp:	15,181
Steal:	Hi-Potion, Ether, Phoenix Pinion

VICE (N/A)

Level:	4
HP/MP:	129/209
Gil:	128
Exp:	48
Steal:	Echo Screen, Potion

WEIMAR (Human)

Level:	1
HP/MP:	38/721
Gil:	73
Exp:	0
Steal:	N/A

WHALE ZOMBIE (Undead/Flying)

Level:	32
HP/MP:	3730/1066
Gil:	1528
Exp:	6609
Steal:	Antidote, Magic Tag

WORM HYDRA (Dragon)

Level:	37
HP/MP:	4846/1268
Gil:	1345
Exp:	8010
Steal:	Hi-Potion, Antidote

WRAITH (Undead/Flying) (Blue)

Level:	36
HP/MP:	4686/1239
Gil:	1654
Exp:	8950
Steal:	Ore, Hi-Potion

WRAITH (Undead/Flying) (Red)

Level:	37
HP/MP:	4686/1268
Gil:	1345
Exp:	8010
Steal:	Topaz, Hi-Potion, Phoenix Pinion

WYERD (Beast)

Level:	2
HP/MP:	129/183
Gil:	116
Exp:	45
Steal:	Potion, Tent, Phoenix Down

YAN (N/A)

Level:	72
HP/MP:	19,465/3378
Gil:	2218
Exp:	42,673
Steal:	Ore, Elixir

YAN (Friendly)

Level:	61
HP/MP:	13,486/2588
Gil:	0
Exp:	0
Steal:	N/A

YETI (Flying)

Level:	9
HP/MP:	463/342
Gil:	221
Exp:	133
Steal:	Eye Drops, Ore, Hi-Potion

YETI (Flying/Friendly)

Level:	6
HP/MP:	246/265
Gil:	0
Exp:	0
Steal:	N/A

ZAGHNOL (Beast) (Pinn. Rocks)

Level:	16/9 (Hunt)
HP/MP:	1189/499;1574/2342
Gil:	546/0
Exp:	1261/0
Steal:	Ore, Tent, Ether/Mythril Gloves, Needle Fork

ZEMZELETT (Flying)

Level:	20
HP/MP:	1571/625
Gil:	889
Exp:	2093
Steal:	Ore, Hi-Potion, Ether

ZENERO (Human)

Level:	1
HP/MP:	32/149
Gil:	0
Exp:	0
Steal:	N/A

ZOMBIE (Undead)

Level:	19
HP/MP:	973/603
Gil:	708
Exp:	1445
Steal:	Magic Tag, Tent, Ether

ZORN (Human)

Level:	16
HP/MP:	4896/9999
Gil:	0
Exp:	0
Steal:	Partisan, Stardust Rod

ZUU (Flying)

Level:	8
HP/MP:	1149/293
Gil:	384
Exp:	320
Steal:	Potion, Ore, Hi-Potion, Phoenix Pinion

WORLD MAP

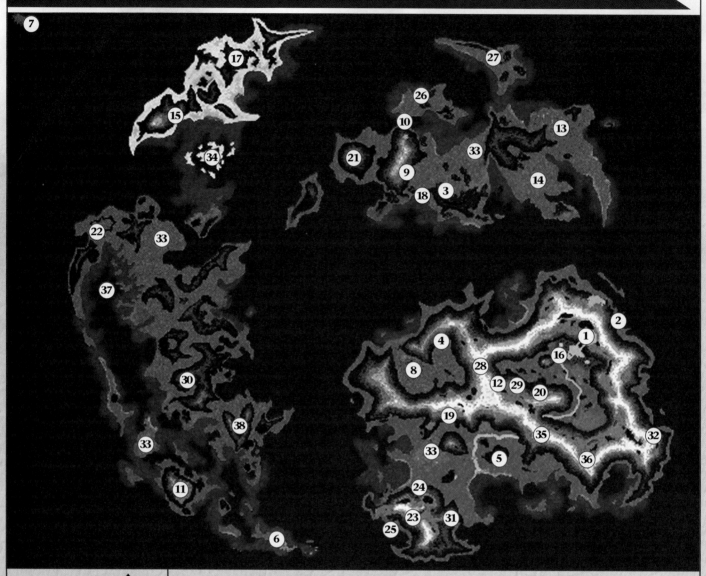

KEYWORD: WOMPS1

PlayOnline.com
WORLD MAPS

For a more detailed look at the world of Gaia, check out PlayOnline.

1. Alexandria
2. Alexandria Harbor
3. Black Mage Village
4. Burmecia
5. Chocobo's Forest
6. Chocobo's Lagoon
7. Chocobo's Paradise
8. Cleyra
9. Conde Petie
10. Conde Petie Mountain Path
11. Daguerreo
12. Dali
13. Desert Palace
14. Earth Shrine
15. Esto Gaza
16. Evil Forest

17. Fire Shrine
18. Fossil Roo
19. Gizamaluke's Grotto
20. Ice Cavern
21. Iifa Tree
22. Ipsen's Castle
23. Lindblum
24. Lindblum Dragon's Gate
25. Lindblum Harbor
26. Madain Sari
27. Mognet Central
28. North Gate
29. Observatory Mountain
30. Oeilvert
31. Pinnacle Rocks
32. Quan's Dwelling

33. Qu's Marsh
34. Shimmering Island
35. South Gate
36. Treno
37. Water Shrine
38. Wind Shrine

NOTES

There are a great deal of noteworthy events that you will encounter throughout your adventure. This page has been provided so that you may include personalized notes as you make your way through FINAL FANTASY IX.

TRUTH IN EVERY DREAM

FINAL FANTASY

COLUMBIA PICTURES
PRODUCED BY
SQUARE USA,
HONOLULU STUDIO

IN THEATRES SUMMER 2001
WWW.FINALFANTASY.COM

SQUARE PICTURES

COLUMBIA
PICTURES